THE CATHOLIC UNIVERSITY OF AMERICA
CANON LAW STUDIES
No. 223

THE REDUCTION OF CLERICS
TO THE LAY STATE

AN HISTORICAL SYNOPSIS
AND COMMENTARY

BY THE

REV. FRANCIS PATRICK SWEENEY, C.SS.R., J.C.L.

Priest of the Baltimore Province

A DISSERTATION

*Submitted to the Faculty of the School of Canon Law
of the Catholic University of America in Partial
Fulfillment of the Requirements for the
Degree of Doctor of Canon Law*

THE CATHOLIC UNIVERSITY OF AMERICA PRESS
WASHINGTON, D. C.
1945

Imprimi Potest:

MICHAEL A. GEARIN, C.SS.R., J.C.D.,
Superior Provincialis.

Brooklynii, die 14 maii, 1945.

Nihil Obstat:

CLEMENS V. BASTNAGEL, S.T.L., J.U.D.,
Censor Deputatus.

Washingtonii, die 15 maii, 1945.

Imprimatur:

✠ MICHAEL J. CURLEY, D.D.,
Archiepiscopus Baltimoriensis-Washingtoniensis.

Baltimorae, die 15 maii, 1945.

Printed by
THE PAULIST PRESS
401 WEST 59TH STREET
NEW YORK 19, N. Y.

51

TO

OUR MOTHER OF PERPETUAL HELP

TABLE OF CONTENTS

PART II

CANONICAL COMMENTARY

CHAPTER III

CHAPTER IV

CHAPTER V

CHAPTER VI

CHAPTER VII

CHAPTER VIII

CHAPTER IX

EFFECTS OF REDUCTION AND THE RETURN TO THE CLERICAL STATE

FOREWORD

The canonical institute of the reduction of clerics to the lay state has been somewhat neglected in the commentaries of the authors. In particular the reduction of minor clerics has received little detailed consideration. Consequently it is time for this field to be explored, for its problems to be indicated and for an attempt to be made at a solution of these problems.

The purpose of this dissertation is twofold: to trace the historical legislation and development which finally evolved into the law of the present Code, and to comment upon the law as it is found today in the Code.

In the historical section it is to be taken for granted that once the cleric had lost his clerical privileges he likewise was reduced to the lay state. The distinction which the present-day Code makes, on the one hand, between a cleric who is deprived of the right to wear the ecclesiastical garb and in consequence loses his privileges, and, on the other hand, a cleric who is reduced to the lay state, was not evident in the pre-Code law. As a matter of fact the phrase "reduction to the lay state" was not of frequent occurrence in the older law. The law rather referred to the loss or forfeiture of the clerical privileges. Hence in the historical section the legal precedents of the present law will be traced rather in relation to the loss of clerical privileges. Any reference to the loss of clerical privileges in that section, then, is to be understood as synonymous with the reduction to the lay state. The historical section will not treat of the law prior to the time of Gratian's Decree. There is no need of it inasmuch as it is well known that degradation was the only mode of reduction to the lay state before that time.

In the canonical commentary it is not proposed to go into any great detail on the penalty of degradation. This penalty received sufficient consideration in a dissertation written a few years ago. But it is intended to explore as thoroughly as the means of the writer permit the legislation regarding reduction with respect to minor clerics and also that which regards major clerics. Particular attention will be given to canon 214, which is perhaps the most important

ix

canon in the entire section which treats of the reduction of clerics to the lay state. As regards the reduction of major clerics by means of an apostolic rescript, an attempt will be made to glean as much information as possible.

Likewise in this dissertation it is proposed to attempt to draw a clear picture of the meaning of the reduction of clerics to the lay state. Possibly this will better be accomplished by means of an indication of what is not meant by the reduction. Lastly there will be indicated the conditions necessary for the return of the erstwhile cleric to the clerical state. It will be pointed out that there is never a re-ordination of any cleric in the event that the cleric was once validly ordained. It will be indicated that re-ordination is repugnant in the case of minor clerics as well as in that of major clerics. This, then, will be the scope of this dissertation. With the help of Her to whom this work is dedicated it is fondly hoped that the dissertation will in some small way aid in crystallizing the import and meaning of the law by which the Mystical Body of Christ is ruled and through which that same Mystical Body guides souls to eternal salvation.

The writer welcomes this occasion to thank the Congregation of the Most Holy Redeemer, the former Provincial of the Baltimore Province, the Most Rev. William T. McCarty, C.SS.R., D.D., Titular Bishop of Anaea and Military Delegate, and the present Provincial, the Very Rev. Michael A. Gearin, C.SS.R., J.C.D., for the opportunity to pursue a course of graduate studies in canon law. He likewise expresses his gratitude to the Faculty of the School of Canon Law of the Catholic University of America for their kindly, considerate and helpful criticism and for their many kindnesses over the past three years.

PART I

HISTORICAL SYNOPSIS

CHAPTER I

FROM GRATIAN'S DECREE (c. 1140) TO THE COUNCIL OF TRENT (1545-1563)

ARTICLE 1. THE MEANING OF REDUCTION

IN the consideration of the reduction of clerics to the lay state it must always be understood that this reduction is only of an external, canonical or juridical character. By the juridical reduction to the lay state is meant the act which takes away the licit use of the power of Orders, deprives the cleric of his rights, privileges and juridical status, and makes the cleric equivalent to laymen.[1] Since the Sacrament of Holy Orders imprints upon the soul an indelible character, it is not within the power of the Church to effect an internal or absolute reduction. That the Sacrament of Holy Orders imprints this character has been the constant teaching of the infallible Church, and its denial was solemnly anathematized in the Council of Trent.[2]

In that portion of the Catholic Church which uses the Roman Rite there are eight steps or grades in the sacred ministry. The possessor of these various Orders, beginning with the lowest, is called respectively a porter, a reader, an exorcist, an acolyte, a subdeacon, a deacon, a priest, a bishop. The first four of these grades are minor Orders; the others are major Orders.[3]

Holy Orders is only one sacrament; yet there is no repugnance

---

[1] Sipos, *Enchiridion Iuris Canonici* (Pécs: Ex Typographia "Haladas R. T.," 1926), p. 160. (Hereafter cited as *Enchiridion*.)

[2] Sess. XXIII, *de ordine*, c. 4, can. 4.

[3] Canon 949.

1

in its being received in the varying degrees of its fulness. The question among theologians is: Is a portion of the Sacrament of Holy Orders conferred in each of the ordination rites, that is, in the ordination to the minor Orders and the subdiaconate as well as in the ordination to the diaconate and the priesthood? It is an article of faith that the Sacrament is conferred in the priesthood, and all theologians agree that it is conferred in the diaconate. In regard to the subdiaconate and the minor Orders there is disagreement among theologians. Some are of the opinion that only the priesthood and the diaconate are of a sacramental nature, while others include the subdiaconate and the minor Orders as truly sacramental, instituted by our Lord implicitly, inasmuch as they are participations of the diaconate. Since the Sacrament of Holy Orders imprints a character, it follows that if the subdiaconate and the minor Orders are of a sacramental nature they also imprint this character. Furthermore, since the character is an indelible sign which can neither be effaced nor taken away,[4] there could never be an absolute reduction of these clerics to the lay state. However, most of the modern theologians deny the sacramentality of Orders below the diaconate. Consequently they think that the Church has the power to reduce absolutely to the lay state any and all clerics who have not received the diaconate. But in view of the dispute the Church *de facto* never exercises this power.[5]

The dogmatical problem whether the subdiaconate and the minor Orders imprint a character is only indirectly an issue in this treatise of the reduction of clerics to the lay state. So far as this treatise is concerned its only object is to point out that, because of the doubt, the Church did not at any time reduce clerics absolutely to the lay state. If it can be shown that, in the period under discussion, this doubt and uncertainty did exist, then the only logical conclusion can be that in this period the reduction of clerics was only of an external, canonical or juridical character.

In the period as here treated, from Gratian's *Concordia Discor-*

---

[4] Conc. Triden., sess. XXIII, *de ordine*, c. 4, can. 4.
[5] Wernz, *Ius Decretalium* (2. ed., 6 vols., Romae et Prati, 1906-1913), II, n. 230.

dantium Canonum (c. 1140) to the Council of Trent (1545-1563), there was, of course, general agreement that Holy Orders imprinted a sacramental character. Thus, Gratian included in his work an objection of St. Augustine (354-430) to Parmenianus (c. 391), Donatist Bishop of Carthage, in which Augustine stated that it was not allowed to repeat either Baptism or Holy Orders.[6] His reason was that neither sacrament should suffer injury.[7]

In the Gregorian Decretals (1234) a letter of Alexander III (1159-1181) mentioned the injury to the sacrament because of re-baptism.[8] Vincentius Hispanus (thirteenth century), in explaining the injury to the sacrament, showed the incongruity of re-baptism by comparing it to the imposition of one picture or character over another, and so apparently obscuring the first sacrament.[9] Ioannes Andreae (1272-1348) simply said that the reason for not repeating Baptism, Confirmation and Holy Orders was that these three sacraments imprint a character.[10]

These are only a few examples picked at random from the unanimous testimony of the canonists of this period. So far all that has been shown is that Holy Orders was known to imprint a character. However, among the canonists there are indications that they understood this of all the Orders, both major and minor. Hostiensis (Henry of Segusia, +1271), for example, compared the character which was imprinted upon the soul by the constitution of the Church to the physical character or mark imprinted upon the arm of a soldier by the constitution of the Emperor. He stated further that this character was not imprinted upon a monk, in consequence of his entrance into the monastic state, since there was no sacrament present, and hence the Pope could again make the monk a layman.[11]

---

[6] C. 97, C. I, q. 1.

[7] ". . . Neutri sacramento iniuria facienda est. . . ."

[8] C. 2, X, *de apostatis et reiterantibus baptisma*, V, 9.

[9] Glossa on *"iniuria"* of c. 2, X, *de apostatis et reiterantibus baptisma*, V, 9.

[10] *In Quinque Decretalium Libros Novella Commentaria* (4 vols., Venetiis, 1581), Lib. I, tit. 16, *de sacramentis non iterandis*, rubrica n. 8 ante c. 1. (Hereafter cited as *Novella Commentaria*.)

[11] *Summa Aurea* (Venetiis, 1586), Lib. I, *de sacramentis non iterandis*, cap. 3, nn. 6-7.

Ioannes Andreae repeated what Hostiensis said,[12] and then, further in his work, stated that Holy Orders was one of the seven sacraments of the Church and its character was not effaced through marriage. Consequently an acolyte could, after the death of his wife, be promoted to sacred Orders without re-ordination to the minor Orders.[13] Again, Ioannes Monachus (Jean le Moyne, +1313) declared that clerics in sacred Orders, in view of the character they had received, did not lose their privileges if they exercised the ignominious art of buffoonery. But Ioannes Andreae replied that this distinction, which exclusively favored major clerics, was not valid, since the same could be said about minor clerics.[14]

Finally, it is well known that some notable theologians of this period held the opinion that minor Orders imprint a character. Among these were St. Albert the Great (+1280), St. Bonaventure (+1274), St. Thomas Aquinas (+1274) and Duns Scotus (+1308).[15]

In view of this opinion the only possible solution regarding the reduction of clerics to the lay state was the same solution as that which is given today, namely, that the reduction was of a merely external, canonical or juridical character. Just as the Church today, for fear of treading on the domain of divine law, does not employ an absolute reduction, so the Church of the late Middle Ages acted the same and for the same reason. Nowhere is the statement found that the act of reduction was meant to be of an absolute character.

The various legal means of reducing a cleric to the lay state will now be considered. Since deposition and degradation were so closely connected with each other as penalties in this period, it is deemed advisable to treat them together. However, once the distinction between these two penalties became clear, degradation alone, and not deposition, included a reduction to the lay state, as will be shown in the following article.

---

[12] *Novella Commentaria,* Lib. I, tit. 16, *de sacramentis non iterandis,* c. 3.

[13] *Op. cit.,* Lib. III, tit. 3, *de clericis coniugatis,* rubrica ante c. 1.

[14] *In Sextum Librum Novella Commentaria* (Venetiis, 1581), Lib. III, tit. 3, *de vita et honestate clericorum,* c. 1 in VI°. (Hereafter cited as *Novella Commentaria in Lib. VI* to distinguish it from the other work of Ioannes Andreae.)

[15] Tymczak, *Quaestiones Disputatae de Ordine* (Premislia, Polonia, 1936), pp. 124-143.

ARTICLE 2. DEPOSITION AND DEGRADATION

When Gratian compiled his *Decree* there was no definite distinction in law between deposition and degradation. It remained for Lucius III (1181-1185),[16] according to Devoti (1744-1820),[17] or Celestine III (1191-1198),[18] according to Benedict XIV (1740-1758),[19] to indicate a clear-cut distinction. Previously the terms had meant the same as long as the deposition was an entire and not merely a partial deposition.[20]

Included in the *Decree* of Gratian and influencing the legislation on degradation was the expression, *"curiae tradere."* This is found in three Pseudo-Isidorian decretals which Gratian incorporated in his *Decree.*[21] As Lega (1860-1935) pointed out, the true meaning of the phrase *"curiae tradere"* implied a person's incorporation in a civil organization which was held responsible for the execution of public services. These burdens were so abhorrent to the citizens that they were forced, as though in punishment, to undertake them.[22]

However, the canonists at and shortly after the time of Gratian, living in a changed society, were unaware of the true significance of this phrase. Consequently they speculated upon its meaning. Gradually the opinion gained force that with reference to incorrigible clerics it meant that they were to be turned over to the civil courts for punishment. This, of course, postulated a reduction to the lay state, including the loss of the clerical privileges.

Lucius III, in 1184, decreed that clerics guilty of heresy were to be deprived of the prerogatives of Orders and of their office and benefice, and were to be relinquished to the judgment of the secular

---

[16] C. 9, X, *de haereticis*, V, 7.

[17] *Institutionum Canonicarum Libri IV* (3 vols., Romae, 1825), Lib. I, tit. IV, 21, n. 2. (Hereafter cited as *Institutiones.*)

[18] C. 10, X, *de iudiciis*, II, 1.

[19] *De Synodo Dioecesana* (Prati, 1844), Lib. IX, cap. 6, n. 3.

[20] Findlay, *Canonical Norms Governing the Deposition and Degradation of Clerics*, The Catholic University of America Canon Law Studies, n. 130 (Washington, D. C.: The Catholic University of America Press, 1941), pp. 41-66. (Hereafter cited as *Deposition and Degradation of Clerics.*)

[21] Cc. 18, 13, C. XI, q. 1; c. 8, C. III, q. 4.

[22] Lega, *De Delictis et Poenis* (2. ed., Romae, 1910), p. 259, not. 2.

court. Here it will be noted that clerics were not actively handed over, but rather were passively relinquished to the secular court in consequence of the deprivation of their privileges.[23]

Celestine III contributed to the distinction between deposition and degradation when he answered that a deposed cleric, if incorrigible, was to be excommunicated. If his contumacy increased, anathemas were to be used against him. Finally, if he still continued in his evil ways, he was to be seized and punished by the secular power.[24]

Innocent III, in 1201, decreed that clerics who used forged Papal letters were to be deposed, while the forgers themselves were to be degraded and delivered to the judgment of the secular court.[25] Here, finally, was the clear terminological distinction between deposition and degradation, and only the latter carried with it the reduction of the cleric to the lay state. This was further clarified by Innocent in 1209 when he referred to the various interpretations of the phrase *"curiae tradere"* and legalized that which indicated the cleric to be deprived of his clerical privileges.[26]

However, there were still some lingering doubts about the procedure to be followed in degradation. In answer to a question from the Bishop of Béziers, Boniface VIII (1294-1303) described the procedure to be followed. Since it is the reduction of clerics to the lay state, not specifically degradation, that is under consideration here, the question of the procedure need not be treated. What is important, though, is the distinction Boniface made between verbal and actual degradation. According to this distinction, verbal degradation connoted a deposition from Orders or from ecclesiastical dignities, while actual degradation carried with it also the deprivation of all clerical privileges. Actual degradation included the reduction to the lay state.[27]

[23] C. 9, X, *de haereticis*, II, 1.
[24] C. 10, X, *de iudiciis*, II, 1.
[25] C. 7, X, *de crimine falsi*, V, 20.
[26] C. 27, X, *de verborum significatione*, V, 40: " . . . ut clericus, qui propter hoc vel aliud flagitium grave, non solum damnabile, sed damnosum, fuerit degradatus, tanquam exutus privilegio clericali saeculari foro per consequentiam applicetur. . . . "
[27] C. 2, *de poenis*, V, 9, in VI°.

With this distinction between actual and verbal degradation another difficulty arose. How did verbal degradation differ from deposition? To the mind of Ioannes Andreae and of Panormitanus (1386-1453) there was no difference; verbal degradation and deposition were identical. Thus Ioannes Andreae declared false the opinion of Petrus de Samsone (+ after 1260) that a degraded cleric enjoyed certain privileges. He then explained that a certain decretal speaks of one verbally deposed, not of one verbally degraded. This is the decretal of Celestine III mentioned above as indicating the difference between deposition and degradation. It should be noted that Ioannes Andreae used the term "verbally deposed" and not "verbally degraded," but he immediately contrasted it with actual degradation.[28]

Again, in commenting on the difference between verbal and actual degradation, he mentioned the definition of actual degradation as given by Innocent IV (1243-1254), namely, as implying the execution of the sentence of deposition. With this definition he agreed. Later canonists based their distinction between verbal degradation and deposition on the argument that a deposition postulated a further sentence if it was to become the equivalent of a degradation, while a verbal degradation did not require any further sentence.[29] Here it is evident that Ioannes Andreae did not demand any further sentence, since according to his views actual degradation was simply the execution of the sentence of deposition. Panormitanus taught that when one who was deposed was also referred to as degraded, the implied status was to be understood in the sense of a verbal degradation.[30]

Verbal degradation, or deposition, in itself did not constitute a reduction to the lay state. However, if after his deposition the cleric was still incorrigible, he lost the clerical privileges and thereby was

---

[28] *Novella Commentaria*, Lib. II, tit. 1, *de iudiciis*, c. 4, n. 10.

[29] Cf., e.g., Schmalzgrueber, *Ius Ecclesiasticum Universum* (5 vols. in 12, Romae, 1843-1845), Lib. V, tit. 33, n. 138.

[30] *Commentaria in Quinque Libros Decretalium* (5 vols. in 7, Venetiis, 1588), Lib. II, tit. 1, *de iudiciis*, c. 10, n. 38. (Hereafter cited as *Commentaria*.)

reduced to the lay state.[31]   Benedict XIV, in referring to this decretal of Celestine III, understood it as implying a degradation.[32] But Ioannes Andreae and Panormitanus had not interpreted the decretal as pointing to a degradation, at least not to an actual degradation.   They argued from the fact that a cleric who was thrice warned, but without the desired effect, to wear the ecclesiastical garb or to cease bearing arms lost the clerical privileges even though he had not been deposed.   *A fortiori,* then, one who had afterwards been warned and still continued in his evil course should be considered as having forfeited the clerical privileges.[33]   This loss of clerical privileges in turn implied a reduction to the lay state.

Panormitanus furthermore denied the necessity of a declaratory sentence of the cleric's incorrigibility, as Zabarella (1335-1417) had required, and the requisition of an ecclesiastical judge as Hostiensis had thought necessary.   He referred to the decretal on heretics, in accord with which their goods were confiscated only after the declaratory sentence of an ecclesiastical judge, but he thought this sentence not to be necessary if the fact of heresy was of a notorious character. According to his mind the case of the reduction of a cleric to the lay state was of a parallel structure, which called for the same interpretation.[34]   Inasmuch as there was not an actual degradation, the reduction necessarily ensued *ipso facto.*

By way of summary it may be concluded that an actual degradation included a reduction to the lay state.   Verbal degradation, or deposition, did not include this reduction, but if a deposed cleric despite a warning continued in his evil course he *ipso facto* lost the clerical privileges and in consequence of this forfeiture was also reduced to the lay state.   Since this *ipso facto* effected reduction of a cleric to the lay state after his deposition was not at all of a unique character, the following article will explore the canonical doctrine with reference to other cases in which the reduction of clerics ensued *ipso facto.*

[31] C. 10, X, *de iudiciis,* II, 1.

[32] *De Synodo Dioecesana,* Lib. IX, cap. 6, n. 3.

[33] Ioannes Andreae, *Novella Commentaria,* Lib. II, tit. 1, *de iudiciis,* c. 10, n. 11; Panormitanus, *Commentaria,* Lib. II, tit. 1, *de iudiciis,* c. 10, n. 28.

[34] *Commentaria,* Lib. II, tit. 1, *de iudiciis,* c. 10, n. 29.

ARTICLE 3. REDUCTION AS EFFECTED *Ipso Facto*

In the decretals of Gregory IX (1227-1241) there is contained a law enacted by Clement III (1187-1191). It treated of the loss of clerical privileges. The case dealt with clerics who divested themselves of the clerical garb to take up the bearing of arms. The law ordained that if they persisted in this even after a third warning they were not to derive any benefit by reason of their clerical privileges.[35] The glossa of Abbas Antiquus (Bernard of Montmirat, + after 1275) on this decretal stated that if the thrice-warned cleric did not relinquish the bearing of arms he lost all the clerical privileges. Panormitanus pointed out that there was no actual degradation in such a case except that which derived from the law itself.[36]

Innocent III (1198-1216) decreed that no one not observing the decorum of a cleric was to profit by the *privilegium fori* in order to escape judgment from a secular tribunal through the subterfuge of representing himself, when his sins caught up with him, by means of tonsure as a cleric. And if a cleric after properly repeated warnings disdained to amend his life, he was to be without the special immunity which was instituted for the protection of clerics against violent attacks by lay persons.[37]

---

[35] C. 25, X, *de sententia excommunicationis*, V, 39: "In audientia nostra talis fuit ex parte tua proposita consultatio, utrum clerici, qui arma militaria relicto habitu clericali gestare nullatenus erubescunt . . . illa clericorum debeant immunitate gaudere. . . . Ad haec tibi breviter respondemus, quod . . . huiusmodi clerici, si a praelatis suis tertio commoniti, militaria noluerint arma deponere, de privilegio clericorum subsidium aliquod habere non debent."

[36] *Commentaria*, Lib. V, tit. 39, *de sententia excommunicationis*, c. 25, nn. 4-5.

[37] C. 45, X, *de sententia excommunicationis*, V, 39: " . . . Sane, sicut accepimus, . . . in dioecesi tua quidam existunt, qui nec in modo tonsurae, nec in vestimentorum forma, nec in qualitate negotiorum de clerico quicquam ostendunt, ad poenae subterfugium se clericos exhibentes. Quum enim super excessibus, quos saeculari luxu committunt, ad publica iudicia pertrahuntur, circumcisis crinibus, ut possint circumvenire vindictam, se pro clericis repraesentant, clericalis fori privilegium labiis allegantes, qui factis paulo ante negaverant clericatum . . . volumus et mandamus, ut tales, si tertio a te commoniti se ipsos contempserint emendare, illius efficiantur immunitatis extorres, quae pro clericorum tutela et laicorum violentia coercenda dignoscitur instituta."

Honorius III (1216-1227) decreed practically the same in a decretal which he issued to the erstwhile queen of England. Here again the situation was one in which clerics resumed the habit and tonsure to escape punishment. Honorius decided they could not claim immunity.[38] The *glossa ordinaria* in its discussion of this decretal stated that, even though the evil-doers had held a clerical status, that status was in no way evident, and so they *ipso facto* had renounced their clerical privileges. It further declared that there was no occasion for any warning in the case, since it was not known that they were clerics.

Gregory X (1271-1276) in the Second Council of Lyons (1274) declared that bigamists were deprived of all their clerical privileges, and forbidden to wear the tonsure or the clerical habit.[39] In this law there was reference to successive and not to simultaneous bigamy. In the next chapter the interpretation of this law will be discussed at greater length.

Boniface VIII (1294-1303) decreed that clerics who exercised the ignominious art of buffoonery for a year lost their clerical privileges *ipso iure*. They likewise forfeited their privileges even after a shorter span of time if upon a previous threefold warning they did not give evidence of the proper emendation of their lives.[40]

In the Council of Vienne (1311-1312) Clement V (1305-1314) commanded local ordinaries to issue a personal threefold warning to clerics who publicly and in their own persons engaged in the work of a butcher or a tavern-keeper that they abandon such pursuits and not resume them in the future. Those who after such warnings did not discontinue the forbidden practice, or who at any time later resumed it, sustained a loss of their clerical privileges. If the cleric was married the forfeiture of his privileges was complete; if the cleric was unmarried the loss of his privileges became effec-

---

[38] C. 27, X, *de privilegiis*, V, 33.

[39] C. un., *de bigamis*, I, 12, in VI°.

[40] C. un., *de vita et honestate clericorum*, III, 1, in VI°: "Clerici, qui, clericalis ordinis dignitate non modicum detrahentes, se ioculatores seu goliardos faciunt aut bufones, si per annum artem illam ignominosam exercuerint, ipso iure, si autem tempore breviori, et tertio moniti non resipuerint, careant omni privilegio clericali."

tive in his goods and possessions, and likewise in his own person if in addition he continued to go about simply as a layman.[41]

In the light of these decretals it may be stated as a general rule that clerics who laid aside their clerical vesture and donned a secular garb lost their clerical privileges if they persisted after a third warning. It may further be asserted that these three warnings were not necessary if the cleric had lived for a long time as a layman, so that the ecclesiastical authorities could not know that he was a cleric. Finally, as was seen in the previous article, deposed clerics who had been warned after their deposition, but who still continued in their evil course, *ipso facto* lost their clerical privileges and thus by implication were reduced to the lay state.

ARTICLE 4. VOLUNTARY REDUCTION OF MINOR CLERICS TO THE LAY STATE

St. Raymond of Pennafort (1175-1275) proposed the doubt whether a cleric with only first tonsure could desert his clerical status. In his reply to the doubt he adopted the negative view. In this he was in accordance with the discipline of the preceding centuries, as expressly stated in the Council of Chalcedon (451),[42] and re-stated by Gregory IX.[43] However, the *glossa* excepted the case wherein a just cause offered a rightful excuse. This was insinuated in a later decretal under the title *De vita et honestate clericorum.* It was a decree of Innocent III, enacted by him in the IV General Council of the Lateran (1215). In this decree it was stated that at the divine office in the church clerics were not to wear tunics fitted with long sleeves, and even elsewhere priests and dignitaries were not

[41] C. 1, *de vita et honestate clericorum,* III, 1, in Clem.

[42] Canon 7: "We have decreed that those who have once been numbered among the clergy or have chosen the monastic state, shall not enter the military service or accept any secular dignity. Those who dare act thus and do not so repent that they return to the vocation they once chose for God's sake, shall be anathematized."—Schroeder, *Disciplinary Decrees of the General Councils* (St. Louis: Herder, 1937), p. 96. (Hereafter cited as *Disciplinary Decrees.*) The Latin translation of the original Greek text appears in c. 3, C. XX, q. 3, of Gratian's *Decree.*

[43] C. 4, X, *de vita et honestate clericorum,* III, 1: "Si quis ex clericis comam relaxaverit, anathema sit."

to wear them unless some justified fear or apprehension dictated this departure from the usual apparel.[44]

Inasmuch as the case here considered was of a temporary import, arising as it did from the exigencies of circumstances, a reduction to the lay state seems not to have been implied.

Raymond continued his treatise, next taking up the question of an acolyte who entered marriage. He decided that the acolyte was still bound to live as a cleric and to perform his clerical duties. He based his decision on a letter sent by Gregory I (590-604) to St. Augustine (+605) in England.[45]

However, he then agreed with the distinction invoked by Tancred (+1235), Ioannes Teutonicus (+1245) and their followers. These canonists distinguished between the cases wherein the cleric performed an act which was or which was not fundamentally contrary to the clerical state. To marry a widow or to become a soldier was considered as incompatible with the clerical state. Such an act deprived the erstwhile cleric of his clerical privileges and dignities. This conclusion was based on the doctrine of Pope Siricius (384-398) in a letter to Himerius, Bishop of Terragona.[46]

If the act or deed was not fundamentally contrary to the clerical state, as when the cleric used secular clothes or entered marriage with a virgin, he was still bound to live as a cleric. However, there were three exceptions to this rule. His obligation to live as a cleric ceased when the cleric in no way wished to retain the clerical privileges. It likewise terminated when a just cause of fear demanded that he put aside the habit and tonsure. Finally the obligation did not exist if the cleric could not without annoyance to his wife continue to wear the tonsure. Under the last mentioned circumstance the wearing of the tonsure was not to be demanded of the cleric unless he received an ecclesiastical benefice by reason of which that

---

[44] Can. 16—Schroeder, *Disciplinary Decrees,* p. 257; c. 15, X, *de vita et honestate clericorum,* III, 1.

[45] C. 3, D. XXXII: "Si qui vero sunt clerici extra sacros ordines constituti, qui se non possunt continere, sortiri uxores debent. . . ."

[46] C. 5, D. LXXXIV: "Quisquis clericus aut viduam, aut secundam uxorem duxerit, omni ecclesiasticae dignitatis privilegio mox denudetur, laica tantum sibi communione concessa. . . ."

particular obligation existed, as Innocent III wrote to the Bishop of Poitiers.[47]   That a married cleric could at all have a benefice seems strange in view of the letter of Alexander III (1159-1181) to the Bishop of Veroli. In this decretal letter the pope declared that minor clerics who were married were to be deprived of their benefice.[48] However, Ioannes Andreae pointed out that a cleric who had married a virgin could by means of a dispensation obtain a benefice if his wife promised the observance of chastity.[49]

From the testimony of Raymond it is clear that a milder discipline was slowly gaining ground. In certain cases the minor cleric could upon his marriage leave the clerical state and be reduced to the lay state of his own accord. Ioannes Andreae asserted that a married cleric who went about in the garb of secular clothes certainly did not enjoy the clerical privileges.[50] Panormitanus agreed to this doctrine, and declared that no warning was postulated as a necessary condition for the loss of these privileges.[51] Both of these authors cited the decretal of Boniface VIII in confirmation of their teaching.[52]

In regard to unmarried minor clerics, Ioannes Andreae cited Innocent IV (1243-1254) as authority for the claim that a minor cleric did not apostatize when he left the clerical state. Again, still citing Innocent IV, he stated that a minor cleric who went about in secular clothes was not punished for so doing. Although he admitted that Huguccio (+1210), Goffredus de Trano (+1245) and Hostiensis (+1271) disagreed, he thought that the decretal of Clement V in the Council of Vienne supported the contention of Innocent. In

[47] C. 7, X, *de clericis coniugatis*, III, 3.
[48] C. 3, X, *de clericis coniugatis*, III, 3.
[49] *Novella Commentaria*, Lib. III, tit. 3, *de clericis coniugatis*, c. 7, n. 11.
[50] *Op. cit.*, Lib. III, tit. 3, *de clericis coniugatis*, c. 7, n. 19.
[51] *Commentaria*, Lib. III, tit. 3, *de clericis coniugatis*, c. 7.
[52] C. un., *de clericis coniugatis*, III, 2, in VI°: "Clerici, qui cum unicis et virginibus contraxerunt, si tonsuram et vestes deferant clericales, privilegium retineant canonis. . . . Et quum iuxta Parisiense concilium nullus clericus distringi aut condemnari debeat a iudice saeculari: praesenti declaramus edicto, huiusmodi clericos coniugatos pro commissis ab eis excessibus vel delictis trahi non posse criminaliter aut civiliter ad iudicium saeculare. . . . In ceteris autem, vel nisi, ut praemittitur, tonsuram vel vestes deferant clericales, etiam in praemissis eos gaudere nolumus privilegio clericali."

this decretal there was no mention of punishment for non-beneficed minor clerics who went about in the garb of secular clothes, if at the same time they did not wear the tonsure.[53]   Boatinus (Bovettino, +1300), also cited by Ioannes Andreae, declared that a cleric who had only the first tonsure could not by just a word renounce his clerical status without the permission of the bishop, but by an act he could.[54]   The converse seems to postulate that by just a word he could renounce the first tonsure with the permission of the bishop, but the doctrine is not so stated explicitly.

Panormitanus stated that a minor cleric, if unmarried and not a soldier, could not be forced to wear the tonsure. He argued that such a person could still choose the life of a layman by contracting marriage, and thus he could also rightfully entertain the hope of contracting marriage. He correspondingly contended that minor clerics had to wear the clerical garb only if they wanted to enjoy the clerical privileges.[55]

From this testimony it appears clear that a minor cleric, married or unmarried, could leave the clerical state and be reduced to the lay state of his own accord. It remains to ascertain whether a major cleric ever had this same option. This point will be considered in the next article which treats of major clerics ordained through grave fear.

ARTICLE 5. CLERICS ORDAINED TO SACRED ORDERS THROUGH GRAVE FEAR

Regarding the validity of the ordination or the reception of the sacramental character when the passive subject of ordination was under constraint, it had to be determined whether the compulsion was of a conditional or of an absolute nature. As long as it was conditional the ordination was considered to be valid.[56]   When the compulsion was absolute the ordination was regarded as invalid, just as in similar circumstances the conferring of Baptism was held to be invalid.[57]

[53] C. 2, *de vita et honestate clericorum,* III, 1, in Clem.
[54] *Novella Commentaria,* Lib. V, tit. 9, *de apostatis et reiterantibus baptisma,* c. 3, n. 3.
[55] *Commentaria,* Lib. III, tit. 3, *de clericis coniugatis,* c. 7.
[56] C. 7, D. LXXIV; c. 5, D. XLV.
[57] C. 3, X, *de baptismo et eius effectu,* III, 42.

St. Raymond gave consideration to the obligation of continence in a major cleric who was ordained through unjust compulsion if it was not absolute in its nature.[58] In such a case it seemed that the cleric nevertheless was bound by the observance of continence, lest sacred Orders in the Church or even religion itself be brought into disrepute, just as in similar cases those forced to embrace Christianity could not afterwards repudiate the faith.[59] The reason advanced for this position was that in spite of the force which was exercised the subject of this force still acted at the command of his own free will.[60] It was also held by some canonists that the vow of continence was implicitly taken in the reception of Sacred Orders, so that once a man was ordained he was bound by the vow unless he had previously protested his inability to observe continence.[61]

Ioannes Teutonicus, however, thought that no one was bound by this obligation if the exerted force or fear was such that it sufficed to influence even a resolute man.[62] Further, he pointed out that virginity and celibacy existed rather as counsels of perfection than as precepts,[63] and that no one was to be held to the observance of continence if he had not willingly undertaken this obligation.[64]

Raymond, upon granting that a cleric ordained under constraint was not obliged to the observance of continence, then proposed

[58] *Summa* (ed. nova, Veronae, 1744), Lib. III, tit. XXII, *de aetate ordinandorum, etc.*, 8.

[59] C. 5, D. XLV: ". . . Qui autem iampridem ad Christianitatem coacti sunt, . . . quia iam constat eos sacramentis divinis associatos, et baptismi gratiam suscepisse, et crismate unctos esse, et corporis Domini extitisse participes, oportet, ut fidem, quam vi vel necessitate susceperint, tenere cogantur, ne nomen Domini blasphemetur, et fides, quam susceperint, vilis ac contemptibilis, habeatur."

[60] C. 1, C. 15, q. 1.

[61] C. 3, D. LXXXIV; c. 8, D. XXVIII: "Diaconi quicumque ordinantur, si in ipsa ordinatione protestati sunt, dicentes, se velle habere uxores, nec posse se continere, hi, si postea ad nuptias venerint, maneant in ministerio, propterea quod his licentiam dederit episcopus. Quicumque sane tacuerint, et susceperint manus inpositionem professi continentiam, si postea ad nuptias convenerint, a ministerio cessare debent."

[62] C. 1, X, *de his quae vi metusve causa fiunt*, I, 40.

[63] C. 13, C. XXXII, q. 1.

[64] C. 1, D. XXXI; c. 4, C. XX, q. 3.

the question whether such a cleric retained his clerical privileges. To him it seemed that as long as the cleric was willing to live according to the clerical state he likewise retained the clerical privileges. Raymond apparently contemplated simply the duties incumbent upon a minor cleric, for he referred to the letter of Gregory I to Augustine in England. In that letter Gregory dealt simply with minor clerics.[65] Raymond accordingly held that a cleric did not forfeit his clerical privileges unless he performed an act fundamentally contrary to or incompatible with the clerical state.[66]

Proposing still another solution, Raymond contended that a cleric ordained subsequent to his marriage was not bound to the observance of continence. This solution, he added, could be understood as paralleling the solution submitted in the previous question. In other words, a man ordained through grave fear was freed from his obligation of continence only if he had married prior to his ordination. In this case, however, if the wife was willing to observe continence but the man was unwilling, he did not retain his privileges and thus was reduced to the lay state. If the man observed continence in the fullest measure that his marital status allowed, he retained his privileges in spite of the unwillingness of his wife to do the same. It must be emphasized here again that this doctrine contemplated simply the man who lived as a minor cleric. This is evident from the letter of Gregory I to Leo, Bishop of Catania, to which Raymond referred.[67] However, if an unmarried man was ordained to major Orders through grave fear, he was bound to the observance of continence.[68]

[65] C. 3, D. XXXII: "Si qui vero sunt clerici extra sacros ordines constituti, qui se non possunt continere, sortiri uxores debent. . . ."

[66] C. 5, D. LXXXIV.

[67] C. 20, C. XXVII, q. 2: ". . . Hi, qui iam uxoribus fuerant copulati, unum e duobus eligerent, id est, aut certe ministrare nulla ratione praesumerent, aut a suis uxoribus abstinerent. Et, quantum dicitur, Speciosus, tunc subdiaconus, pro hac re ab administrationis se suspendit officio, et usque in obitus sui tempora notarii quidem gessit officium, et a ministerio, quod subdiaconum oportuerat exhibere, cessavit. . . ."

[68] C. 5, D. XLV: ". . . Qui autem iampridem ad Christianitatem coacti sunt . . . oportet, ut fidem, quam vi vel necessitate susceperint, tenere cogantur, ne nomen Domini blasphemetur, et fides, quam susceperunt, vilis ac contemptibilis, habeatur."

Raymond distinguished between the case of a man married previous to his ordination to sacred Orders and a man not married previous to his ordination to sacred Orders. If the man married previous to his ordination was ordained through grave fear he was not obliged to countenance. If the man not married previous to his ordination was ordained through grave fear he was obliged to continence. Hostiensis adopted the same argumentation and arrived at the same conclusion.[69]

Ioannes Andreae, although he cited Vincentius Hispanus and Philip of Aquilliia (both of the early thirteenth century) for the opinion that no cleric who was ordained to major Orders through unjust grave fear was obliged to the observance of continence, nevertheless held with Hostiensis that grave fear did not take away this obligation except for those who had married previous to their ordination.[70] Panormitanus was of the same opinion. It seems that this doctrine constituted the prevailing opinion of the fourteenth century.[71]

In regard to the ratification of the Orders received Hostiensis pointed out that, if the ordained cleric, vested in liturgical dress and free from coercion, solemnly read the epistle even once, he could never rightfully impugn his obligations.[72] Still, even though he ratified his ordination, if his wife did not know of it or was unwilling to lead a life of continence, he could be reduced to the lay state. This conclusion was simply a deduction from the fact that a man who was ordained to major Orders without the knowledge or permission of his wife was bound to return to her.[73]

By way of recapitulation, then, it may be stated that an unmarried cleric, if ordained to major Orders through unjust grave fear,

[69] *Summa Aurea*, Lib. I, *de aetate et qualitate et ordine praeficiendorum*, nn. 4-5.

[70] *Novella Commentaria*, Lib. III, tit. 42, *de baptismo et eius effectu*, c. 3, n. 17.

[71] *Commentaria*, Lib. III, tit. 42, *de baptismo et eius effectu*, c. 3, n. 7.

[72] *Commentaria in V Libros Decretalium* (Venetiis, 1581), Lib. III, tit. 42, *de baptismo et eius effectu*, c. 3, nn. 35-38.

[73] Ioannes Andreae, *Novella Commentaria*, Lib. III, tit. 32, *de conversione coniugatorum*, c. 3, n. 4; Lib. I, tit. 33, *de tempore ordinationum et qualitate ordinandorum*, c. 2, n. 8.

was still bound to the observance of continence. A married cleric thus ordained, but unwilling to practice continence, could return to his wife. There seemed to be implied here a reduction to the lay state. However, the canonists did not indicate how the reduction occurred, nor did they state whose permission it was necessary to obtain before the man could return to his wife. In the event that the man was willing to practice continence, but his wife was unwilling, he could live as a minor cleric and thereby retain his privileges. But if he freely, though only tacitly, ratified his ordination by a single act, he was bound to the observance of continence if his wife knew about his act and did not express unwillingness about it.

ARTICLE 6. RETURN TO THE CLERICAL STATE

Degradation of its very nature was always a perpetual vindictive penalty. As a general rule there was no return to the clerical state. The pope, however, could grant a dispensation which allowed the former cleric to return to his former state.[74] The bishop could dispense clerics who had lost their privileges for exercising the ignominious art of buffoonery and thus allow them to return to the clerical state.[75]

Those who were reduced *ipso facto* because of incorrigibility, for example after deposition, could regain their privileges through penance and reconciliation.[76]

Clerics, married or unmarried, could lose their privileges for not wearing the ecclesiastical garb and the tonsure. But they also could regain them by resuming the ecclesiastical garb and the tonsure.[77]

---

[74] Ioannes Andreae, *Novella Commentaria in Lib. VI*, Lib. V, tit. 9, *de poenis*, c. 2, n. 7.

[75] Ioannes Andreae, *op. cit.*, Lib. III, tit. 1, *de vita et honestate clericorum*, c. 1, n. 2.

[76] Ioannes Andreae, *Novella Commentaria*, Lib. III, tit. 1, *de vita et honestate clericorum*, c. 16, n. 5.

[77] C. 1, *de vita et honestate clericorum*, III, 1, in Clem. In this decretal it is stated that clerics lose their privileges as long as they go about as laymen (*quamdiu praemissis institerint*). Ioannes Andreae drew this conclusion in consequence of this qualifying clause. Cf. *Novella Commentaria*, Lib. III, tit. 3, *de clericis coniugatis*, c. 7, n. 19.

CHAPTER II

FROM THE COUNCIL OF TRENT (1545-1563) TO THE CODE OF CANON LAW (1918)

ARTICLE 1. DEPOSITION AND DEGRADATION

IN the history of Canon Law subsequent to the Council of Trent, the discipline regarding deposition and degradation, as far as reduction to the lay state was concerned, suffered very little change. Degradation still included the reduction of the cleric to the lay state, while deposition did not include this reduction. However, there are two developments of interest.

In the first place, the famous decretal of Celestine III, regarding deposed clerics who were afterwards warned and remained incorrigible,[1] gradually received an interpretation different from that offered by Ioannes Andreae and Panormitanus. The point under discussion was whether a real degradation was postulated before the deposed and incorrigible cleric lost all his privileges and thereby was reduced to the lay state. As was shown previously, Ioannes Andreae and Panormitanus did not think a real degradation necessary. Rather, they held that the fact of incorrigibility after deposition constituted an automatic reduction to the lay state.

After the Council of Trent many canonists still held this opinion. In fact, Carolus de Grassis (fl. 1617) cited Covarruvias (1512-1577) for the statement that almost all who treated the question held this opinion.[2] Barbosa (1589-1649) explained this opinion by stating that there was an assumed degradation, which derived from the law itself.[3] Fagnanus (1598-1678) held that no real degradation was necessary for the forfeiture of the clerical state, though he termed

---

[1] C. 10, X, *de iudiciis*, II, 1.

[2] *Tractatus de Effectibus Clericatus* (Venetiis, 1674), Effectus I, n. 797.

[3] *Collectanea Doctorum tam Veterum quam Recentiorum in Ius Pontificium Universum* (Lugduni, 1716), Lib. II, tit. 1, c. 10, n. 9. (Hereafter cited *Collectanea Doctorum*.)

the opposite opinion more secure.[4]   Reiffenstuel (1642-1703) also held that no real degradation was necessary, though he called attention to the statement of Fagnanus that the more secure opinion was that which demanded a real degradation.[5]

Whatever may be said about the probability of the opinion that no real degradation was necessary to effect a cleric's forfeiture of his status for a century or more after the Council of Trent, it cannot be denied that this opinion gradually lost more and more of the recognition that had formerly been accorded to it by canonical authors. Thus, in the eighteenth century, Van Espen (1648-1728),[6] Schmalzgrueber (1663-1735),[7] Benedict XIV (1740-1758)[8] and apparently Giraldi (1692-1775)[9] interpreted the decretal of Celestine III as postulating a real degradation as a condition for the forfeiture of their clerical status on the part of deposed incorrigible clerics. In the nineteenth century it was by far the more common opinion that a real degradation was necessary under the mentioned circumstances to effect the loss of clerical status.[10]

Consequently, in contrast to the discipline of the Church immediately preceding the Council of Trent, no longer was there an *ipso facto* effected reduction to the lay state for deposed clerics who afterwards remained incorrigible. A real degradation was now required before they could be apprehended by the civil courts in view of their loss of the *privilegium fori*.

The distinction between deposition and verbal degradation developed along similar lines in this period. Boniface VIII had intro-

---

[4] *Commentaria in Quinque Libros Decretalium* (Venetiis, 1697), Lib. II, tit. 1, c. 10, nn. 25-26. (Hereafter cited as *Commentaria*.)

[5] *Ius Canonicum Universum* (Maceratae, 1760), Lib. II, tit. 2, n. 255.

[6] *Ius Ecclesiasticum Universum* (5 vols. in 2, Coloniae Agrippinae, 1729), Pars III, tit. II, n. 46.

[7] *Ius Ecclesiasticum Universum*, Lib. V, tit. 37, n. 151.

[8] *De Synodo Dioecesana*, Lib. IX, cap. 6, n. 3.

[9] *Expositio Iuris Pontificii* (2 vols., Romae, 1769), Pars I, sect. 219.

[10] Santi-Leitner, *Praelectiones Iuris Canonici* (4. ed., 5 vols. in 2, Ratisbonae, 1903-1905), II, n. 32; Soglia, *Institutiones Iuris Publici et Privati Ecclesiastici* (Buscoduci, 1853), Lib. I, cap. 1, 8; Lega, *De Delictis et Poenis*, n. 210; Devoti, *Institutiones*, tit. IV, 21, n. 2; Craisson, *Manuale Totius Iuris Canonici* (6. ed., 4 vols., Pictavii, 1880), n. 6348.

duced into law the distinction between verbal and real degradation.[11] While this distinction was immediately accepted, confusion arose in distinguishing between verbal degradation on the one hand and deposition on the other. As was shown previously, Ioannes Andreae and Panormitanus had considered these two penalties identical. After the Council of Trent many canonists continued to hold this opinion.[12]

On the other hand many authors preserved a real distinction between verbal degradation and deposition,[13] and this opinion eventually prevailed.[14]

According to this distinction, verbal degradation was complemented by real degradation and, in order to proceed from verbal to real degradation, no further sentence was required. Deposition, however, required no further complement. It was a penalty complete in itself and, in order to proceed to real degradation, a new sentence was required. The sentence of deposition did not, of itself, suffice for proceeding to real degradation.

So far as reduction to the lay state was concerned, neither verbal degradation nor deposition included this reduction. Actual or real degradation, however, did carry with it the reduction of the cleric to the lay state.

ARTICLE 2. REDUCTION AS EFFECTED *Ipso Facto*

In the Council of Trent the old discipline which forbade minor clerics to leave the clerical state was not renewed. Nevertheless the

---

[11] C. 2, *de poenis*, V, 9, in VI°.

[12] Barbosa, *Collectanea Doctorum*, Lib. V, tit. 9, c. 2, n. 4, in VI°; Reiffenstuel, *Ius Canonicum Universum*, Lib. V, tit. 39, n. 22; Ferraris, *Prompta Bibliotheca, Canonica, Iuridica, Moralis, Theologica necnon Ascetica, Polemica, Rubricistica, Historica* (8 vols., Parisiis, 1860-1863), v. *Degradatio*, n. 1; Fagnanus, *Commentaria*, Lib. V, tit. 1, c. 6, n. 76.

[13] Schmalzgrueber, *Ius Ecclesiasticum Universum*, Lib. V, tit. 37, n. 138; Benedictus XIV, *De Synodo Dioecesana*, Lib. IX, cap. 6, n. 3; Lega, *De Delictis et Poenis*, n. 207; Santi-Leitner, *Praelectiones Iuris Canonici*, V, 116; Aichner, *Compendium Iuris Ecclesiastici* (6. ed., Brixinae, 1887), p. 748.

[14] Chelodi, *Ius Poenale et Ordo Procedendi in Iudiciis Criminalibus iuxta Codicem Iuris Canonici* (4. ed., recognita et aucta a Vigilio Dalpiaz, Tridenti; Ardesi, 1935), n. 53.

Council did state that the minor Orders constituted the gateway to the higher Orders. The Council likewise decreed that no one should be admitted to the higher Orders if a secure hope and a good promise of sufficient knowledge on his part did not show him to be worthy of major Orders.[15]

Again, the Council declared that no one who had received the first tonsure or who was constituted in minor Orders was to enjoy the privilege of the forum unless he had an ecclesiastical benefice, or, wearing the clerical garb and tonsure, served in some church by order of the bishop, or was in an ecclesiastical seminary or, with the permission of the bishop, in some school or university on the way, as it were, to the reception of major Orders.[16]

The Council was referring only to unmarried minor clerics. It will be noted, too, that the Council spoke disjunctively in relation to the conditions requisite for the enjoyment of the privilege of the forum. Consequently, as long as any one of the conditions was fulfilled, the minor cleric enjoyed this privilege according to the rule of law, "In alternatives . . . it is sufficient that one be fulfilled." [17]

Thus, as long as an unmarried cleric had a benefice he enjoyed the privilege of the forum even though none of the other conditions were fulfilled. Likewise, an unmarried minor cleric without a benefice enjoyed this privilege if he wore the clerical garb and tonsure and fulfilled any one of the three conditions further outlined by the Council. This was the common interpretation of the canonists.

Benefices could be conferred to minor clerics only when they were unmarried. The conferral of a benefice to a married minor cleric, unless a dispensation intervened, was invalid.[18] Furthermore, an unmarried minor cleric who had a benefice lost that benefice *ipso iure* by marrying.[19] Consequently, to retain the privilege of the forum a married cleric had to comply with the conditions outlined

[15] Sess. XXIII, *de ref.*, c. 11; Schroeder, *Canons and Decrees of the Council of Trent* (St. Louis: Herder, 1941), p. 171.

[16] Sess. XXIII, *de ref.*, c. 6; Schroeder, *op. cit.*, p. 168.

[17] Reg. 70, R. J., in VI°: "In alternativis . . . sufficit alterum impleri."

[18] C. 2, X, *de clericis coniugatis*, III, 3.

[19] C. 1, 3, X, *de clericis coniugatis*, III, 3.

by the Council of Trent for married clerics. These conditions will be indicated presently.

The Council of Trent decreed that clerics possessing a benefice who, after an admonition of their bishop, did not wear a clerical dress conformable to their dignity were to be compelled thereto by suspension from their benefices and the fruits of their benefices, and also if, having been once rebuked, they offended again, even by deprivation of their benefices.[20]

Sixtus V (1585-1590) in his Constitution *"Cum Sacrosanctam"* of January 9, 1589, decreed that clerics who did not wear the clerical garb and the tonsure were *ipso facto* deprived of their benefices without any warning, citation, decree or ministry of a judge.[21]

Benedict XIII (1724-1730) in the Constitution *"Apostolicae Ecclesiae"* of May 2, 1725, tempered the Constitution of Sixtus V somewhat when he decided that clerics guilty in this manner were to be deprived of their benefices according to the process of law by means of a declaratory sentence of deprivation.[22]

Gradually, however, a contrary custom arose against the stricter decrees of Sixtus and Benedict, so that in accord with this custom it was sufficient to observe the discipline of the Council of Trent.[23]

Again, it should be noted that once the cleric had lost his benefice he was subject to the conditions laid down by the Council of Trent for minor clerics in the matter of retaining the privilege of the forum. This was true no matter how the cleric lost his benefice. However, once a minor cleric *ipso facto* lost his benefice in accordance with the law of the Constitution *"Cum Sacrosanctam"* of Sixtus V there was required a further declaratory sentence of the fact that he had not worn the clerical garb and the tonsure. The necessity of the declaratory sentence stood confirmed by a decision of the Sacred Congregation of the Council on October 6, 1612.[24] However, as was

---

[20] Sess. XIV, *de ref.*, c. 6; Schroeder, *op. cit.*, p. 110.

[21] *Codicis Iuris Canonici Fontes, cura Emi Petri Card. Gasparri editi* (9 vols., Romae: Typis Polyglottis Vaticanis, 1923-1939; vols. VII, VIII, IX ed. cura et studio Emi Iustiniani Card. Serédi), n. 167. (Hereafter cited as *Fontes.*)

[22] *Fontes*, n. 286.

[23] Wernz, *Ius Decretalium*, II, n. 177, not. 29.

[24] Fagnanus, *Commentaria*, Lib. II, tit. 2, c. 1, n. 25.

already seen, by a contrary custom this Constitution eventually lost its force.

In specifying the conditions requisite for a minor cleric to retain the privilege of the forum the Council of Trent said nothing about the other clerical privileges. Consequently there was speculation as to whether a cleric who did not observe these conditions and thereby lost the privilege of the forum lost also the other clerical privileges.

Some authors were of the opinion that such a cleric lost the privilege of the canon and the other clerical privileges and thereby became reduced to the lay state.[25] They reasoned that the Council of Trent mentioned only the privilege of the forum, since that was the principal privilege, and hence the other privileges were included in it. This opinion was followed also in some decisions of the Sacred Roman Rota.[26]

The majority of the authors, however, held the opposite opinion. They argued that previous to the Council of Trent the guilty cleric had lost no privilege. Consequently, since the Council of Trent mentioned only the privilege of the forum, the other privileges were to be treated according to the discipline preceding the Council. In addition, as an onerous law this particular enactment was to receive a strict interpretation.[27] This opinion had been previously followed in a decision of the Sacred Congregation of the Council,[28] and pre-

[25] Suarez, *Opera Omnia* (ed. nova, a Carolo Berton, 28 vols., Parisiis: Apud Ludovicum Vivès, 1856-1861), Tom. XXIII, p. 548; Engel, *Collegium Universi Iuris Canonici* (ed. nova; post omnes alias recognita et iocupletata; cui nunc primum adjectae sunt annotationes Caspari Bethel, Beneventi, 1760), Lib. III, tit. 1, n. 9; De Luca, *Theatrum Veritatis et Iustitiae* (15 lib. in 5 vols., Venetiis, 1734), Lib. XIV, Annot. ad Sac. Concil. Trid., Disc. XXIV, nn. 33-34.

[26] *Sacrae Romanae Rotae Decisiones Recentiores Nuncupatae* (18 partes, pars 18 in duobus tomis distincta; novissime editae a Ioanne Baptista Campagno Iuris-consulto Romano; Romae, Typis Reverendae Camerae Apostolicae, 1681), Pars 18, Dec. 10, nn. 10-11 (Jan. 16, 1673); Pars 17, Dec. 392, n. 12 (Dec. 12, 1672) et Dec. 304, nn. 19-23 (April 4, 1672).

[27] Reg. 15, R. J., in VI°; Schmalzgrueber, *Ius Ecclesiasticum Universum*, Lib. III, tit. 1, n. 39; Benedictus XIV, *De Synodo Dioecesana*, Lib. XII, cap. 2, n. 2; Reiffenstuel, *Ius Canonicum Universum*, Lib. III, tit. 1, nn. 80-81.

[28] S. C. C., October 16, 1582; cf. Fagnanus, *Commentaria*, Lib. II, tit. 2, n. 75.

vailed until September 20, 1860, when the Sacred Congregation of Ecclesiastical Immunity issued a declaratory letter which decided the question.[29] The prelude to this letter was the case of a certain minor cleric who had not observed the conditions of the Council of Trent for preserving the privilege of the forum, and furthermore had committed two great crimes. Having been apprehended by the civil authorities he was condemned to death, whereupon he appealed to the Church authorities on the ground that he still enjoyed the privilege of the canon. Previously his appeal on the ground of the privilege of the forum had been denied. After great deliberation and not a little hesitation, the consultor who reviewed the case concluded that this cleric still possessed the privilege of the canon.[30]

While this was the law according to the prevalent opinion, the Holy See was unwilling that its application should thus continue. Consequently, on September 20, 1860, a declaratory letter regarding the status of the non-conforming minor clerics was sent to the ordinaries of the Papal States. According to this declaration both married and unmarried minor clerics who did not observe the conditions of the Council of Trent lost the privilege of the forum and *ipso iure* and *ipso facto* were to be considered as deprived of all the clerical privileges and to be treated as lay people even in criminal causes and for penal effects. Furthermore, from then on there was no need of a threefold warning or of any particular declaration that they had incurred this punishment.[31] While this letter was sent only to the ordinaries of the Papal States, it was none the less a declaration of the common law and hence it affected all non-conforming minor clerics.[32]

In regard to married clerics the Council of Trent had stated that the Decretal *"Clerici, qui cum unicis"* of Boniface VIII was to be observed provided that these clerics, having been assigned by the bishop to the service or ministry of some church, served or ministered in that church and wore the clerical garb and tonsure; privilege

---

[29] *Acta Sanctae Sedis* (41 vols., Romae, 1865-1908), III (1867-1868), 433. (Hereafter cited *ASS*.)

[30] *ASS*, III (1867-1868), 444-448.

[31] *ASS*, III (1867-1868), 433.

[32] Wernz, *Ius Decretalium*, II, n. 165, not. 78.

or custom was to avail no one in this matter.[33]   This decretal of
Boniface VIII had described the conditions necessary for the retention of the privilege of the canon as well as the privilege of the
forum.[34]   Consequently, for a married cleric to retain these privileges it was postulated that he have married a single girl who was a
virgin, that he wore the clerical garb and the tonsure, and that he
served in some church by deputation of the bishop.   These conditions all had to be fulfilled concurrently, so that if one condition
was lacking the cleric no longer possessed the clerical privileges.[35]

In 1840 a certain married minor cleric who had discarded the
clerical garb and neglected to wear the tonsure was condemned to
death.   He appealed first to the privilege of the forum, and then,
when that was denied, to the privilege of the canon.   However, the
second appeal was decided in like manner, namely, that he had lost
also the privilege of the canon.[36]

With reference to married minor clerics the pre-Tridentine discipline remained in force, as far as bigamists were concerned.   A clerical bigamist was *ipso facto* deprived of all clerical privileges throughout the entire period here considered.[37]   It should be explained here
that bigamy did not imply that the cleric had two wives at the same
time.   Rather, it implied that the cleric had married a second time
after the death of his first wife, and had consummated this second
union.   If he had not consummated the union he was not a bigamist.

There were certain cases which the canonists classified under

---

[33] Sess. XXIII, *de ref.*, c. 6; Schroeder, *Canons and Decrees of the Council
of Trent*, p. 168.

[34] C. un., *de clericis coniugatis*, III, 2, in VI°: "Clerici, qui cum unicis et
virginibus contraxerunt, si tonsuram et vestes deferant clericales, privilegium
retineant canonis. . . . Et quum iuxta Parisiense concilium nullus clericus
distringi aut condemnari debeat a iudice saeculari: praesenti declaramus edicto,
huiusmodi clericos coniugatos pro commissis ab eis excessibus vel delictis trahi
non posse criminaliter aut civiliter ad iudicium saeculare. . . . In ceteris autem,
vel nisi, ut praemittitur, tonsuram vel vestes deferant clericales, etiam in praemissis eos gaudere nolumus privilegio clericali."

[35] Schmalzgrueber, *Ius Ecclesiasticum Universum*, Lib. III, tit. 3, n. 40;
Reiffenstuel, *Ius Canonicum Universum*, Lib. III, tit. 3, n. 23.

[36] *ASS*, III (1867-1868), 443.

[37] C. un., *de bigamis*, I, 12, in VI°.

interpretative bigamy. These included any case in which the wife of the cleric, either before or after her marriage, had carnal relations with another man. Thus widows also were included. As far as the law was concerned both true and interpretative bigamy was stigmatized so that any minor cleric who even in good faith contracted a marriage with a woman whom he mistakenly thought to be a virgin was *ipso facto* deprived of his clerical privileges and thus beeame reduced to the lay state.[38]

There were other cases of *ipso facto* effected reduction which persisted in law according to the discipline which prevailed before the Council of Trent. It has been previously indicated that a cleric who, upon donning secular dress, took up arms as a soldier and then persisted in this practice even after three warnings *ipso facto* lost the clerical privileges.[39] Likewise a cleric who in secular garb immersed himself in worldly business and then neglected to desist from it even after a third warning lost his privileges, so that he could not hope by resuming the clerical garb to escape punishment for any crime he had in the meantime committed.[40]

According to the interpretation of most of the canonists after the Council of Trent these laws applied only to clerics in minor Orders. Inasmuch as the cleric by wearing a secular dress had already lost the privilege of the forum, since he had neglected to observe all the conditions of the Council of Trent, it is evident that these laws, superfluous in regard to that privilege, applied particularly to the privilege of the canon. As is evident from the wording of the laws, and as all the canonists pointed out, three warnings were required. However, by virtue of the declaration of the Sacred Congregation of Ecclesiastical Immunity on September 20, 1860, these warnings were no longer required and the cleric was *ipso facto* reduced to the lay state.[41]

The discipline preceding the Council of Trent had also inculcated an *ipso facto* effective loss of the privilege of the canon for any

[38]Reiffenstuel, *Ius Canonicum Universum*, Lib. I, tit. 21, nn. 12-27; Schmalzgrueber, *Ius Ecclesiasticum Universum*, Lib. V, tit. 39, n. 218.

[39] C. 25, X, *de sententia excommunicationis*, V, 39.

[40] C. 45, X, *de sententia excommunicationis*, V, 39.

[41] *ASS,* III (1867-1868), 433.

cleric, major or minor, who went about in secular dress and engaged in atrocious or outrageous excesses.[42]   There ensued a discussion among canonists in relation to the number of enormous crimes that was necessary before this law became operative in its full effect. Most of the writers demanded more than one crime, for the law postulated a certain degree of persistent repetition in the evil-doing. Consequently, in the review of the cases leading up to the declaratory letter of the Sacred Congregation of Ecclesiastical Immunity, it was decided that three crimes were necessary, both because a threefold repetition was necessary for constituting a persistent recurrence of acts, and because it was necessary to follow the safer opinion inasmuch as the privilege of the canon was instituted for the benefit of the entire clerical order.[43]

This discipline continued after the Council of Trent. Consequently, since by not wearing the clerical garb the minor cleric had already lost the privilege of the forum, by the further loss of the privilege of the canon he became reduced to the lay state.

Major clerics who went about and engaged in outrageous excesses after three unheeded warnings lost the privilege of the canon and likewise the privilege of the forum. This was the interpretation of Suarez (1548-1617) [44] and Schmalzgrueber (1663-1735),[45] which Wernz (1842-1914), with some hesitation, likewise adopted.[46]

The other laws of the old discipline remained in force throughout the post-Tridentine period. Hence clerics who exercised the ignominious art of buffoonery, under certain conditions, were *ipso facto* reduced to the lay state. This reduction of status or cessation of the clerical privileges applied to both major and minor clerics.[47] Likewise clerics who engaged in the butcher's trade or the tavernkeeper's business were under similarly recounted conditions *ipso facto* reduced to the lay state.[48]   It was the unanimous opinion of

---

[42] C. 14, 23, X, *de sententia excommunicationis*, V, 39.

[43] *ASS,* III (1867-1868), 448.

[44] *Opera Omnia,* Tom. XXIII, p. 546.

[45] *Ius Ecclesiasticum Universum,* Lib. V, tit. 39, n. 218 et Lib. II, tit. 11, n. 90.

[46] *Ius Decretalium,* II, n. 172, V, f.

[47] C. un., *de vita et honestate clericorum,* III, 1, in VI°.

[48] C. 1, *de vita et honestate clericorum,* III, 1, in Clem.

the authors that this law also applied to both major and minor clerics.

Throughout the entire post-Tridentine period a minor cleric was allowed a free departure from the clerical state. It has already been seen that a married minor cleric who did not wear the clerical garb or tonsure, or who failed to fulfill any of the other conditions prescribed by the Council of Trent, was *ipso facto* reduced to the lay state. This reduction of status or cessation of the clerical privileges for a cleric who was married and lived as a layman was not meant as the punishment of an abuse. Rather, it was decreed, as Schmalzgrueber pointed out, for the simple reason that the purpose which was to be served by the privileges had ceased.[49]

The condition of unmarried minor clerics who had no benefice and who did not wear the clerical garb and the tonsure was rather anomalous until the declaration, in 1860, of the Sacred Congregation of Ecclesiastical Immunity. Before that time they could live as laymen and still possess the privilege of the canon as long as they were not deprived of their privileges after three unheeded warnings, administered by the bishop,[50] or as long as they did not contract marriage. This at least was the prevalent opinion. However, with the declaration of September 20, 1860, the continued retention of the clerical privileges no longer had force. Once the cleric had lost the privilege of the forum for the non-observance of the conditions specified by the Council of Trent, he lost also the privilege of the canon, and correspondingly became reduced to the lay state. Nevertheless the cleric did have the option of continuing in the clerical state, being free of course at the same time to effect his return to the lay state in consequence of his non-compliance with the conditions prescribed by the Council of Trent for the maintenance of clerical status. For such a return to the lay state there was no need of any authoritative concession or special indult. Likewise this manner of forfeiting clerical status for lay status did not imply or connote the perpetration of any crime or the presence of any delict.[51]

[49] *Op. cit.*, Lib. V, tit. 33, n. 201.
[50] Benedictus XIV, *De Synodo Dioecesana*, Lib. V, cap. 11, n. 1.
[51] Wernz, *Ius Decretalium*, II, n. 235.

Article 3. Reduction by Dispensation

This article will be concerned only with clerics in major Orders. In the period before the present-day Code of Canon Law minor clerics needed no dispensation to leave the clerical state, as was seen in the previous article.

Clerics in major Orders could be divested of their clerical status and thus return to the lay state only by means of a dispensation of the Holy See.[52] To preserve clarity it is proper to mention again that this change of status implied only an external, canonical reduction from the clerical state; it did not mean that the character of Holy Orders was taken away, for this was impossible, as the Council of Trent declared.[53]

There can be no doubt of the power of the pope to effect a reduction from the clerical to the lay state by means of a dispensation. If by the law of the Church a cleric could be degraded and thus reduced to the lay state, *a fortiori,* the pope as supreme legislator in the Church could for a just cause validly and licitly dispense a cleric and thus reduce him to the lay state.

For clerics the reception of sacred Orders seemed to imply a tacit vow of celibacy. Besides the reception of major Orders gave rise to a diriment impediment to marriage.[54] In relation to major Orders as a diriment impediment to marriage the pope could validly grant a dispensation even apart from the existence of a just cause for so doing. Regarding the vow of celibacy, however, the pope could not dispense from the vow without a just cause.[55] Consequently, if a major cleric had been dispensed by the pope without benefit of a just cause, such a cleric could have contracted a valid marriage, but his marriage would have been contracted illicitly because of the undispensed vow. On the contrary, if a major cleric had been dispensed by the pope for a just cause, he could have contracted a marriage both validly and licitly.

[52] Wernz, *Ius Decretalium,* II, n. 237.

[53] Sess. XXIII, *de ordine,* c. 4, can. 4.

[54] Wernz, *Ius Decretalium,* IV, n. 393; Schmalzgrueber, *Ius Ecclesiasticum Universum,* Lib. III, tit. 3, nn. 29-30.

[55] Schmalzgrueber, *loc. cit.*

History presents some instances in which the pope used this power of dispensing for reducing major clerics to the lay state. That these instances are isolated and that they became actual—at least when there was question of a general indult—only in consequence of the ravages and chaos of war, or of a religious upheaval attended with a calamitous depreciation of moral standards, reveals the abiding reluctance of the Church to depart from her avowed course of insistence on clerical celibacy. For a more complete understanding the review of some cases seems indicated.

In 1801 the Catholic Church in its hierarchy was re-established in France through the aid of a concordat ratified between Pope Pius VII and Napoleon Bonaparte. In the process of this re-establishment the problem of the major clerics who had contracted invalid marriages presented itself. Pius VII, having in mind the eternal welfare of so many souls, settled the question by delegating to his Legate the faculty to dispense major secular clerics, even priests, in order to allow them to contract a marriage which would be valid in the eyes of the Church. However, these clerics were never again to exercise their sacred Orders, they were to be dispossessed of all their ecclesiastical benefices, rights and privileges, and they were thenceforth to be considered as laymen. This dispensation was to be granted only to clerics who had already contracted an invalid marriage. Furthermore, a valid dispensation could be granted only with reference to the woman with whom the cleric had already contracted marriage invalidly. After her death the beneficiary of the dispensation was forbidden to marry again.[56]

It is interesting to note that in the dispensation granted to a certain French priest in 1802 the pope declared that any sin committed by this priest against the sixth commandment was also a sacrilege. Hence this priest, had he resorted to the practice of birth control, for example, would have committed three distinct sins, sins against chastity, justice and religion.[57]

[56] Roskovány, *Coelibatus et Breviarium: duo gravissima clericorum officia e monumentis omnium saeculorum demonstrata* (13 Toms., Toms. I-V, Pestini, 1861; Toms. VI-XIII, Nitriae, 1877-1888), III, Monitiones 1966-1967. (Hereafter cited as *Coelibatus et Breviarium.*)

[57] Roskovány, *op. cit.*, III, Mon. 1969.

This power of dispensing had been used previously by Pope Julius III in 1554. At that time, due to the religious upheaval in England, the conditions were somewhat the same as those later verified after the French Revolution. Julius III granted his Legate the power to dispense major secular clerics who were already invalidly married, but in this instance too the dispensation was granted only with regard to the woman whom the cleric had married invalidly, and there was to be no other marriage after her death.[58]

Regarding the reduction of a bishop to the lay state there was, in 1802, the case of Charles Talleyrand (1754-1838), erstwhile Bishop of Autun in France. This bishop had been one of those clerics in France who, in disobedience to the prohibition of the pope, had taken the solemn oath of allegiance to the "civil constitution of the clergy." Having become repentant he applied for a dispensation, so that he might be reduced to the lay state and thus be allowed to fulfill secular offices in the government of France. This dispensation was granted, but in the dispensation there was no permission for marriage. He was still bound by the law of clerical celibacy.[59]

ARTICLE 4. MAJOR CLERICS ORDAINED THROUGH GRAVE FEAR

Again, in this article there is question only of major clerics. Even though a cleric was ordained to minor Orders through grave fear, he still had the choice either of continuing in the clerical state or of embracing the lay state. Furthermore, the cleric in minor Orders had the freedom to marry, since the obligation of celibacy came only with the subdiaconate.

By grave fear is not understood absolute grave fear as a result of which the will of the one ordained remains set against his ordination, so that the ordination itself would be invalid. It is evident that one so ordained would contract none of the clerical obligations. Rather, there is question of that kind of relatively grave fear which suffices merely to influence the act of even a resolute man. This influence is of such a nature that the will which is beset with it still operates by means of its own decision. The candidate for major

---

[58] Roskovány, *op. cit.*, II, Mon. 1333.
[59] Roskovány, *op. cit.*, III, Mon. 1970.

Orders really intends the reception of Orders, but he feels driven to this intention through grave fear.

Regarding the nature of the effect of grave fear when it was justly brought to bear upon an individual to constrain him to perform an incumbent duty there was no dispute or difference of opinion among the canonists or theologians. For example, if a cleric was the holder of a benefice for the active incumbency of which the law postulated a cleric's ordination to major Orders, the cleric could be constrained to receive the called-for major Orders under threat of being deprived of the beneficial revenues, or even of the benefice itself, if he refused to comply with the demand of the law. If he was ordained under this kind of constraint, the cleric was none the less subject to the obligations which derive from the reception of major Orders. Accordingly the present consideration is concerned with only that kind of grave fear which its victim sustains as a thing of injustice.[60]

It has been seen that during the pre-Tridentine period the majority of the canonists restricted the freedom from celibacy on the part of such clerics as were ordained through grave fear to only those clerics who had already contracted marriage prior to their ordination. The testimony of Hostiensis was somewhat ambiguous, for in his *Summa Aurea*[61] he restricted the application of this freedom to clerics already married prior to their ordination, but in his *Commentaria*[62] he made no such restriction. After considering this conceivable divergency in the canonical doctrine of Hostiensis, the present writer nevertheless inclines to the view that the doctrine of the *Commentaria* is to be understood in the light of the teaching of the *Summa Aurea,* that is, as restricting the application of the freedom from celibacy to those clerics who had contracted marriage prior to their ordination. It was in this same manner that Ioannes Andreae seemed to evaluate and accept the doctrine of Hostiensis.[63]

In the period after the Council of Trent, however, it became the common opinion that any major cleric who had been ordained

[60] Schmalzgrueber, *Ius Ecclesiasticum Universum,* Lib. I, tit. 11, n. 24.

[61] Lib. I, *de aetate et qualitate et ordine praeficiendorum,* nn. 4-5.

[62] Lib. III, tit. 42, *de baptismo et eius effectu,* c. 3, nn. 35-38.

[63] *Novella Commentaria,* Lib. III, tit. 42, *de baptismo et eius effectu,* c. 3, n. 17.

through grave fear was not subject to the obligation of celibacy. It is of interest to note here that Barbosa cited Hostiensis among the others for this opinion.[64]

On January 15, 1575, the Sacred Roman Rota considered the case of a subdeacon who had been ordained through grave fear. It decided that this cleric was bound to the observance of continence unless he had entered marriage prior to his ordination to subdeaconship. Here the opinion of Goffredus of Trani (+1245) and of most of the canonists before the Council of Trent was followed.

However, on March 22, 1575, this case was again brought before the Sacred Roman Rota. This time it was decided that the subdeacon was not obliged to the observance of continence regardless of whether or not he was previously married. The reason adduced for the decision was this: Any act, such as the act of the vow of continence, which postulates not only a will which is not disinclined but also a will which is freely and spontaneously elicited, is not to be held as valid if the will was under serious duress or constraint. This time the Sacred Roman Rota followed the opinion of Ioannes Teutonicus (+1245) and his followers.[65]

With this decision the opinion of the authors who distinguished between absolute grave fear and conditional grave fear was confirmed. When the fear was absolute the ordination was invalid; when the fear was conditional the ordination was valid, but the cleric contracted none of the obligations arising from major Orders.[66]

Nevertheless, as all the authors indicated, the cleric was bound by the obligations arising from major Orders if, after his ordination through grave fear, and at a time when this fear no longer persisted, he ratified his ordination either expressly or tacitly, by word or by deed, for example, by ministering in the order which he had received.[67]

In the period after the Council of Trent, and especially after

[64] *Collectanea Doctorum,* Lib. III, tit. 42, c. 3, n. 18.

[65] Fagnanus, *Commentaria,* Lib. III, tit. 42, c. 3, nn. 103-108.

[66] *ASS,* I (1865-1866), 330, not. 1.

[67] Schmalzgrueber, *Ius Ecclesiasticum Universum,* Lib. I, tit. 11, n. 24; St. Alphonsus, *Theologia Moralis* (ed. L. Gaudé, 4 vols., Romae, 1905-1912), Lib. VI, n. 811.

the above-mentioned decision of the Sacred Roman Rota, practically every author who treated the question held the opinion that a cleric who was ordained to major Orders through unjust grave fear was not obliged to observe celibacy even though the ordination was valid.[68]

While it was admitted by all that the cleric ordained through grave fear, whether that fear was conditional or absolute, did not contract the obligations arising from major Orders, it was also stated by most of the authors that this liberation could be acknowledged for the cleric only in and for the internal forum.[69] To vindicate his liberation in the external forum it was necessary that the cleric establish proof before an ecclesiastical tribunal that he did not contract these obligations. In the case of one who was ordained through absolute grave fear it was necessary for him to establish proof that he did not intend to receive major Orders. In the case of one who was ordained through conditional grave fear it was required of him to prove that, though he intended to receive major Orders, his will was under constraint in his seeming acceptance of the obligations arising from the reception of major Orders.

The legal process was conducted according to the norms outlined by Benedict XIV in his Constitution *"Si datam,"* originally enacted as the mode of procedure which was to be observed by those who impugned the validity of their religious profession on the ground of grave force or fear.[70]

The cases in which a cleric who had been ordained through conditional grave fear was declared free of his obligation of celibacy by the Holy See were very few. In a case of this kind on July 28, 1866, the cleric's advocate diligently searched the records of the Sacred Congregation of the Council for similar cases. He succeeded in finding but two.[71]

[68] Barbosa, *Collectanea Doctorum,* Lib. III, tit. 42, c. 3, n. 18; Fagnanus, *Commentaria,* Lib. III, tit. 42, c. 3, nn. 101-118; Schmalzgrueber, *Ius Ecclesiasticum Universum,* Lib. I, tit. 11, n. 25; Benedictus XIV, *De Synodo Dioecesana,* Lib. XII, cap. 4, n. 2; St. Alphonsus, *Theologia Moralis,* Lib. VI, n. 811; Wernz, *Ius Decretalium,* II, n. 83.

[69] Cf., e. g., Suarez, *Opera Omnia,* XV, p. 799; Wernz, *op. cit.,* II, n. 201, IV.

[70] March 4, 1748—*Fontes,* n. 385; *ASS,* II (1866-1867), 443.

[71] *ASS,* II (1866-1867), 450, not. 2.

As is evident from the nature of such a case it was quite difficult to prove that the cleric, while receiving major Orders, did not take upon himself the obligation of the vow of celibacy. In order to be declared free of this obligation a double conformable sentence, in the tribunal of the bishop and the tribunal of the metropolitan, was necessary.[72]

If the cleric could not prove his case conclusively, either with regard to the presence of grave fear or with regard to the absence of his ratification, it was regularly decided that he was still bound by the obligation of celibacy in the external forum. But there still remained open for such a cleric the possibility of applying for a dispensation from these obligations.[73] This dispensation was sometimes granted, but more frequently it was denied.[74] However, if the cleric did prove his case, then there was no need of asking the Holy See for a dispensation.[75] Once the cleric was declared free in the external forum from the obligations which normally arise with the reception of major Orders, he was reduced to the lay state and thus became free to contract marriage.[76]

ARTICLE 5. CELIBACY AND DIVINE OFFICE

Only major clerics were obliged to observe celibacy. When a major cleric was reduced to the lay state this obligation ordinarily continued. The obligation ceased, of course, for those major clerics who were expressly dispensed.[77]

A major cleric who was ordained through grave fear, whether that fear was absolute or conditional, was not under obligation in

---

[72] Wernz, *Ius Decretalium*, II, n. 201, IV.

[73] Wernz, *loc. cit.*

[74] *ASS,* II (1866-1867), 450-451, not. 1-2.

[75] *ASS,* VI (1871-1872), 90-91; *Decisiones Sacrae Rotae Romanae coram bon: mem: Reverendissimo P. D. Jacobo Emerix eiusdem Sacrae Rotae Decano, ac Sacrae Poenitentiariae Regente in Tres Partes Distinctas* (Romae, 1701), Pars II, dec. 870 (Jan. 10, 1689).

[76] Wernz, *Ius Decretalium,* IV, n. 397.

[77] Roskovány, *Coelibatus et Breviarium,* II, Mon. 1333; III, Mon. 1966-1967.

the internal forum regarding the observance of celibacy.[78] However, he was bound in the external forum until he had received two conformable and favorable decisions from ecclesiastical tribunals, or, in the case of doubtful grave fear, until he was dispensed.[79] But, if clerics were reduced to the lay state through degradation, or if they were *ipso facto* reduced to the lay state, they were still obliged to observe celibacy.[80]

All major clerics and all minor clerics who possessed a benefice were obliged to recite the divine office.[81] This obligation ceased for a minor cleric when he lost his benefice, since it was only by reason of his holding of a benefice that he was obliged to recite the office. Major clerics who were degraded or who were *ipso facto* reduced to the lay state were still obliged to recite the office.[82] But major clerics who were ordained through grave fear, conditional or absolute, were under no obligation in the internal forum. However, they were obliged in the external forum until they received two favorable decisions or until they were dispensed.

---

[78] Suarez, *Opera Omnia,* Tom. XV, p. 799; Wernz, *Ius Decretalium,* II, n. 201, IV.

[79] Wernz, *loc. cit.*; *ASS,* II (1866-1867), 450-451, not. 1-2.

[80] Wernz, *Ius Decretalium,* II, n. 201, V.

[81] Schmalzgrueber, *Ius Ecclesiasticum Universum,* Lib. III, tit. 41, nn. 54-56; Wernz, *op. cit.,* III, n. 563.

[82] Schmalzgrueber, *loc. cit.*

PART II

CANONICAL COMMENTARY

CHAPTER III

THE MEANING OF REDUCTION

In order to understand the true meaning of the reduction of clerics to the lay state it is helpful to recall some preliminary notions which will greatly aid in the clarification of the discussion. To begin with, there are in the Catholic Church, by divine institution, clerics distinct from laymen, although not all clerics are of divine institution.[1] Here there is presented a dogmatic difficulty which, if one prescinds from a decision of the Church, appears to defy solution. Does canon 107 mean that all clerics are by divine institution distinct from laymen, even though the specific grades among the clergy are not all of divine institution? In other words, does the ceremony of first tonsure, a ceremony which all agree was instituted by the Church, distinguish the recipient from laymen by divine institution? Or does this canon mean that there are in the Church some clerics by divine institution distinct from laymen, and other clerics who are not of divine institution and who consequently are not distinct from laymen by divine institution?

Chelodi (1880-1922) seemed to think that all clerics are by divine institution distinct from laymen. He pointed out that whoever receives first tonsure is a cleric, and by the clergy is understood the universal ecclesiastical hierarchy distinct from laymen by divine institution.[2] On the other hand Toso declares that, just as not all

---

[1] Canon 107.—Ex divina institutione sunt in Ecclesia *clerici* a *laicis* distincti, licet non omnes clerici sint divinae institutionis. . . .

[2] *Ius de Personis* (ed. altera a Sac. Ernesto Bertagnolli recognita et aucta, Tridenti: Libr. Edit. Tridentum, 1927), n. 105.

clerics are of divine institution, so also not all are distinct from laymen by divine institution.[3]

Canon 948 declares that Orders distinguish clerics from laymen in the Church for the government of the faithful and the ministry of divine worship, and this from the institution of Christ.[4] According to canon 950 in the law of the Code the words, *ordain, orders, ordination* and *sacred ordination* comprehend besides episcopal consecration the Orders mentioned in canon 949 (the three major and the four minor Orders) and also first tonsure, unless the nature of the case or the context shows that the words are to be taken in a stricter sense. In the interpretation of Chelodi canon 948 would embrace all the Orders mentioned in canon 950 as well as first tonsure.[5]

This interpretation is the only logical interpretation for those who hold that all clerics are distinct from laymen by divine institution. According to canon 948 by divine institution Orders are the efficient cause of the distinction between clerics and laymen. Consequently those who hold this opinion must postulate first tonsure also as an efficient cause. The theologians and canonists who deny that all clerics are distinct from laymen by divine institution must exclude first tonsure as the efficient cause of this distinction; in other words, they must admit that from the nature of the case first tonsure is not included under the word *Orders* in canon 948. Furthermore, any theologian or canonist who does exclude first tonsure from this canon likewise must deny that all clerics are distinct from laymen by divine institution.

Some authors are of the opinion that canon 948 refers only to the Sacrament of Holy Orders, and hence does not include first tonsure.[6] Consequently these authors must deny that clerics in first

[3] *Ad Codicem Iuris Canonici Commentaria Minora* (5 vols. in 2, Romae: Marietti, 1920-1927), II, 59. (Hereafter cited as *Commentaria Minora*.)

[4] Canon 948: Ordo ex Christi institutione clericos a laicis in Ecclesia distinguit ad fidelium regimen et cultus divini ministerium.

[5] Chelodi, *loc. cit.*: In statum clericalem quis ingreditur per sumptionem ordinis (can. 948). Cuius octo sunt gradus: episcopatus . . . ostiariatus; quibus praevia accedit et iuridice accensetur (can. 950) prima tonsura.

[6] Cappello, *Tractatus Canonico-Moralis de Sacramentis* (3 vols. in 5, Romae: Marietti, Vol. II, Pars III [*De Sacra Ordinatione*], 1935), Vol. II, Pars III,

tonsure are by divine institution distinct from laymen. Though they do not treat the question, that can be their only logical solution. Whether or not they include subdeaconship and the minor Orders in this canon depends upon their opinion regarding the sacramentality of these Orders, a question which will shortly be treated.

Finally, Vermeersch (1858-1936) stated that the use of the term *Sacrament of Orders* was deliberately avoided in canon 948.[7] Evidently, then, the Code prefers not to settle this question, since it is primarily a question for the dogmatic theologians.

In the opinion of this writer it is difficult to prove that clerics in first tonsure are distinct from laymen by divine institution. According to the Council of Trent (1545-1563) Christ instituted a sacred hierarchy which consists of bishops, priests and ministers.[8] Prümmer (1866-1931), writing before the Code, called it the more probable opinion that by ministers are also understood those in first tonsure.[9] However, writing after the Code, he declared that, according to some, ministers include those in first tonsure.[10] It seems that it is by far the more common, if not also the certain, opinion today that this term does not comprehend those in first tonsure.[11] Canon

---

n. 3. (Hereafter cited as *De Sacra Ordinatione*.) Noldin-Schmitt, *De Sacramentis* (Oeniponte: Typis et Sumptibus Fel. Rauch, 26 ed., 1940), n. 449; Merkelbach, *Summa Theologiae Moralis ad Mentem D. Thomae et ad Normam Iuris Novi* (3. ed., aucta et emendata, 3 vols., Parisiis: Typis Desclée de Brouwer et Soc., 1938-1939), III, n. 715. (Hereafter cited as *Summa*.)

[7] *Theologia Moralis Principia-Responsa-Concilia,* Vol. III, *De Personis, de Sacramentis, de Legibus Ecclesiae et Censuris* (2. ed., auctior et emendatior, Brugis-Parisiis-Romae, 1927), n. 669.

[8] Sess. XXIII, *de ordine,* canon 6. Cf. canon 108, § 3.

[9] *Manuale Iuris Ecclesiastici* (Friburgi Brisgoviae, 1909), Q. 57.

[10] *Manuale Iuris Canonici in Usum Scholarum* (ed. 4. et 5., Friburgi Brisgoviae, 1927), p. 79. (Hereafter cited as *Manuale*.)

[11] Cf., e. g., Aertnys-Damen, *Theologia Moralis iuxta Doctrinam S. Alfonsi De Ligorio Doct. Ecclesiae* (13. ed., 2 vols., Taurini: Marietti, 1939), II, n. 553. (Hereafter cited as *Theologia Moralis*.) Cappello, *De Sacra Ordinatione*, n. 100; Blat, *Commentarium Textus Codicis Iuris Canonici* (5 vols. in 7, Vol. II, *De Personis,* Romae, 1921), II, n. 40. (Hereafter cited as *De Personis*.) Marc-Gestermann-Raus, *Institutiones Morales Alphonsianae* (19. ed., 2 vols., Lugduni: Emmanuel Vitte, 1933-1934), II, n. 1888. (Hereafter cited as *Institutiones Morales*.)

108, § 3, reiterates the statement of the Council of Trent and further states that other grades are added to the hierarchy by the institution of the Church. In the hierarchy of Orders ecclesiastical institution is understood at least of those in first tonsure. Consequently it seems that clerics in first tonsure are distinct from laymen not by divine but by ecclesiastical institution. It may be alleged by the proponents of the opposite opinion that Christ established two general classes, the clergy and the laity, thereby determining the genus, but allowed the Church to determine further the various species which come under this genus.[12] Nevertheless it appears that no convincing proof has been brought forth for this opinion.

So far as reduction to the lay state is concerned both opinions would admit the possibility of a complete and absolute reduction for those in first tonsure. This is evident in the case of those who hold that there is no divinely instituted distinction between those in first tonsure, on the one hand, and laymen on the other. As regards the other opinion, its defenders would admit that, just as Christ gave the Church the power to include tonsured clerics in the general class of the clergy, He likewise gave the power to exclude or expel these from that general class.

It is an article of divine faith that the Sacrament of Holy Orders imprints upon the soul a character, that is, a certain spiritual and indelible mark. It is also an article of divine faith that this character is imprinted in the reception of the priesthood, and consequently a priest could never again become a layman.[13] Since a bishop is also a priest, it is evident that this applies also to bishops. While it is not an article of divine faith that this character is received in the reception of the diaconate, it is the unanimous opinion of theologians that deacons also receive the character of Holy Orders. Once a man becomes a deacon he can never again become a layman. There is no question about this; all theologians agree on it.

In regard to tonsure also there is no dispute. Tonsure is numbered neither among the major nor among the minor Orders. It is

---

[12] Ojetti (*Commentarium in Codicem Iuris Canonici* [4 vols., Romae: Apud Aedes Universitatis Gregorianae, 1927-1931], II, 214-215) seems to hold this opinion.

[13] Conc. Triden., sess. XXIII, *de ordine*, canon 4.

certain that no character is imprinted in its conferral.   Therefore, just as the Church by virtue of the power received from God can determine that a man become a cleric by first tonsure, she can likewise determine that this man be ejected absolutely from the clerical state and become once again, in the true sense, a layman.   Some of the older canonists [14] thought that tonsure was a minor Order, but this opinion is not tenable today.

Subdiaconate and the minor Orders present a problem about which the theologians have been in disagreement for centuries.   The dispute revolves around the question whether these Orders are truly Sacraments, implicitly instituted by Christ in the institution of Holy Orders and explicitly determined by the Church, or merely sacramentals instituted by the Church in imitation of the Sacrament of Holy Orders.   The Council of Trent did not solve the difficulty, and the Code of Canon Law uses the terminology of the Council of Trent.[15]   Cappello, defending the more common opinion today, namely that these Orders are only sacramentals, declares that to himself and others this opinion appears certain.[16]   Tanquerey (1854-1932), however, held that these Orders are Sacraments.[17]   Prümmer, citing Wernz, preferred to leave the question open as a controverted point.[18]   So far as the reduction of clerics to the lay state is concerned, if these Orders are Sacraments, there can never be an intrinsic theological reduction, that is, the cleric can never become a layman, since he has received the indelible character imprinted in Holy Orders; if these Orders are sacramentals, then the cleric can be absolutely reduced to the lay state, so that he is again a layman.

Canon 211 states unequivocally that sacred ordination, once validly received, is never taken away.   According to canon 950 the term *sacred ordination,* when used in law, is to be understood of all the Orders both major and minor, and also first tonsure, unless the contrary is plain either from the nature of the matter or from the

---

[14] Cf., e. g., Reiffenstuel, *Ius Canonicum Universum,* Lib. I, tit. 11, n. 10-25.

[15] Canon 108, § 3.

[16] *De Sacra Ordinatione,* n. 93.

[17] *Synopsis Theologicae Dogmaticae* (3 vols., Vol. III, 23. ed., quam recognovit J. B. Bord, Parisiis-Tornaci-Romae, 1934), III, n. 1006.

[18] *Manuale,* p. 82, footnote 37.

words in the context. Canon 211 seems to offer no reason why either
the nature of the matter or the words in the context should demand
that first tonsure be excluded.[19] Vermeersch-Creusen seem to limit
the meaning to the sacrament of Orders, but they allege no reason
for the restriction.[20] The canon refers certainly to major clerics,
and, while all grant that bishops, priests and deacons have received
the Sacrament, it is disputed whether the subdiaconate, which is also
a major Order, is a Sacrament. The Code did not intend to solve
this dogmatic difficulty. Consequently it does not appear that sacred
ordination is to be understood in a restricted sense in this canon.
Practically, however, whatever opinion is held does not make much
difference, since Vermeersch-Creusen admit with all that the Church,
as a matter of fact, does not wish to take away even that power
which she alone confers.[21] Therefore, as all agree, the reduction of
clerics to the lay state is not to be understood as an intrinsic, theological reduction, but rather as an external, canonical or juridical
reduction, that is, in the eyes of the law the person in question is considered a layman.

It has been seen in the law prior to the Code that the loss of
clerical privileges, at least in the case of a minor cleric, constituted
a reduction to the lay state. In the Code, however, a cleric may
be deprived, even perpetually, of his clerical privileges, and still not
be reduced to the lay state.[22] Consequently, though every reduction to the lay state includes the loss of the clerical privileges,[23] it
cannot be asserted that the loss of the clerical privileges necessarily
entails a reduction to the lay state.

By a cleric is understood one who has been assigned to or enrolled in the divine ministry at least by first tonsure.[24] A layman is
a member of the Church who has not received any such assignment.

---

[19] Maroto, *Institutiones Iuris Canonici ad Normam Novi Codicis* (2 vols.,
Romae, 1919), I, n. 733. (Hereafter cited as *Institutiones*.)

[20] *Epitome Iuris Canonici* (3. ed., 3 vols., Mechliniae et Romae, 1927-1928),
I, n. 286. (Hereafter cited as *Epitome*.)

[21] *Epitome, loc. cit.*

[22] Cf. canon 2304, §§ 1-2.

[23] Canons 123 and 213.

[24] Canon 108, § 1.

Both clerics and laymen can be religious,[25] and this fact in no way detracts from the fundamental and all-inclusive distinction in the Church between clerics and laymen.

By a state is understood a condition of life arising from a cause which is permanent and not easily changeable.[26] Sacred ordination then, in its widest sense, that is, including first tonsure, is the permanent and not easily changeable cause of the clerical state or condition of life. The fact that a cleric may be reduced to the lay state does not detract from the objective stability of this state.

The most obvious definition of the clerical state is that which points to the state of those who have been assigned to the divine ministry at least through first tonsure. The lay state is the state of those members of the Church who have not been assigned to the divine ministry, not even through first tonsure. It is necessary to emphasize here that by the lay state is not understood the condition of those people who are outside the Church, but that the terms *clerical state* and *lay state* are used in this dissertation only in regard to members of the Church.

With these preliminary notions it is now easier to arrive at a definition of the reduction of clerics to the lay state. Coronata defines the reduction as a perpetual and juridical loss of the licit use of the power of Orders and the forfeiture of the clerical rights and obligations.[27] This definition is not fully satisfactory, for a major cleric ordinarily retains the obligation of celibacy.[28] Vermeersch-Creusen define reduction as the act by which the cleric, having already been forbidden the use of the power of Orders, loses all the rights of the clerical state and is not bound by some or all of his obligations, save the obligation of celibacy in a cleric not forcibly ordained.[29] This definition likewise is not fully satisfactory, since a minor cleric may leave the clerical state without being previously forbidden the use of his power of Orders.[30]

[25] Canon 107.

[26] Wernz, *Ius Decretalium*, III, n. 588.

[27] *Institutiones Iuris Canonici* (5 vols., Vols. I and II, 2. ed., 1939, Taurini: Marietti, 1933-1939), I, 358. (Hereafter cited as *Institutiones.*)

[28] Canon 213, § 2.

[29] *Epitome*, I, n. 286.

[30] Canon 211, § 2.

Sipos defines the juridical reduction to the lay state as the act which takes away the licit use of the power of Orders, deprives the cleric of his rights, privileges and juridical status, and makes the cleric equivalent to a layman.[31] This is a definition which is exclusive. It can refer to no other process of law but the reduction of clerics to the lay state. It is stated that the reduction takes away the *licit* use of the power of Orders. As was seen previously, the Church is powerless to take away the *valid* use of those Orders which are of divine institution. In the Sacrament of Penance, where jurisdiction is required, the Church revokes this jurisdiction and thereby renders the attempted administration of the Sacrament invalid, but in doing this the Church does not touch Holy Orders. The power both of Orders and of jurisdiction is essential for the valid administration of the Sacrament of Penance. The Church revokes an essential element and thereby the administration of the Sacrament is rendered null and void, but so far as the power of Orders alone is concerned the Sacrament would not be administered invalidly.

In certain cases a priest who has been reduced to the lay state is not only allowed but also has an obligation to administer the Sacraments. Such a case could occur if the priest came across a dying person, and that person wished to make a sacramental confession and to receive Holy Viaticum and Extreme Unction. In this case the priest would acquire the jurisdiction for the valid and licit administration of the Sacrament of Penance from the common law.[32] It may be objected that this special provision of the common law weakens the definition of Sipos. However, the definition does cover the ordinary cases; any attempt to cover also all possible extraordinary cases would result in unduly lengthening an already long definition. The exception for extraordinary cases being properly noted, then, the reduction to the lay state will be understood in this dissertation according to the definition of Sipos.

[31] *Enchiridion,* p. 160.
[32] Canon 882.

CHAPTER IV

REDUCTION OF MINOR CLERICS AS EFFECTED
IPSO IURE

ACCORDING to canon 211, § 2, a cleric in minor Orders may return to the lay state in various ways. The first method mentioned points to an operation inherent in the law itself.[1] In other words, once the minor cleric places an act which, according to law, calls for an immediate return to the lay state, he loses the clerical state. The placing of this act is not necessarily a delict, though it can be such, nor is it necessarily a prohibited act, though again it may be such. Since the cleric himself performs the act, the principal cause of the reduction is the will of the cleric. Hence this method of reduction is rather termed a return to the lay state or a fall from the clerical state. Considered as an operation of law it may be regarded as a reduction in which the law itself is the effective agent of it, and so this operation is included under the general title in the Code, *"De reductione clericorum ad statum láicalem."* However, in the canons themselves which speak of this reduction the phrase, "fall from the clerical state," is used. Consequently, in these canons it is evident that the agent is considered rather from the side of the person who places the act. In the three canons which treat of this method of reduction this terminology is consistently used.[2]

ARTICLE 1. REDUCTION BY MARRIAGE OF THE MINOR CLERIC

Canon 132, § 2, refers to clerics in minor Orders who marry. Minor Orders are neither a prohibitive nor a diriment impediment to marriage. Consequently, as the canon points out, minor clerics can indeed marry, but, unless the marriage is null and void because of force or fear inflicted upon them, they *ipso iure*, that is, by a disposition of law, fall from the clerical state.[3]

---

[1] Canon 211, § 2: Clericus minor ad statum laicalem regreditur, non solum ipso facto ob causas in iure descriptas. . . .

[2] Cf. canons 132, § 2; 136, § 3; 141, § 2.

[3] Canon 132, § 2: Clerici minores possunt quidem nuptias inire, sed, nisi matrimonium fuerit nullum vi aut metu eisdem incusso, ipso iure e statu clericali decidunt.

46

Chastity indeed must be observed by all clerics. This observance includes a twofold obligation. The one is negative, to refrain from marriage; the other is positive, to observe the moral law.[4] It is evident that minor clerics are obliged by the positive obligation, an obligation which arises from the natural law. However, they are also bound by the obligation of refraining from marriage. Yet, this is not an absolute obligation. It is conditional, that is, either they abstain from marriage or they fall from the clerical state.[5] This is a departure from the law existing prior to the Code, since in the former law a minor cleric who had married a virgin could still rightfully wear the clerical cassock and tonsure, and at the same time could serve or minister in some church by assignment of the bishop, and thus retain his clerical status.[6]

The second paragraph of canon 132 begins by stating that minor clerics can marry. This refers certainly to the validity of the marriage, for minor Orders are not a diriment impediment to marriage. However, does this mean that they can also licitly marry? Prümmer somewhat restricted the licitness of such a marriage inasmuch as he stated that minor clerics can licitly marry *sometimes*.[7] Chelodi and Cappello make no such restriction. They simply state that minor clerics can validly and licitly marry.[8] Blat and Vermeersch-Creusen hold the same opinion. They point out that there is no prohibition in the canon.[9] Wernz-Vidal maintained that there is no direct prohibition in the canon, but that such clerics are indirectly hindered from marrying insofar as they fall from the clerical state for so acting.[10]

Most of the authors are content with a simple re-statement of the canon. Actually it is difficult to see how the marriage of these minor clerics would inherently be illicit. The canon is clearly worded.

[4] Chelodi, *Ius de Personis*, n. 117.
[5] Chelodi, *loc. cit.*; Cappello, *De Sacra Ordinatione*, n. 578.
[6] Conc. Trident., sess. XXIII, *de ref.*, c. 6.
[7] *Manuale*, p. 92.
[8] Chelodi, *Ius de Personis*, n. 117; Cappello, *De Sacra Ordinatione*, n. 578.
[9] Blat, *De Personis*, n. 69; Vermeersch-Creusen, *Epitome*, I, n. 219.
[10] *Ius Canonicum* (7 vols. in 8, Romae: Apud Aedes Universitatis Gregorianae, 1923-1938), II, n. 110.

There is no hint of illicitness in its statement. Here, of course, the question is considered purely in itself, in complete abstraction from external circumstances which, if present in an individual case, must always be taken into consideration. Thus, in repeated cases there would perhaps be present the danger of scandal; but the giving of scandal must always be avoided according to the precept of the natural law. It is quite likely that this is what Prümmer had in mind when he restricted the licitness of the marriage with his use of the word *sometimes*.

Again, it does not seem that canon 132, § 2, should be understood as granting the minor cleric a choice of means in leaving the clerical state, that is, either by marrying or by means of a declaratory notification sent to the ordinary. The discipline of the seminary at which the cleric is resident demands the observance of the latter method at least as a more fitting means.

Clerics in the seminary are on their way to the reception of sacred Orders. Consequently such a cleric is presumed to have a divine vocation. To act contrary to a presumably present vocation might be sinful, and to decide against it without the advice and consultation of a spiritual director might be imprudent. Finally, granted that the cleric has no vocation, and granted also that he has not imprudently decided this, the question still arises: In what circumstances of time and place did the cleric meet and court the person he is to marry, or, if the marriage as proposed is the result of an impetuous decision, is it reasonable for the cleric to enter upon the state of married life without further and more mature consideration? Evidently, then, some fault or neglect could readily precede the proposed marriage. Nevertheless, in prescinding from circumstances which would render the marriage illicit, one must admit that a cleric in minor Orders can contract a marriage both validly and licitly. The argument of Vidal (1867-1938) has weight only if the cleric wishes to remain in the clerical state. In that supposition he is indirectly hindered from marriage. However, if it be supposed that the cleric is willing to forfeit the clerical state, then he may marry both validly and licitly, as Vidal agrees.[11]

---

[11] *Ius Canonicum*, II, n. 110.

By virtue of canon 592, canon 132 may be applied also to religious minor clerics.[12] However, in the case in which the cleric is a religious it need hardly be remarked that the marriage is illicit because of the vow.

Prümmer was of the opinion that clerics who have benefices are obliged to the observance of celibacy. He based his contention on a comparison of canon 132, § 2, with canon 118.[13] Canon 118 states that only clerics may obtain benefices. However, the cleric is not absolutely obliged to the observance of celibacy, but only by way of condition for preserving his clerical status; through his marriage or also through his attempt at marriage he is regarded by the law as having tacitly renounced his benefice.[14] It may consequently be stated that he is only indirectly hindered from marrying, for it is in the event that he wishes to retain his benefice that he may not marry, just as a minor cleric who wishes to retain the clerical state may not marry. Nevertheless, if he does marry, the marriage is both valid and licit, but he likewise loses his benefice.

The fall from the clerical state as mentioned in canon 132 is in no wise to be considered a penalty. By a penalty is understood the privation of some good, inflicted by legitimate authority, for the correction of the culprit or the punishment of the delict.[15] Here there is question neither of correction nor of punishment, since the cleric has not committed any delict. The reduction to the lay state is rather an administrative measure arising from the present-day policy of the Church to exclude married persons from the clerical state.

Any valid marriage brings about the fall from the clerical state. Again, any marriage though it be null and void for any reason other than that of force or fear inflicted upon the cleric himself, likewise causes this reduction to the lay state. If the marriage is null

[12] Canon 592: Obligationibus communibus clericorum, de quibus in can. 124-142, etiam religiosi omnes tenentur, nisi ex contextu sermonis vel ex rei natura aliud constet.

[13] *Manuale*, p. 92.

[14] Canon 188, 5°; De Meester, *Iuris Canonici et Iuris Canonico-Civilis Compendium* (3 vols. in 4, Brugis, 1921-1928), I, n. 363, footnote 2. (Hereafter cited as *Compendium*.)

[15] Canon 2215.

because of force or fear inflicted upon the woman in the case then the cleric falls from the clerical state. This is quite clear from canon 132 which indicates that the marriage must be null because of force or fear inflicted upon the cleric if he is to escape the fall from the clerical state. Augustine (1872-1943) mentions only a valid marriage as causing this fall from the clerical state.[16] However, the wording of the canon appears to favor the opinion that any marriage or attempt at marriage will cause the forfeiture of the clerical state. The canon explicitly mentions the excepted case, namely a marriage which is null and void because of force or fear inflicted upon the cleric. It seems to follow that a marriage which is null and void for any other reason causes the fall from the clerical state. This interpretation is held by most of the authors.[17] Finally, there is no exception made for ignorance of or inadvertence to the fall from the clerical state, since there is no question of a penalty here.

If the marriage is invalid for several reasons, but among them is present also the force or fear inflicted upon the cleric, then there is no fall from the clerical state. Here the consideration is solely that of canon 132, that is, simply the consideration of marriage as the cause of the fall from the clerical state, but with the exception there noted. It may well be that the attempt at marriage will offer a reason for the reduction of the cleric to the lay state, e. g., if the marriage was attempted before a non-Catholic minister acting as a sacred minister. Still, as long as the marriage is null and void because of force or fear, the cleric does not immediately fall from the clerical state.

The declaration of the nullity of the marriage must be made in accordance with the procedure outlined in the Code.[18] Until this

[16] *A Commentary on the New Code of Canon Law* (8 vols., Vol. II, 5. ed., 1928, St. Louis: Herder), II, 80.

[17] Coronata, *Institutiones*, I, 223; Vermeersch-Creusen, *Epitome*, I, n. 219, 2; Prümmer, *Manuale*, p. 92; Blat, *De Personis*, n. 69; Raus, *Institutiones Canonicae iuxta Novum Codicem Iuris pro Scholis vel ad Usum Privatum synthetice Redactae* (2. ed., Lugduni: Parisiis: Typis Emmanuelis Vitte, 1931), p. 112. (Hereafter cited as *Institutiones Canonicae.*) Ayrinhac, *General Legislation in the New Code of Canon Law* (London-New York-Toronto: Longmans, Green & Co., 1933), p. 278; Wernz-Vidal, *Ius Canonicum*, II, n. 110; Cappello, *De Sacra Ordinatione*, n. 578, and others.

[18] Canons 1960-1989.

declaration of nullity is given, the cleric is to be considered as having fallen from the clerical state, since a marriage is to be presumed valid until the contrary is proved.[19]

If the sentence of the court states that the marriage is not evidently null and void, then the cleric is considered to have lost the clerical state. A difficulty arises when the marriage is declared null for some reason other than force or fear, though at the same time it might have been declared null because of force or fear inflicted upon the cleric. In this case it must be judged that the cleric has fallen from the clerical state. The cleric could afterwards present his case to the legitimate authorities, and leave it to their judgment to re-admit him to the clerical state. It does not seem practical to go through another procedure on the score of force or fear when the marriage has already been declared null, and when the re-admittance to the clerical state will have the same practical effect as the declaration of nullity because of force or fear, namely, that the cleric is again reinstated in the clerical state. If the ordinary decides not to re-admit the cleric, the latter is not to consider himself as unjustly deprived of his status, for the unwillingness of the ordinary seems to indicate his judgment that, in consideration of the dignity of the clerical state, this cleric cannot be promoted to sacred Orders, which judgment is a sufficient reason for the ordinary to reduce any minor cleric to the lay state by means of a decree.[20]

The reason for a minor cleric to fall from the clerical state when he marries or attempts marriage consists, according to Ojetti (1862-1932), in the statement of the law that the will of contracting marriage and the will of remaining in the clerical state cannot co-exist.[21] The will of taking a wife becomes actual when the marriage is celebrated, even when the act of contracting marriage remains inefficacious. But when force or fear is present in such a degree as to render the marriage invalid, then the preponderant will is presumed by law to be the will of remaining in the clerical state.

Ojetti then goes on to point out that it seems strange that an exception is made for a marriage which is null because of force or

---

[19] Canon 1014.
[20] Canon 211, § 2.
[21] *Commentarium*, III, 107.

fear, while no exception is made for a marriage which is null because of substantial error or defect of consent, since the latter two also affect the validity of the contractual consent. However, he declares, though in the case of substantial error a valid consent is excluded, still the will to contract marriage is actually present, even if the person involved in the ceremony be not the partner of the matrimonial contract. Consequently the cleric really fosters a will incompatible with the will of remaining in the clerical state.

In the case of defect of consent the matter stands altogether different. Here there is question of a marriage which is not only null and void, but which does not even exist. And since an act which does not juridically exist affirms nothing, but is a mere negation, the marriage cannot have even the appearance of an act which juridically exists. *A fortiori,* then, from the very nature of the case, a minor cleric who goes through such a ceremony does not fall from the clerical state.

By an act which does not exist is understood an act in which there is lacking some element altogether essential, either by inherent necessity or by legislative demand, for constituting an act as juridically valid. An act which is null and void is an act which juridically exists, but in which there is found some defect which affects the validity. In a contract two things are required for its existence, namely, the consent and the matter or the object of the contract. If one of these is lacking, then the contract in question is not only null and void, but juridically simply does not exist.

In marriage, then, if the couple does not express consent, there is not present and there does not exist any marriage, not even one whose validity is vitiated. On the contrary, if there be found in the consent some defect arising from force or fear, then there is present a marriage which indeed is null and void, but which nevertheless juridically exists and of which the law can take cognizance.

Again, the contract of marriage must encompass the specific object-matter which is properly inherent in the institution of marriage, namely, the mutually possessed right, exercisable between a determinate man and woman, whereby the purpose of human procreation is served through the physical union of their bodies. Thus any attempted contract of marriage between two males, or between two females, is not only a contract which is null and void, but like-wise an act which has no existence whatsoever as a matrimonial con-tract.

Some writers think that a marriage is not merely null and void, but does not even exist, when there is a defect in the substantial form. In the law of the Code, the observance of the substantial form of marriage postulates that the marriage be celebrated before the pastor and witnesses. Hence, so they argue, a marriage which is celebrated before a pastor who has no juridical competence for assisting thereat, that is, one who is without authorization inasmuch, for instance, as he is outside his parochial territory, is a mar-riage which is null and void, while a marriage which is contracted without the presence of a priest is a marriage which does not jurid-ically exist. But to this contention one must reply that a juridical non-existence or nullity which derives not from the inherently defi-cient constitution of the contract itself, but from a positive precept of law, is not contemplated in the assertion of the general principle that laws generally do not recognize acts which have no juridical existence, for the reason that the legislator takes cognizance only of that which exists and not of that which does not exist. Hence the Code often gives consideration to an act which is merely attempted, for example, to a merely civil ceremony of marriage on the part of a cleric in sacred Orders, or of a religious in solemn profession.[22]

This explanation concerning the non-recognition by the law of an act which does not juridically exist is the explanation of Ojetti.[23] Several authors, without attempting such a detailed explanation, apply the same principle to other canons.[24] However, these authors extend the application also to those instances in which the consent is vitiated through grave fear or substantial error. Furthermore, they point out, it does not make any difference on whose part the

[22] Cf. canon 2388.

[23] *Commentarium,* III, 107-108, footnote 11.

[24] In relation to canon 2388 cf. Vermeersch-Creusen, *Epitome,* III, n. 592; Coronata, *Institutiones,* IV, 633; Cappello, *Tractatus Canonico-Moralis de Censuris* (3. ed., Augustae Taurinorum et Romae: Marietti, 1933), n. 355. (Hereafter cited as *De Censuris.*) In relation to canon 188, 5°, cf. Coronata, *Institutiones,* I, 316; Augustine, *A Commentary,* II, 161; with reference to the pre-Code law cf. Wernz, *Ius Decretalium,* II, n. 532, II.

consent is vitiated. An attempt at marriage must be made by two persons. It is impossible for one person to attempt marriage. Hence no matter on whose part the consent is vitiated, there is no attempt at marriage for either of the parties.

Canon 132, on the other hand, seems directly to exclude any extension of the principle enunciated by Ojetti. The canon states that clerics do not fall from the clerical state if the marriage is invalid because of force or grave fear inflicted upon them. Hence it seems implicitly to contemplate a fall from the clerical state if the grave fear is inflicted upon the contemplated partner of the marriage. Since grave fear is excluded in canon 132 as an instance in which the principle of Ojetti may be applied, substantial error is also excluded no matter on whose part this error arises. The reason is that while both grave fear and substantial error vitiate the consent, there is consent there which can be vitiated.

When there is no consent at all, however, the cleric does not fall from the clerical state. In this case there is not even the appearance of a marriage, and there is certainly no attempt at marriage. Furthermore, it does not seem to make any difference on whose part the consent is lacking. The reason is that one person cannot attempt marriage. Consequently, if on either part there is no consent at all— and this would be the case if either party feigned consent—there is no fall from the clerical state.

In this interpretation the force referred to in canon 132 cannot be understood as force in the sense of canon 103, that is, extrinsic force which cannot be resisted. If this force were contemplated by the canon, then the argument of Ojetti would be devoid of any foundation. The reason is that in this instance also consent would be absolutely absent, and not simply vitiated. Force in canon 132 is rather to be taken in the same sense as it is used in canons 1087 and 572. In canon 1087 force is considered as moral coercion, which gives rise to fear in the person upon whom the force is exercised.[25] Similarly, in canon 572 force is rather to be understood as moral coercion. In this canon the far more common opinion, as will be

---

[25] Cf. Vermeersch-Creusen, *Epitome,* II, n. 375; Aertnys-Damen, *Theologia Moralis,* II, n. 821; De Smet, *Tractatus Theologico-Canonicus de Sponsalibus et Matrimonio* (4. ed., Brugis: Beyaert, 1927), p. 468.

shown when canon 2387 is considered, is that the force therein mentioned as invalidating the profession refers only to force exercised upon the candidate for profession, and not also to that exercised on the superior. Nevertheless, no one would deny that if absolute force was brought to bear upon the superior the profession would be invalid. Hence force in canon 572 must be considered as moral coercion.

By way of summary it may be stated that a minor cleric who enters a valid marriage immediately falls from the clerical state. A minor cleric who enters an invalid marriage also immediately falls from the clerical state, unless the marriage is invalid because of force or fear brought to bear on him, or also because of defective consent in either of the seeming contractants, provided that the consent is absolutely absent, and not simply vitiated as in the case of grave fear or substantial error. Finally, it may be well to mention that, even though the cleric in such cases does not immediately fall from the clerical state by reason of canon 132, his manner of acting may well convince the ordinary that this cleric, in view of the dignity of the clerical state, should not be promoted to sacred Orders. This is a sufficient reason for the ordinary to reduce any minor cleric to the lay state by means of a decree.[26]

Article 2. Reduction for Neglecting to Wear the Clerical Dress and Tonsure

The second case of the reduction of minor clerics to the lay state as effected *ipso iure* is mentioned in canon 136, § 3. Clerics in minor Orders who, on their own authority and without a legitimate cause, do not wear the clerical dress and the tonsure and, after being admonished by the local ordinary, do not amend within a month, *ipso iure* fall from the clerical state.[27] In the fifth book of the Code the observance of this prescription is urged.[28]

---

[26] Canon 211, § 2.

[27] Canon 136, § 3: Clerici minores qui propria auctoritate sine legitima causa habitum ecclesiasticum et tonsuram dimiserint, nec, ab Ordinario moniti, sese intra mensem emendaverint, ipso iure e statu clericali decidunt.

[28] Canon 2379: Clerici, contra praescriptum can. 136, habitum ecclesiasticum et tonsuram clericalem non gestantes, graviter moneantur; transacto inutiliter

In order to understand this law it is first necessary to decide the precise obligations of clerics in the wearing of the ecclesiastical dress and the tonsure. Canon 136, § 1, states that all clerics must wear an appropriate ecclesiastical garb in accordance with the legitimate customs of the region and the prescriptions of the local ordinary. They must also wear the clerical tonsure, unless the custom of the country directs otherwise.

In the pre-Code law, Pope Sixtus V (1585-1590), in his Con-stitution *Cum sacrosanctam* of January 9, 1589, had commanded that clerics wear the *talaris,* that is, a clerical garb which extended to the ankles.[29] However, by approved custom the interpretation that the *talaris* be used at least in sacred and public functions prevailed. Outside of these functions a shorter garb was permitted according to the accepted usage in the various regions.[30]

Canon 136 refers only to the dress worn outside of liturgical functions, since there is another canon regulating the vesture to be worn in liturgical functions.[31] The use of the *talaris* outside of liturg-ical functions is not prescribed,[32] but the garb must be of a modest character, appropriate to the clerical state, quite distinct from the dress of laymen, and either black or at least of a dark color.

In the United States the III Plenary Council of Baltimore (1884) legislated regarding the ecclesiastical garb. The clergy were to wear the *talaris* or cassock and the Roman collar at home and in the church, while outside the house they were to wear the Roman collar and a black coat extending to the knees. Furthermore, inasmuch as religious customarily did not wear the community garb or habit outside of their houses, they too were obliged when outside of their houses to conform to the prescribed usage.[33]

---

mense a monitione, quod ad clericos minores attinet, servetur praescriptum eiusdem can. 136, § 3. . . .

[29] *Fontes,* n. 167.

[30] Wernz, *Ius Decretalium,* II, n. 177.

[31] Canon 811, § 1; cf. Coronata, *Institutiones,* I, 227.

[32] Coronata, *loc. cit.*; Cocchi, *Commentarium in Codicem Iuris Canonici ad Usum Scholarum* (5 vols. in 8, Vol. II, *De Personis,* Taurinorum Augustae: Marietti, 1922), II, n. 48. (Hereafter cited as *De Personis.*)

[33] *Acta et Decreta Concilii Plenarii Baltimorensis Tertii* (Baltimorae: Typis Ioannis Murphy Sociorum, 1886), n. 77.

Augustine thought that the obligation of wearing a coat extending to the knees is still binding.[34]   Barrett does not think so.   He points out that the law from the very beginning received a broad interpretation, namely, that the clergy should conform somewhat to the style followed by conservative laymen.   With this interpretation as the basis, there now seems to be a custom against the law.   Again, *epikeia* seems to justify the shorter coat.   The III Plenary Council itself modified the prescription of the II Plenary Council (1866), that is, that the coat extend below the knees.   Hence it may well be conjectured that its intention was that clerics could follow the style of conservative laymen.[35]

The opinion of Barrett appears to be correct.   In 1916 a writer in an American Catholic periodical testified to the "almost universal" custom sanctioning for the clergy the use of the dress of the ordinary civilian, with the sole difference that they wore clothes of a black color.[36]   In regard to this statement it should be noted that in the pre-Code law the more common opinion held that ten years was a sufficient period of time to establish any custom with legal consent.[37] The tacit consent of the legislators seemed to be present from the continued silence of both the Holy See and the bishops collectively regarding this custom.

In line with this opinion, then, the ecclesiastical garb in the United States consists of the cassock and the Roman collar inside the house for secular priests.   Religious are not bound by this law, since they have their own legislation in canon 596.[38]   Outside the house, however, since in this country the custom which was recognized in law in the Baltimore Council was that of not having to wear the cassock or the habit, both secular priests and religious are to

[34] *A Commentary*, II, 84.

[35] *A Comparative Study of the Councils of Baltimore and the Code of Canon Law*, The Catholic University of American Canon Law Studies, n. 83 (Washington, D. C.: The Catholic University of America, 1932), pp. 48-49.

[36] *The Ecclesiastical Review* (originally *The American Ecclesiastical Review*, Philadelphia, Pa., 1889—), LV (1916), 87.

[37] Guilfoyle, *Custom*, The Catholic University of America Canon Law Studies, n. 105 (Washington, D. C.: The Catholic University of America, 1937), p. 62.

[38] Raus, *Institutiones Canonicae*, n. 68.

wear a black suit and the Roman collar. The Council mentioned only priests. Minor clerics are not obliged by the Baltimore Council to wear the Roman collar outside the house. They are to follow the usage of the place and the prescripts of the ordinary. In many places an ordinary collar with a black tie is worn instead of the Roman collar.

Again, attention must be called to a decree of the Sacred Congregation of the Council on July 28, 1931. The decree referred to abuses which were prevalent in certain countries in the matter of wearing the clerical dress, and then provided for the enforcement of ecclesiastical discipline. The Sacred Congregation ordered that all clerics, in addition to the clerical tonsure, wear in public always, even during the summer vacation, a decent ecclesiastical dress, that is, such a dress as the lawful custom and the prescripts of the local ordinary recognize as proper to the clerical order in their own country. Lastly, in order that this decree might be exactly observed by all whom it concerned, the Sacred Congregation called upon the local ordinaries for special diligence and watchfulness. In particular cases those who disobeyed were to be dealt with in accordance with the special provisions enacted in canons 136, § 3, 188, 7°, and 2379 of the Code.[39]

Finally, mention may also be made of the circular letter of the Sacred Congregation of the Council on July 1, 1926. This letter called attention to certain abuses, among which was that of discarding the clerical garb during vacation. However, since the latter was concerned solely with priests, it is not of an equally comprehensive interest with the later decree which concerned clerics in general.[40]

All clerics are bound to wear the clerical tonsure unless the custom of the region rules otherwise. This prescript binds all, even religious, though the religious are to follow their rules and customs regarding the form of the tonsure.[41] In the United States there is a custom which prescinds from the wearing of the tonsure.

[39] *AAS*, XXIII (1931), 336-337; Bouscaren, *The Canon Law Digest* (2 vols., Milwaukee: Bruce, 1934-1943), I, 125.

[40] *AAS*, XVIII (1926), 312-313; Bouscaren, *The Canon Law Digest*, I, 138.

[41] Coronata, *Institutiones*, I, p. 229.

Consequently clerics in this country are not bound by this obligation.[42]

As was seen previously, canon 136, § 3, states that clerics in minor Orders who, on their own authority and without a legitimate cause, do not wear the ecclesiastical garb and the tonsure and, after being admonished by the local ordinary, do not amend within a month, *ipso iure* fall from the clerical state. Before he will incur this fall from the clerical state, then, the cleric must (1) have acted on his own authority; (2) have proceeded in his act without a legitimate cause; (3) have discarded the ecclesiastical garb and the tonsure; (4) have received a previous admonition from the local ordinary; and (5) have not amended within a month. All these circumstances must be verified before the cleric falls from the clerical state. If even only one is left unverified the cleric does not fall from the clerical state.

1. First of all, the cleric must act on his own authority. If he is commanded, advised or permitted by his superior to discard the ecclesiastical dress and the tonsure, he does not fall from the clerical state by complying with the superior's command, advice or permission.[43] Blat regards a cleric as not to be acting on his own authority when he acts on the illegitimate command of civil authority. However, since its command is illegitimate, the civil authority bestows no authority whatsoever on the cleric. Hence he acts not on any authority granted him by another, but simply on his own. This is sufficient, if the other conditions are present, for a cleric to incur the fall from the clerical state.

2. The cleric likewise must act without a legitimate cause. Blat refers to canon 84, § 1, to substantiate the claim that the cause must be a proportionate one. But canon 84 does not have any direct application to the case. Canon 84 has reference to the granting of a dispensation, but in the present case there is no question of such a grant. If a dispensation were granted, then the cleric would be acting on the authority of the one dispensing. The case is rather concerned with an excusing cause. Certainly the cause must be propor-

---

[42] Augustine, *A Commentary*, II, 84-85.

[43] Toso, *Commentaria Minora*, II, 100; Ojetti, *Commentarium*, III, 146; Blat, *De Personis*, p. 96.

tionate to the obligation from which it excuses. This is precisely what the canon postulates in its mention of a legitimate cause. If the cause were not proportionate, it would not be legitimate. If there is question of discarding the clerical dress for any great length of time, for example during a time of persecution, then the avoidance of the danger of death or the escape from serious loss would certainly constitute a legitimate cause.[44] Since the discarding of the clerical dress for a period of five or six days constitutes a relatively lighter matter, it is clear that a less serious cause would be sufficient to excuse the cleric for that length of time from wearing the clerical garb.[45]

3. The cleric must discard the clerical garb *and* the tonsure. If he did not wear the clerical garb but wore the tonsure, or if he neglected to wear the tonsure but wore the ecclesiastical garb, he would not incur the fall from the clerical state. This is evident from the wording of the canon, which clearly demands both, and from the interpretation of the authors.[46] Toso requires that the discarding of the clerical dress and the neglect to wear the tonsure be a public act, since there is no obligation for any cleric to wear them privately.[47] Iorio states that the obligation of wearing the clerical dress is to be understood in relation only to the public or social life, to the performance of the sacred functions and works of the sacred ministry, and to certain associations and dealings with others. He points out that the obligation is not to be urged when the cleric is at home, when he is engaged in manual labor, when he is by himself, or when he is indulging in honorable recreation with a few friends.[48] These opinions appear reasonable, for the purpose of the law is fulfilled simply by its public observance. The discarding of the clerical dress

---

[44] St. Alphonsus, *Theologia Moralis*, Lib. VI, n. 825; Aertnys-Damen, *Theologia Moralis*, I, n. 1105.

[45] Iorio, *Theologia Moralis iuxta Methodum Compendii Ioannis P. Gury, S. I. et Raphaelis Tummolo, S. I.* (6. ed., 3 vols., Neapoli: M. D'Auria, 1938-1939), II, n. 1080. (Hereafter cited as *Theologia Moralis*.) Cf. also Vermeersch-Creusen, *Epitome*, I, n. 221.

[46] Cf., e. g., Blat, *De Personis*, p. 96; Ojetti, *Commentarium*, III, 146; Vermeersch-Creusen, *Epitome*, III, n. 583; Iorio, *Theologia Moralis*, II, n. 1081.

[47] *Commentaria Minora*, II, 100.

[48] *Theologia Moralis*, II, n. 1080.

for a short period of time is a relatively light matter, and hence it seems that a proportionate cause could readily be present in the cited instances.   However, the custom of the place and the particular local statutes must be taken into consideration.   Thus, in the United States, the law of the III Plenary Council of Baltimore (1884) requires that the *talaris* or the cassock be worn at home.[49]

4. To incur the fall from the clerical state, the cleric must have been previously admonished by the local ordinary to resume the wearing of the clerical garb and the tonsure.   This warning must be given in the nature of a canonical admonition, as outlined in the Code.[50] An admonition is the act of a superior calling upon his subject to amend or change something in his behavior which is at least exteriorly reprehensible.[51]   The ordinary should admonish, either personally or through a properly authorized delegate, whoever is in a proximate occasion of committing a delict, or anyone on whom, in view of a previous inquiry, there falls the grave suspicion of an already perpetrated commission of a delict.[52]   In canon 136, which treats of the cleric who has discarded the clerical garb and neglected to wear the tonsure, the Code seems to presume on his part a proximate occasion for the committing of a delict, for it prescribes that an admonition be administered to him.[53]

The admonition may be given either publicly or secretly.[54]   A public admonition is made before a notary or two witnesses, or it may be made by means of a letter, but always in such a manner that from some document it is plain what was contained in the letter and that the letter reached its desired destination.[55]   Even if the admonition be given secretly, the fact of its administration to the cleric must be plainly vouched for in some document which is to

---

[49] *Acta et Decreta*, n. 77.

[50] Coronata, *Institutiones*, IV, 621.

[51] Ayrinhac-Lydon, *Penal Legislation in the New Code of Canon Law* (2. ed., New York: Benziger Brothers, 1936), n. 180.   (Hereafter cited as *Penal Legislation*.)

[52] Canon 2307.

[53] Canon 2379.

[54] Canon 2309, § 1.

[55] Canon 2309, § 2.

be deposited and preserved in the secret archives of the diocesan curia.[56]

In the pre-Code law, before the issuance in 1860 of the declaratory letter of the Sacred Congregation of Ecclesiastical Immunity, the prevalent opinion held that three admonitions had to precede the cleric's ultimate forfeiture of his status. However, this declaratory letter explained that no admonition was required, and that as long as the minor cleric did not observe the conditions enacted by the Council of Trent for the retention of the clerical privileges he was *ipso iure* reduced to the lay state.[57] According to the Code an admonition is indeed necessary, but a single admonition also suffices to lead up to the loss of the clerical state on the part of a cleric who proves recalcitrant.

5. Finally, the cleric must have postponed his amendment beyond a month from the time of the admonition if he is to fall from the clerical state. The duration of the month is to be computed in accordance with the divers rules contained in canon 34, § 3, 1°, 2°, 3°, 4°, in relation to the particular rule pertinent in the case.

Augustine demanded a declaratory sentence for this penalty to ensue.[58] He argued that, because of the public character of the clergy and of the clerical privileges, the public welfare is concerned. Therefore a declaratory sentence must be issued.[59] Other authors, however, do not think a declaratory sentence to be necessary.[60] Actually, although in particular cases the sentence should perhaps be issued, it does not seem that it can be demanded as a general rule. According to canon 6, 3°, insofar as the canons of the Code are in agreement with the previous law they should receive their proper interpretation in the light and understanding of the previous law. In the law prior to the Code there was no need of a declaration that

---

[56] Canon 2309, § 5.

[57] *ASS*, III (1867-1868), 433.

[58] *A Commentary* (8 vols., Vol. VIII, 2. ed., St. Louis: Herder, 1924), VIII, 459.

[59] Canon 2223, § 4: Poenam latae sententiae declarare generatim committitur prudentiae Superioris; sed . . . bono communi ita exigente, sententia declaratoria dari debet.

[60] Coronata, *Institutiones*, IV, 621; Toso, *Commentaria Minora*, II, 100.

the cleric had incurred this penalty.[61]   Consequently, in the law of
the Code there seems to be no compelling reason which demands this
declaration.   But in countries which recognize the privilege of immunity and in which at the same time military conscription is in
force, it seems the part of prudence to declare the penalty and thereby
inform the civil government of the cessation of the privileges formerly enjoyed by the person in question.   However, in other countries the declaration could unnecessarily occasion injury to the
reputation of the erstwhile cleric.   It seems that no general invariable
rule can be invoked.   Circumstances will determine the better method,
and hence it is to be left to the judgment of the superior to decide
when circumstances warrant the declaration.

The reduction of clerics to the lay state as enacted in canon 136,
§ 3, has been referred to as a penalty.   An ecclesiastical penalty implies the privation of some good.   This privation is inflicted by legitimate authority either for the correction of the delinquent or for
the punishment of the delict committed by him.[62]   By a delict is
understood an external and morally imputable violation of a law
to which at least an indeterminate canonical sanction has been added.[63]
According to canon 136, § 1, all clerics are obliged to wear the
ecclesiastical dress and also the tonsure, unless the custom of the
people rules otherwise.   Consequently the minor clerics mentioned
in the third paragraph of this canon commit a delict inasmuch as
they violate a law to which a determined sanction, the reduction to
the lay state, is added.   Furthermore, the reduction to the lay state
implies the privation of the clerical status as inflicted by the law
for the punishment of the delict.   Consequently, this reduction to
the lay state is a penalty.[64]

Granted that the reduction to the lay state is a penalty, what
kind of penalty is it?   Certainly it is not a censure, otherwise once
the cleric receded from his contumacy the ordinary would be obliged
to absolve him and the absolution would mean a reinstatement

[61] S. C. Immunitatis Ecclesiasticae, *Epistola declaratoria circa privilegia
clericorum,* 20 sept. 1860—*ASS,* III (1867-1868), 433.

[62] Canon 2215.

[63] Canon 2195.

[64] Cf. De Meester, *Compendium,* I, n. 370; Coronata, *Institutiones,* IV,
621; Ayrinhac-Lydon, *Penal Legislation,* n. 349; and others.

in the clerical state. From canon 212, § 1, which treats of the return to the clerical state of minor clerics who have been reduced to the lay state, it seems that there is no obligation on the part of the ordinary to allow them to resume their state. Consequently this penalty cannot be a censure. Hence it must be a vindictive penalty.

Though this penalty is not explicitly listed as a separate penalty among the vindictive penalties which can be applied only to clerics, it does not seem that the list as given is meant to be an exhaustive or complete enumeration.[65] Moreover among these penalties degradation is mentioned.[66] According to canon 2305, § 1, degradation entails (1) deposition; (2) the permanent deprivation of the wearing of the ecclesiastical garb; and (3) reduction to the lay state. In accordance with the rule of law *"Plus semper in se continet quod est minus,"* it appears that there is at least an implied mention made of the penalty of reduction to the lay state in canon 2298.[67]

A vindictive penalty is one which is directly intended for the expiation of the delict, so that its relaxation does not depend on the cessation of contumacy on the part of the delinquent.[68] While the remittance of the penalty brings about the return of the delinquent to the clerical state, it seems preferable to postpone all future discussion on this specific point until the return of those who have been reduced to the lay state is specifically considered.

Canon 136, § 3, points to the second instance of reduction to the lay state as effected *ipso iure* in the Code. The present instance differs from the first, which is that of the minor cleric who marries or attempts a marriage, inasmuch as the fall from the clerical state as enacted in canon 136, § 3, is a penalty. In the case of the minor cleric who marries, and thereby falls from the clerical state, his forfeiture is not in the nature of a penalty; rather, it simply connotes the operation of an administrative measure.

ARTICLE 3. REDUCTION FOR VOLUNTEERING FOR MILITARY SERVICE

The third instance of reduction to the lay state as effected *ipso iure* is mentioned in canon 141, § 2. This canon states that clerics

---

[65] Coronata, *Institutiones,* IV, 258; Augustine, *A Commentary,* VIII, 255.
[66] Canon 2298, 12°.
[67] Reg. 35, R. J., in VI°.
[68] Canon 2286.

may not volunteer for military service, unless they do so with the permission of their ordinary in order that they may the sooner become free from the obligation of military service. The second paragraph of this canon declares that a minor cleric who, contrary to the prescript of the first paragraph, freely joins the military *ipso iure* falls from the clerical state.[69] The military here is not to be understood as referring only to soldiers in the service in the army. Rather, it connotes the armed service in any form, so that the naval and marine services are likewise connoted under the term "military."

The only exception the law makes is for those clerics who, with the permission of their ordinary, volunteer in order that thereby they may the sooner be free from their obligation of military service. The case arises in those countries where a period of military service is obligatory for all youths attaining a certain age.

Both the permission of the ordinary and the motive that the cleric may the sooner be free from his military obligation appear to be essential conditions which must be verified in a case if a cleric's enlistment is not to entail automatically his reduction to the lay state. As long as either of these conditions is not present the minor cleric transgresses the prescription and consequently falls from the clerical state. The ordinary has the right to give permission only in order that the cleric may the sooner be free from his obligation of military service. If the ordinary gives permission for some other reason, it appears that the permission thus granted is invalid, but, since the cleric would most likely be acting in good faith, he would not incur the fall from the clerical state.[70] This, of course, prescinds from any particular faculty the ordinary may have received from the Holy See. The permission of the proper ordinary of the cleric is necessary. The permission of another ordinary is not sufficient. Finally, if the cleric volunteers for the purpose of so much the sooner becoming free from his obligation, but does so without the needed permission of his ordinary, he likewise falls from the clerical state.

[69] Canon 141, § 1. Saecularem militiam ne capessant voluntarii, nisi cum sui Ordinarii licentia, ut citius liberi evadant, id fecerint; . . .

§ 2. Clericus minor qui contra praescriptum § 1 sponte sua militiae nomen dederit, ipso iure e statu clericali decidit.

[70] Cf. canon 2218, § 2.

The Church permits clerics to volunteer, despite her explicit vindication of clerical immunity,[71] in order to avoid greater evils.[72] Some functions in the military are less opposed to the clerical dignity than others. Thus, a cleric who can choose to volunteer for the medical or the administrative branch of the military should not offer himself for the ordinary service which entails the bearing of arms. Vermeersch-Creusen think that a cleric who is already enrolled in military service in a medical or an administrative capacity transgresses the canon if he freely and without the permission of his ordinary offers himself for the ordinary service.[73] In advancing their statement these authors seem to embrace the opinion offered by some, namely, that the military service in canon 141, § 2, is to be understood only of that service which entails the bearing of arms. However, it does not seem that the canon is to be considered in such a restricted sense.

The essential characteristic of military service as contemplated in canon 141 seems rather to be the fact that the clerics are taken away from the direct supervision of their superiors and placed under military discipline so that they are considered soldiers in the common estimation.[74] Hence, granted in the case proposed by Vermeersch-Creusen that the cleric transgresses the spirit of the law, it is not clear that he incurs the fall from the clerical state. He does not freely join the military, since he has already been inducted. He does transfer from one branch of the service to another which is less in accord with the clerical state, but it does not seem that the penalty of reduction to the lay state is specified for a transfer, but rather for the initial act of joining the military in any branch. While such an act on the part of the cleric probably offers a sufficient reason for his reduction to the lay state by means of a decree of the

---

[71] Canon 121.

[72] Blat, *De Personis*, p. 104.

[73] *Epitome*, I, n. 223.

[74] Cf. Fanfani, *De Iure Religiosorum ad Normam Codicis Iuris Canonici* (2. ed., Taurini-Romae: Marietti, 1925), pp. 277-278. (Hereafter cited as *De Iure Religiosorum.*) Schäfer, *Compendium de Religiosis ad Normam Codicis Iuris Canonici* (3. ed., Roma: S. A. L. E. R., 1940), pp. 622, 627, 628. (Hereafter cited as *De Religiosis.*) Coronata, *Institutiones*, I, 215.

ordinary, it does not seem that the cleric *ipso iure* forfeits his clerical status.

In the event that the cleric is bound to serve in the medical or administrative branch, the ordinary may still give him permission to join the ordinary service, provided that thereby the cleric may the sooner be free from his military obligation. In such a case it is left to the judgment of the ordinary to determine whether a shorter period of time in the ordinary service would be less detrimental than a longer period in the medical or administrative branch. In the various countries circumstances will probably alter cases; consequently no general rule is indicated.

If the cleric is to be drafted for the ordinary service, but by volunteering he may enter the medical or administrative branch which will require a longer period of service, it does not seem that the ordinary may permit him to volunteer for the latter service. By this is meant that the law does not give the ordinary this specific faculty. Still, in a particular case, after carefully considering the effects of each service on the cleric, and if there is not sufficient time to consult the Holy See, the ordinary could probably indicate to the cleric that in his judgment the use of *epikeia* would provide a safe norm of action. Whether the ordinary can dispense according to canon 81 in a particular case of this kind the writer is not in a position to say, since he does not know if the Holy See is accustomed to dispense in these instances. That is why the use of *epikeia* is indicated as a probably justified means for indicating what particular action is to be taken.

In the United States, a country in which religion has quite generally been held in high respect, clerics are not required to perform military service. Although it appears probable that the future will bring some form of military conscription, there is no reason to think that this country will depart from its traditional practice of exempting clerics. Consequently, any minor cleric in the United States who volunteers for military service *ipso iure* falls from the clerical state.

The fall from the clerical state as enacted in canon 141, § 2, appears to be a penalty. The delict is the external and morally imputable violation of canon 141, § 1, to which a determined sanction is added in canon 141, § 2. The penalty is the deprivation of the clerical state inflicted by the law itself in punishment of the delict. In this canon, as in canon 136, § 3, the penalty appears to be a vindictive penalty. Even upon quitting the military service for which he unlawfully volunteered the cleric has no rightful claim upon being received again into the clerical state. This law concerns religious as well as secular minor clerics, but the law as affecting religious clerics will be considered shortly under a special heading.

On October 25, 1918, the Holy See issued a decree concerning clerics returning from the military service. Certain rules were established in accordance with which the ordinaries were to repair, as well as possible, the damage inflicted upon ecclesiastical discipline by the fact that clerics were constrained to bear arms. The decree required all priests to present themselves to their ordinaries within ten days after their return. Furthermore, they were to bring letters from their military ordinary, or at least from their military chaplain, along with other documents which bore testimony to their life and conduct. When the students of seminaries returned they were to report to their ordinaries exactly in the manner in which provision was made for priests. When the ordinary questioned them in regard to the external or public manner of life they had led while in the service, what they had done and where they had been, they had to reply conscientiously and truthfully. If from the examination and from other sources and documents it appeared that the student had not behaved well while in the service, the bishop, upon previous consultation with the prefects of discipline and the rector, was called on to exclude such a person from re-entering the seminary.[75]

The decree does not expressly state that minor clerics who have been excluded from the seminary should be reduced to the lay state. However, that seems to be the spirit of the decree. Otherwise, despite the fact that the cleric is still in cardinated in his diocese and so *de iure* is not a vagrant cleric, from a practical standpoint such a cleric would differ little from a vagrant cleric.

If it was found that the student had behaved well while in the service, then the bishop, upon previous consultation with the prefects of discipline and the rector, could admit the student to the

---

[75] S. C. Consist., decr. *De clericis a militia redeuntibus,* 25 oct. 1918, n. 10, c)—*AAS,* X (1918), 484. The decree in its entirety is contained on pp. 481-486.

seminary. However, first of all, the student was to be ordered to make a spiritual retreat according to the time, place and manner decided by the bishop. After the spiritual exercises had been completed the bishop at his discretion, and after taking advice as previously mentioned, was to decide whether it was better to admit the student at once with the others, or to keep him apart for a time under special surveillance with those who had returned from military service. Finally, as regarded the ordination, the bishop had to take care not to advance his students, especially to major Orders, before he had duly tested them for some months. This obligation the bishop was called upon to regard as a very grave responsibility for which he was held accountable in conscience.[76]

Regarding the decree *Redeuntibus* the question was raised whether clerics who returned from the military service on "unlimited furlough" were bound to present themselves to their ordinaries in the same way as those who had received an unconditional discharge. The answer was given in the affirmative.[77]

In treating of the decree *Redeuntibus* and of the response to the question about this decree this dissertation has here limited itself only to the parts which concerned minor clerics. Furthermore, in this decree there was no consideration of a cleric's reduction to the lay state as effected *ipso iure*. The reduction of those who returned from military service was to be effected by the ordinary, if he thought it necessary, in a decree issued according to canon 211, § 2, which will be considered later. It was thought a better arrangement to include under the present article the enactments of the decree regarding those who returned from military service in order to confine the discussion concerning secular minor clerics and their military service in the same section.

Canon 141, § 2, points to the third and last instance of reduction of minor clerics as effected *ipso iure*. In the first instance the reduction was considered as connoting simply an administrative measure. In the other two instances the reduction was considered to be in the nature of a vindictive penalty.

---

[76] *Ibid.*, nn. 10 d)-12—*AAS*, X (1918), 484-485.

[77] S. C. Consist., declar. (circa decr. *Redeuntibus*), 21 dec. 1918—*AAS*, XI (1919), 6-7.

CHAPTER V

REDUCTION OF RELIGIOUS MINOR CLERICS AS EFFECTED *IPSO FACTO*

Article 1. Reduction By Dismissal of a Religious in Temporary Vows

Canon 647, § 1, states that the supreme moderator of a religious institute or the abbot of an independent monastery, each with the consent of his respective council, obtained by a secret ballot, may dismiss one who is professed in temporary vows in an Order or in a Congregation of pontifical approval; in a Congregation of diocesan approval the local ordinary may dismiss one who is professed in temporary vows. However, the local ordinary should not use this right apart from the knowledge, or in the face of the just dissent of the moderator.[1]

It is further stated in the law, with insistence on the accompanying serious responsibilities of conscience, that these superiors cannot dismiss a religious unless the causes of his dismissal are of a grave character.[2] These reasons may arise in relation to the religious institute or with reference to the religious himself. The lack of a religious spirit which is a source of scandal to others is a sufficient reason for dismissal if a repeated admonition together with a salutary penance has produced no effect. Poor health is no reason, unless it is known with certainty that it was fraudulently concealed or disguised before profession.[3]

---

[1] The Pontifical Commission for the Interpretation of the Code answered on March 1, 1921, that in the dismissal of those who pronounce vows with the following or a similar condition; "as long as I shall live in the Congregation," canons 646, 647 and 648, which relate to the dismissal of those who have made temporary vows, are to be observed.—*AAS*, XIII (1921), 137; Bouscaren, *The Canon Law Digest*, I, 308-309.

[2] Canon 647, § 2, 1°.

[3] Canon 647, § 2, 2°.

The reasons for dismissal must be known with certainty to the superior who decrees the dismissal, but a formal canonical trial to establish the reasons is not necessary. The religious, however, must be informed of the reasons for the dismissal, and must likewise be given an ample opportunity to answer the charges; his replies to the charges must be truthfully submitted to the superior who has the right of dismissal.[4] The religious has the right of recourse to the Holy See against the decree of dismissal and, pending the recourse, the dismissal has no juridical effects.[5]

A religious minor cleric who is dismissed according to the norm of canon 647 is *ipso facto* reduced to the lay state.[6]

It is not intended here to give any detailed commentary on canon 647. Only insofar as the various parts of this canon influence the reduction of the cleric to the lay state will they be considered. Thus, any neglect of the specifications of this canon which would suffice to invalidate the dismissal would suffice also to suspend any of the effects of the dismissal. Hence an invalid dismissal would not cause the reduction of the religious minor cleric to the lay state.

The first requisite of canon 647 is that the dismissal be effected by the supreme moderator in Orders and in Congregations of pontifical approval, and by the abbot in an independent monastery. If any and all special faculties be prescinded from, then a dismissal decreed by any other superior is invalid.

In canon 653, special provision is made for the case of grave external scandal or of very grave harm threatening the community. In this case the major superior with the consent of his council or, if delay would be dangerous and time does not permit an approach to the major superior, the local superior with the consent of his council and of the local ordinary, may send the religious back to the world with the obligation on his part of immediately discarding the religious habit. However, the case should then without delay be submitted through the local ordinary or the major superior, if he is

---

[4] Canon 647, § 2, 3°.

[5] Canon 647, § 2, 4°.

[6] Canon 648.—Religiosus dimissus ad normam can. 647 ipso facto solvitur ab omnibus votis religiosis . . . ; clericus autem in minoribus ordinibus constitutus eo ipso redactus est in statum laicalem.

available, to the judgment of the Holy See. This provision concerns the dismissal of those who are professed with perpetual vows in a non-exempt clerical religious institute.

A similar provision is made for the dismissal of those who have taken perpetual vows, whether solemn or simple, in a clerical exempt religious institute.[7] But in this latter case a trial, if it has not yet been instituted, is to be immediately begun in accordance with the canons regulating trials for dismissal. Furthermore, canon 668 does not demand that the major superior have the consent of the local ordinary, nor that the local superior have the consent of the local ordinary. According to some authors it seems that this provision, with the necessary changes, can be applied to religious in temporary vows.[8] Hence, under certain conditions, superiors other than those mentioned in canon 647 may send back to the world a religious in temporary vows.

However, in these cases there is not actually a decree or a sentence of dismissal, the decree or sentence being pronounced later. Hence this is not a true juridical dismissal. It is rather the fact of the sending of the religious from the religious institute into the world. Dismissal of the religious in temporary vows is accomplished when the decree is issued. Only then the juridical effects of dismissal are present. The cleric in minor Orders is not reduced to the lay state until there is a true juridical dismissal.[9]

The supreme moderator and the abbot must have the consent of the council obtained by a secret ballot. In accordance with the norm of canon 105 the required consent is demanded for validity. If it is not present the dismissal is invalid, and is devoid of any juridical effects. It does not seem, however, that a secret ballot is required for the validity of the action.[10] In a Congregation of diocesan ap-

---

[7] Canon 668.

[8] Coronata, *Institutiones,* I, 877; Fanfani, *De Iure Religiosorum,* p. 497; O'Neill, *The Dismissal of Religious in Temporary Vows,* The Catholic University of America Canon Law Studies, n. 166 (Washington, D. C., The Catholic University of America Press, 1942), p. 102.

[9] Coronata, *loc. cit.;* O'Neill, *loc. cit.*

[10] Coronata, *Institutiones,* I, 868, footnote 5; O'Neill, *The Dismissal of Religious in Temporary Vows,* p. 94.

proval the ordinary of the place in which the religious house is situated should not, apart from the knowledge or in the face of the just dissent of the moderator, dismiss one who is in temporary vows. Nevertheless, if he did so, the dismissal would be valid and entail all its juridical effects.

Finally, according to the opinion of many authors, this power of dismissal may be delegated. It appears to be an ordinary power, since it is annexed by law to the office.[11]   An ordinary power, however, may be delegated unless the law states the contrary.[12]   But nowhere in the law is there a statement denying this right to grant a delegation on the part of the superiors who are empowered to effect a dismissal.[13]

Superiors have a grave obligation in conscience which stands in the way of their dismissal of a religious unless the causes of the dismissal are of a grave character. Coronata thinks that the formalities of canon 647, with the exception of the decisive vote of the council, are not required for validity.[14]   Schäfer, however, maintains that a grave cause is required for validity.[15]   Practically, whatever opinion is held does not seem to make much difference. Unless the cleric has recourse to the Holy See, the dismissal must be considered as valid, and the minor cleric as reduced to the lay state. If the cleric does have recourse, the dismissal, pending the recourse, has no juridical effect.

In the opinion of Schäfer, if the cause is not grave, the dismissal will be declared invalid, and the minor cleric will not have been reduced to the lay state. In the opinion of Coronata, if the cause is not grave, the dismissal is not invalid, but may nevertheless be rescinded. He thinks that the Holy See will rescind the dismissal. In that event the cleric will of course not be reduced to the lay state.

---

[11] Canon 197, § 1.

[12] Canon 199, § 1.

[13] Cf. Coronata, *Institutiones,* I, 869; Tabera, "De dimissione religiosorum" —*Commentarium pro Religiosis* (Romae, 1920—), XII (1931), 148. (Hereafter cited as *CpR.*)

[14] *Institutiones,* I, 869.

[15] *De Religiosis,* p. 989.

Finally, it should be pointed out that it is difficult to determine the sufficiency of a cause. In 1873 the Holy See answered that it should not be asked what constitutes a just and reasonable cause in this matter, since that was a question left to the judgment and conscience of the superiors.[16] In the present legislation also it seems that judgment regarding the sufficiency of a cause is left in great part to the judicious discretion and conscience of the superiors.

The dismissal according to the norm of canon 647 effects the reduction of the minor cleric to the lay state.[17] While canon 648 mentions clerics who are in minor Orders, it seems to comprehend also those clerics who have received only the first tonsure, for the term "minor Orders" is evidently employed in contradistinction to the term "major Orders" as used in the first part of the canon, and not with a view to excluding those who have received only the first tonsure.[18]

It will be noticed that canon 648 refers to religious who have been dismissed *"ad normam can. 647."* Does this mean that minor clerics who have been dismissed according to the norm of canon 646 are not contemplated in canon 648? If it does, then minor clerics who have been dismissed in accordance with the rule of canon 646 are neither released from their vows nor reduced to the lay state. Several authors maintain that minor clerics in temporary vows who have been dismissed in accordance with the norm of canon 646 are released from their vows and reduced to the lay state in consequence of the ruling of canon 648.[19] Yet it hardly seems that they offer any sufficiently compelling reason for their conclusion.

---

[16] S. C. Ep. et Reg., resp. 15 sept. 1873. This response is found embodied in another response of the same Congregation given on May 13, 1904.—*Fontes,* n. 2048.

[17] Canon 648.

[18] Blat, *Ius de Religiosis et Laicis iuxta Codicis Ordinem* (3. ed., Romae: Apud Angelicum, 1938), n. 668. (Hereafter cited as *De Religiosis*.)

[19] Vermeersch-Creusen, *Epitome,* I, n. 762; Pejška, *Ius Canonicum Religiosorum* (3. ed., Friburgi Brisgoviae: Herder, 1927), p. 191; Creusen-Garesché-Ellis, *Religious Men and Women in the Code* (3. English ed., Milwaukee: Bruce, 1940), p. 269; Coronata, *Institutiones,* I, 871; Fanfani, *De Iure Religiosorum,* pp. 514-515; O'Neill, *The Dismissal of Religious in Temporary Vows,* p. 126.

The present writer, not without some hesitation, thinks that religious minor clerics who have been dismissed according to the norm of canon 646 are neither released from their vows nor reduced to the lay state in consequence of their dismissal. The reason for this assertion derives from the insertion in canon 648 of the phrase *"ad normam can. 647."* It seems difficult, if not also impossible, to bring forward a reason for the insertion of this phrase if the minor clerics who have been dismissed in accordance with the ruling of canon 646 are also contemplated in canon 648.

An objection to the opinion as here maintained by the writer may arise from the answer of the Sacred Congregation of Religious on March 1, 1921. As was previously seen, the question concerning religious who had pronounced vows with the following or a similar condition: "as long as I shall live in the Congregation," was whether the dismissal of such religious was to be governed according to canons 647-648, as relating to the dismissal of those who are in temporary vows, or by canon 649 and the following canons, as relating to the dismissal of those who are in perpetual vows. The Sacred Congregation answered that in regard to those who have already made vows under the aforesaid condition, canons 646, 647 and 648 should be observed.

In the answer, then, canon 646 did receive mention, whereas in the question it did not. It may be argued that canon 646 was mentioned in order to point out that the effects of dismissal as enumerated in canon 648 were to be extended to those also who were dismissed in accordance with the ruling of canon 646. However, this objection may be countered by the contention that canon 646 was mentioned simply in order to comprehend every method of the dismissal of such religious. It does not follow necessarily that inasmuch as canon 646 was mentioned the effects of canon 648 must be applied to those who were dismissed for the reasons listed in canon 646. The Sacred Congregation mentioned canon 646 to integrate the comprehensiveness of its answer. But it left canon 648 to be applied according to the wording of the canon, that is, to those who have been dismissed *"ad normam can. 647."* Hence those who have been dismissed for the reasons which are listed in canon 646 are not by that very fact reduced to the lay state.

According to canon 648 the dismissal which has been effected by the method indicated in canon 647 entails the reduction of the religious minor cleric to the lay state. At first sight canon 648 appears to present no difficulty. It appears to state clearly that any religious minor cleric by the very fact of his dismissal is reduced to the lay state. Some of the authors, however, employ a distinction.[20]

According to this distinction the reduction to the lay state is specified only for those religious who received minor Orders in the religious institute. If a secular minor cleric becomes a religious and is later dismissed from the institute while he is still in temporary vows, these authors claim that he is not by the fact of his dismissal reduced to the lay state. They argue that a cleric is by law affiliated either with a religious institute or with a diocese,[21] which affiliation with a diocese is called incardination.[22] Since by the fact of dismissal the affiliation with the religious institute is broken for all clerics,[23] and since, on the one hand, the Code does not contemplate vagrant or unattached clerics and, on the other, it seems equitable that minor Orders, if they were conferred with the sole authoritative consent of the religious superior and only for the benefit of the religious institute, should cease when the religious profession for the sake of which they were conferred ceases, then clerics ordained in the religious institute are reduced to the lay state. Otherwise the local ordinary who had no part in authorizing the ordination would be obliged to accept among his clergy the dismissed cleric.

The case is altogether different, according to these authors, when the cleric is ordained prior to his entrance into a religious institute. Such a cleric has not lost the diocese which he had in the world [24] and into which he was incardinated through his reception of first tonsure. Further, it is quite possible that the cleric continues *de iure*

---

[20] Goyeneche, "Consultatio"—*Commentarium pro Religiosis et Missionariis* (previously, i. e., before 1935, *Commentarium pro Religiosis*), XIX (1938), 163-166. (Hereafter cited as *CpRM*.) Schäfer, *De Religiosis*, p. 1000.

[21] Canon 111, § 1.

[22] Canon 111, § 2.

[23] Canon 648.

[24] Canon 585.

to hold a benefice in that diocese, for his benefice does not become vacant until three years after any religious profession.[25]   Moreover, the sanction of canon 648 for religious minor clerics who have been dismissed is applied in the case wherein the dismissal was decreed not only when the causes were grave on the part of the religious, but also when there were grave causes solely in relation to the institute, even though these causes did not pertain to the moral order.[26]   Wherefore it is clear, contrary to what some authors say,[27] that the sanction of canon 648 has not the character of a penalty, but denotes merely the privation of the clerical state, as required according to the principles which regulate the discipline of ordination.   Nevertheless it is a privation of rights, and therefore as a *lex odiosa* is subject to a strict interpretation.[28]

As a further argument these authors point out that a juridical abnormality would seem to follow if all dismissed minor clerics without distinction were reduced to the lay state by reason of the rule expressed in canon 648.   For in that event a cleric when dismissed in temporary vows, although he has committed no delict, is not only punished the same as a cleric who has been dismissed in perpetual vows upon the commission of three delicts, but even more severely. He not only loses the clerical state as does the cleric in perpetual vows, but he also loses his incardination in his diocese and the possession of his benefice, if he has one.   Finally, it does not seem fitting that a cleric who has been accepted into the diocese by the bishop, and has been further bound to it by the possession of a benefice, should be deprived of his diocese and his benefice, without any consultation of the bishop, simply by the action of the religious superior, and quite possibly also for a cause which does not determine his unsuitability for the clerical state but only his unfitness for the religious life.

[25] Canon 584.

[26] Cf., e. g., Fanfani, *De Iure Religiosorum,* p. 497; O'Neill, *The Dismissal of Religious in Temporary Vows,* p. 142.

[27] Palombo, *De Dimissione Religiosorum* (Taurini-Romae: Marietti, 1931), p. 257; Schaaf, "Episcopus proprius ordinationis religiosorum"—*ER,* XC (1934), 495.

[28] Canon 19; cf. Goyeneche, "Consultatio"—*CpRM,* XIX (1938), 165.

O'Neill does not agree with this distinction. He thinks that the arguments advanced in support of it are not sufficiently compelling to counter-balance the apparently clear wording of canon 648. He argues first of all that the wording of the canon in itself does not seem to admit this distinction.[29] Even if it be granted that the canon *in itself* does not seem to admit the distinction, still this canon taken in conjunction with canons 111, § 1, and 584 does seem not only to admit but, in equity, to demand this interpretation.

He counters the argument that canon 648 is a corollary of canon 111, § 1, by saying that it is rather a parallel and particularized statement of canon 211, § 2.[30] While nobody would deny that canon 648 is a particularized statement of canon 211, § 2, it can still be a corollary of canon 111, § 1, inasmuch as the latter canon determines the reason for the law of canon 648. To the argument that the cleric in temporary vows suffers a greater loss than the cleric in perpetual vows O'Neill answers that it does not follow strictly that the condition of the former is worse than that of the latter. However, the argument is not that his condition is rendered worse, for the ultimate condition of both is the same, namely, they are reduced to the lay state. The argument of Goyeneche is rather that, for a cause which is not necessarily a delict and which may even be devoid absolutely of culpability, there is nevertheless decreed the same sanction, which has for its effect in the case of the cleric in temporary vows both the loss of his incardination and the forfeiture of his benefice, which losses the cleric who is perpetually professed does not suffer.

Finally, O'Neill states that in reply to the argument that the Code does not wish the bishop to lose his cleric by the sole authoritative action of the religious superior it can be answered that he does not really lose his cleric, since on the one hand he lost the services of the cleric when the latter entered the institute, and since on the other hand he can easily regain this person as a cleric by readmitting him to the clerical state. But the argument of Goyeneche is that it is not fitting that a cleric, incardinated and given a benefice

---

[29] *The Dismissal of Religious in Temporary Vows,* p. 149.

[30] Canon 211, § 2: Clericus minor ad statum laicalem regreditur . . . ipso facto ob causas in iure descriptas.

by the bishop, should lose that incardination and that benefice, without consultation of the bishop, simply by the action of the religious superior who dismisses the cleric for a cause which by no means affects his clerical status, but only his fitness for the religious life. This argument becomes even stronger when the cleric is dismissed not because of his ineptitude for the religious life, but for some reason in relation to the institute, such as the latter's inability to support its members.

Consequently it appears to this writer that Goyeneche has the better interpretation. Canon 648 refers only to those religious clerics in temporary vows who were ordained after their entrance into the religious institute. By the fact of their dismissal they are reduced to the lay state. Minor clerics in temporary vows ordained prior to their entrance into the religious institute are not reduced to the lay state by the simple fact of their dismissal.

However, according to a joint decree of the Sacred Congregation of Religious and the Sacred Congregation of Seminaries and Universities on July 25, 1941, before a religious who has by any title belonged to a religious family may be admitted to a seminary, the ordinary must have recourse to the Sacred Congregation of Seminaries and Universities which, after all the accompanying requirements of the case have been duly met, will inform the ordinary of its judgment in the case.[31]

The question concerning the juridical status of those religious in minor Orders who freely leave at the expiration of their temporary vows, or whom the institute excludes from further profession, now arises. A religious professed in temporary vows can freely leave the institute at the expiration of these vows; similarly the institute for a just and reasonable cause can exclude the religious from the renewal of his temporary vows or from the profession of perpetual vows, but not because of illness, unless it is certainly proved that the illness was maliciously concealed or disguised prior to profession.[32]

In contrast to the dismissal of a religious in temporary vows there is no reduction to the lay state specified for those religious who

---

[31] *The Clergy Review*, XXI (1941), 364; Bouscaren, *The Canon Law Digest*, II, 426.

[32] Canon 637.

freely leave the institute at the expiration of their temporary vows, or whom the institute excludes from another profession. As a result the authors are at variance regarding the juridical status of these clerics. Here again, to clarify the discussion, the distinction must be made between clerics ordained prior to their entrance into the religious institute and clerics ordained after their religious profession. Most of the authors agree that clerics ordained before their entrance into the religious institute, if they freely leave at the end of their temporary profession or are excluded from further profession, remain clerics and retain the incardination they had in the diocese before their entrance into the religious institute.[33] The reasons for this contention are the same as those which were given for the analogous opinion previously supported when the dismissal of religious was discussed. The force of these reasons is greatly strengthened by the fact that the law does not expressly decree a reduction to the lay state in canon 637.

The controversy is rather concerned with the juridical condition of the clerics who were ordained in the institute. One solution proposed is that such clerics are reduced to the lay state.[34] The basis of this contention is that the Code does not admit vagrant or unattached clerics,[35] or, together with this reason, that the Code sets up a restriction in its prescript of canon 641, § 1, which states exclusively that clerics in sacred Orders should return to their proper diocese and be received by their proper ordinary.[36] A second solu-

---

[33] Cf., e. g., Blat, *De Religiosis,* p. 552 (Blat, however, is speaking only of major clerics. He does not express his opinion regarding minor clerics); Coronata, *Institutiones,* I, 203, footnote 3; Schäfer, *De Religiosis,* p. 949; Fanfani, *De Iure Religiosorum,* p. 515; Goyeneche, "Consultatio"—*CpR,* IV (1923), 146-147; Schaaf, "Episcopus proprius ordinationis religiosorum"—*ER,* XC (1934), 494-495; Oesterle, "De domicilio religiosorum"—*CpR,* V (1924), 168-169; O'Neill, *The Dismissal of Religious in Temporary Vows,* p. 179; cf. also canons 115 and 585.

[34] Wernz-Vidal, *Ius Canonicum,* II, n. 66; Palombo, *De Dimissione Religiosorum,* p. 261; Oesterle, "De domicilio religiosorum"—*CpR,* V (1924), 169; Moeder, *The Proper Bishop for Ordination and Dimissorial Letters,* The Catholic University of America Canon Law Studies, n. 95 (Washington, D. C.: The Catholic University of America, 1935), pp. 105-106.

[35] Canon 111, § 1; Moeder, *loc. cit.*

[36] Oesterle, *loc. cit.*

tion contends that such clerics are vagrant or unattached.[37]   Finally, some authors are of the opinion that these clerics are incardinated in the diocese of their proper bishop.[38]   These authors argue from an analogy with canon 641, § 1, which refers to religious in sacred Orders who are secularized or who leave the institute at the expiration of their temporary vows, and from the general principles of law.[39]   They point out that canon 648 cannot be applied here, since as a *lex odiosa* it requires a strict interpretation.[40]   Hence these clerics remain clerics and are incardinated in the diocese of their proper bishop according to the general rules of canons 90, 92, 93, § 2, 94, § 1.   To the objection that it is not equitable that the ordinary, without whose permission the religious received minor Orders, be obliged to receive the cleric into his diocese, it may be answered that the ordinary is free to reduce this cleric to the lay state by means of a decree to that effect.[41]

Which of these opinions is the most satisfactory?   It seems that the first must be considered as the least probable, for its proponents are arguing from parallel cases on a point which limits the free exercise of rights and hence demands a strict interpretation.   The second opinion, which considers these clerics as vagrant or unattached, is clearly at variance with canon 111, § 1, which intimates that the public existence of vagrant clerics is by no means to be admitted. The third opinion avoids these difficulties but it encounters the particular difficulty of explaining why it is not inequitable to acknowl-

---

[37] Coronata, *Institutiones*, I, 203, footnote 3; Chelodi, *Ius de Personis*, n. 108.   It should be noted, however, that Chelodi applied this solution only to exempt religious; he thought that the non-exempt religious are to return to their proper diocese and bishop.

[38] Schäfer, *De Religiosis*, p. 949; Goyeneche, "Consultatio"—*CpR*, IV (1923), 146-147; VII (1926), 449-450; XIV (1933), 352-354; Schaaf, "Episcopus proprius ordinationis religiosorum"—*ER*, XC (1934), 494-495; Fanfani, *De Iure Religiosorum*, p. 515; O'Neill, *The Dismissal of Religious in Temporary Vows*, p. 182.

[39] Canon 20: Si certa de re desit expressum praescriptum legis sive generalis sive particularis, norma sumenda est, nisi agatur de poenis applicandis, a legibus latis in similibus. . . .

[40] Canon 19.

[41] Canon 211, § 2.

edge as attached to the diocese of an ordinary a cleric about whom the ordinary knows nothing, and regarding whom he is nevertheless held responsible. However, inasmuch as it can answer to this that the ordinary has the option of reducing such a cleric to the lay state, this opinion may perhaps be regarded as embodying the most satisfactory of the various explanations offered.

By means of the same argumentation it is concluded that the juridical condition of those who are dispensed from their temporary vows is the same as that of those who are excluded from further profession at the end of their temporary vows, or who freely leave the institute at the termination of their temporary vows. The Holy See may reduce the cleric to the lay state when the dispensation is granted; but in the absence of this special reduction the juridical condition of the cleric is the same as that of the cleric excluded from further profession.

Finally, there remains the consideration of the juridical status of exclaustrated and secularized minor clerics. The indult of exclaustration or the permission for a temporary sojourn outside the cloister [42] presents no problem, since the cleric remains bound by his vows and other religious obligations inasmuch as they are compatible with his state.[43] Consequently he is still a member of his institute and in no way is to be considered as reduced to the lay state.

The indult of secularization or the permission for perpetually remaining outside the cloister is a different matter.[44] In this case the cleric is separated from his institute and freed from his vows. He would have to make a new novitiate and profession if he returned to his institute.[45] The law makes no explicit provision regarding the status of secularized minor clerics. However, it does not seem that their condition differs substantially from that of those who are dispensed from their vows. Consequently the same solution is proposed. Arguing from a similar case, that of secularized major clerics as considered in canon 641, § 1, the cleric must return to his proper diocese, since the link between him and his diocese has

---

[42] Canon 638.
[43] Canon 639.
[44] Canon 638.
[45] Canon 640.

not been broken, for the simple reason that he has not made a per-petual religious profession.[46]   In this case it is left to the judgment of the ordinary to receive him or to reduce him to the lay state.

ARTICLE 2. REDUCTION FOR VOLUNTEERING FOR MILITARY SERVICE

Canon 141, § 1, states that clerics may not volunteer for military service, unless they do so with the permission of their ordinary in order that they may the sooner become free from the obligation of military service.   The second paragraph of this canon declares that a minor cleric who, contrary to the prescript of the first paragraph, freely joins the military *ipso iure* falls from the clerical state.   This canon has already been considered in relation to secular minor clerics. It applies also to religious minor clerics.   There is no need of a detailed commentary on the canon here, for what has been said about secular minor clerics can, in general, be understood as applicable also to religious minor clerics.   However, it is necessary to indicate such differences as do exist.

The ordinary whose permission it is necessary to secure before the religious minor cleric may volunteer is the ordinary of the place in which the religious house is situated if the religious belongs to a non-exempt clerical or lay institute; the major superior, if the re-ligious is a member of a clerical exempt institute.[47]   As far as canon 141 is concerned, this appears to be the only distinction be-tween secular and religious clerics in the discipline regulating minor clerics with reference to their obligation of military service.   How-ever, the Holy See has made certain specific provisions for religious who are under obligation in the matter of military service.   It is now necessary to consider these.

On January 1, 1911, the Sacred Congregation of Religious saw fit to issue the decree *Inter reliquas* concerning religious who were obliged to enter the military service.[48]   After the promulgation of the Code of Canon Law a doubt arose whether this decree was still in effect.   The Sacred Congregation of Religious replied, on July 15,

[46] Canon 585.
[47] Cf. canons 198, § 1; 488, 8°. Cf. also Coronata, *Institutiones*, I, 231.
[48] *AAS*, III (1911), 37-39; Bouscaren, *The Canon Law Digest*, I, 106-108.

1919, that the decree was still in effect.[49]   The Sacred Congregation pointed out that, since the Code declares religious exempt from military service,[50] the decree which regulated their conduct while they were in such service was of its nature temporary.   However, because the conditions which gave rise to the decree still existed in 1919, that is, religious were still in many countries subject to military service, the decree was still in effect.   Since these conditions are present even at the present time, it appears that the decree *Inter reliquas* has correspondingly remained in effect.

There are certain provisions in the decree and in the response which pertain to the reduction of these minor clerics to the lay state. First of all it should be stated that, after the response of the Sacred Congregation in 1919, the religious in military service is no longer bound by his vows, even though during this period of service he remains a member of his institute under the authority of his superiors.   This is provided for when the religious takes his vows.   He makes only a temporary profession, and the vows are not taken for the three years which canon 574 prescribes when the circumstances are not unfavorable.   The vows are taken as binding the religious until he enters the military service, at which time they cease.

Generally the duration of the vows will be less than three years, but it can happen that they will continue to bind longer than three years, namely, if the religious is not called for military service at the end of three years.   During his military service the cleric in accordance with canon 637 may freely leave the society, notifying his superiors by means of a statement made in writing or before witnesses, which statement shall be carefully kept in the archives of the institute.   However, as was seen in the consideration of canon 637, it does not seem that the cleric by his free egress from the institute is reduced to the lay state.   In the decree *Inter reliquas* it was provided that, if the religious in military service wished or asked for a release from his vows, the superior general, with the consent of his council, could release him from his vows.   In lay institutes the vows were released by means of a letter of the superiors who gave the religious permission to return to the world.   However,

---

[49] *AAS*, XI (1919), 321-323; Bouscaren, *The Canon Law Digest*, I, 105-106.
[50] Canons 614; 121.

as has just been seen, the provision of the response of 1919, in harmony with the Code of Canon Law, has rendered these specifications of the decree unnecessary.

The decree *Inter reliquas* further provided that the superior general with the consent of his council should dismiss religious who, during or after their military service and before their solemn or perpetual vows, showed signs of faltering in their vocation, or failed to obey the prescriptions laid down for them during their military service, or turned aside from the right way of faith or of morals. This provision also has been supplanted by canon 637, so that the response of 1919, after referring to canon 637, states that the society may, for just and reasonable causes, declare the religious dismissed.[51]

Though the response refers to a dismissal, there seems rather to be question here of an exclusion from profession.[52] The word "dismissal" is evidently used in a broad sense in the response, since it refers to canon 637, which in turn is concerned with the exclusion from profession. In harmony, then, with the opinion previously sponsored, it does not seem that the religious who is in this manner excluded from profession is reduced to the lay state.

ARTICLE 3. REDUCTION BY DISMISSAL OF A RELIGIOUS IN PERPETUAL VOWS

Canon 669, § 2, declares that a religious minor cleric in perpetual vows when he is dismissed from the institute is by that very fact reduced to the lay state.[53] The dismissal of religious who take vows in a non-exempt clerical institute or in a lay institute is effected according to the norms outlined in canons 649-653. The dismissal of religious who take perpetual vows, whether solemn or simple, in a clerical exempt institute is effected according to the norms of

---

[51] *AAS,* XI (1919), 322; Bouscaren, *The Canon Law Digest,* I, 106.

[52] Coronata, *Institutiones,* I, 773, footnote 1.

[53] Canon 669, § 1. Professus qui vota perpetua emisit, a religione dimissus, votis religiosis manet adstrictus, salvis constitutionibus aut Sedis Apostolicae indultis quae aliud ferant.

§ 2. Si clericus est in minoribus ordinibus constitutus, eo ipso reducitur ad statum laicalem.

canons 654-663. Regarding these canons as regulating the dismissal
it will suffice to say that an invalid dismissal begets no juridical
effect.   Hence any minor cleric so dismissed is not reduced to the
lay state.   However, in a non-exempt clerical or lay institute, as
long as the religious has not had recourse to the Holy See,[54] the
dismissal must be considered to have begotten its juridical effect so
that the cleric is reduced to the lay state.   In a non-exempt clerical
or lay institute of pontifical approval and in a clerical exempt institute it is very rare that the dismissal will be invalid, since for its
effectiveness the dismissal must be previously confirmed by the
Holy See.[55]

All men religious are *ipso facto* dismissed if they publicly apostatize from the Catholic faith or if they attempt flight with a woman
or finally if they attempt or contract marriage or even a so-called
civil bond, or union.[56]   In these cases it is sufficient that the major
superior with his chapter or council make a declaration of the fact
according to the norm of the constitutions.   Moreover, according
to a decision of the Pontifical Commission for the Interpretation of
the Code on July 30, 1934, it is not necessary that the fact be
declared before the religious is considered as *ipso facto* legitimately
dismissed.[57]

Once any religious minor cleric in perpetual vows is dismissed
from his institute he is reduced to the lay state.   The distinction between clerics ordained prior to their entrance into religion and clerics
ordained in the institute does not enter here, since by his perpetual
profession the cleric loses the proper diocese he had in the world
and also his attendant incardination.[58]   Furthermore, if he had a
benefice before he entered the religious institute he loses that benefice at the time of his perpetual profession.[59]

---

[54] Canons 650, § 2, 1°; 647, § 2, 4°.

[55] Canons 650, § 2, 2°; 666.

[56] Canon 646, § 1.

[57] *AAS*, XXVI (1934), 494; Bouscaren, *The Canon Law Digest*, II, 175.

[58] Canons 585; 115.

[59] Canon 574 demands a three-year temporary profession before the perpetual profession; canon 584 declares that three years after any profession non-
parochial benefices become vacant.

While the religious minor cleric in temporary vows when dismissed according to the norm of canon 647 is by that very fact released from his vows in religion,[60] the same is not true of the religious who is dismissed in perpetual vows, unless the constitutions of his institute or indults of the Holy See state the opposite.[61] Consequently the religious dismissed in perpetual vows who is not released from those vows remains a religious.[62]

Canon 614 states that all religious, even lay members, enjoy the clerical privileges enumerated in canons 119-123. O'Leary thinks that the minor cleric, in spite of his reduction to the lay state, retains the clerical privileges for the reason that he is still a religious.[63] Most of the authors, however, maintain that such a religious loses his clerical privileges.[64] This seems to be the better opinion in view of canons 123 and 213, which state that *all* who are reduced to the lay state lose the clerical privileges. This opinion is also more in harmony with the axiom, *ubi lex non distinguit nec nos distinguere debemus.*[65] Finally, O'Leary admits that a major cleric who is reduced to the lay state does lose his clerical privileges. Yet, if his former distinction is valid, the major cleric, as a religious, has the same title to the clerical privileges as the minor cleric. Hence it appears that it is a more probable opinion that the minor cleric who is dismissed after perpetual profession does lose his clerical privileges by reason of his reduction to the lay state.

There now remains to be considered the juridical status of a perpetually professed minor cleric who is dispensed from his vows or who receives an indult of secularization. The case differs from that of a cleric in temporary vows, for by virtue of the perpetual profession the cleric loses the diocese which he had in the world.

---

[60] Canon 648.

[61] Canon 669, § 1.

[62] Coronata, *Institutiones*, I, 886.

[63] *Religious Dismissed after Perpetual Profession*, The Catholic University of America Canon Law Studies, n. 184 (Washington, D. C.: The Catholic University of America Press, 1943), p. 95.

[64] Vermeersch-Creusen, *Epitome*, I, n. 772; Fanfani, *De Iure Religiosorum*, p. 367; Coronata, *Institutiones*, I, 821; Schäfer, *De Religiosis*, p. 1023; Maroto, *Institutiones*, I, 610; Cocchi, *De Religiosis*, n. 157.

[65] Cf. Wernz, *Ius Decretalium*, I, n. 131, I.

Piontek thinks that the secularized cleric is reduced to the lay state.[66] Yet such does not seem to be the case. Nowhere in law is this reduction decreed for secularized clerics, nor does it appear that canon 669, § 2, can be applied here, inasmuch as any reduction as a *res odiosa* is subject to a strict interpretation.[67]

Arguing from canon 641, § 1, which treats of secularized religious in major Orders, one will hold that the secularized religious in minor Orders should endeavor to find a bishop who will receive him into his diocese. If the cleric cannot find such a bishop, then it seems that he should return to his former diocese. In this event it is left to the judgment of the ordinary to receive him or to reduce him to the lay state. Otherwise the cleric would become a vagrant or unattached cleric, which possibility the law in no way admits.[68]

Again, the joint decree of the Sacred Congregation of Religious and the Sacred Congregation of Seminaries and Universities must be observed. Hence, before the ordinary may admit the ex-religious cleric into his seminary, he must have recourse to the Sacred Congregation of Seminaries and Universities and abide by the judgment of this Congregation.[69] If the Sacred Congregation decides that the ex-religious is not to be admitted to the seminary, then it seems indicated that the ordinary should reduce him to the lay state.

---

[66] *De Indulto Exclaustrationis necnon de Indulto Saecularizationis,* The Catholic University of America Canon Law Studies, n. 29 (Washington, D. C.: The Catholic University of America, 1925), p. 204.

[67] Canon 19; cf. Ellis, "De religiosi minoristae saecularizati incardinatione" —*Periodica de Re Canonica et Morali utili praesertim Religiosis et Missionariis* (Brugis, 1905—), XXV (1936), 53-55. (Hereafter cited *Periodica.*)

[68] Canon 111, § 1.

[69] *The Clergy Review,* XXI (1941), 364; Bouscaren, *The Canon Law Digest,* II, 426.

CHAPTER VI

REDUCTION FOR CERTAIN DELICTS

The treatment of the reduction of minor clerics to the lay state in the preceding chapters has been concerned only with immediate reduction, that is, reduction as effected *ipso iure* or *ipso facto*. In this chapter the consideration of the reduction of minor clerics will proceed to cases wherein the reduction is the result of the action of the competent superior. The fifth book of the Code contains two canons in which the reduction of the minor cleric to the lay state is effected by the competent superior as a punishment for certain delicts. Canon 2379 also mentions the penalty of the reduction of the cleric to the lay state. However, this is the same case as the one mentioned in canon 136, wherein the reduction is effected *ipso iure*. The other cases treated of in the fifth book will now require some commentary.

ARTICLE 1. FOR DELICTS AGAINST THE SIXTH COMMANDMENT

According to canon 2358, clerics in minor Orders guilty of some delict against the sixth commandment are to be punished in accordance with the gravity of the fault, and even with the dismissal from the clerical state if the circumstances of the delict warrant such a penalty.[1] The canon refers to clerics in minor Orders. By these are generally understood acolytes, exorcists, lectors and porters to the exclusion of those who have received only first tonsure.[2] However, it appears that the phrase *"clerici in minoribus ordinibus"* was used in contradistinction to the phrase *"clerici in sacris"* of the following canon, and it therefore embraces also those who have received

---

[1] Canon 2358: Clerici in minoribus ordinibus constituti, rei alicuius delicti contra sextum decalogi praeceptum, pro gravitate culpae puniantur etiam dimissione e statu clericali, si delicti adiuncta id suadeant, praeter poenas de quibus in can. 2357, si his locus sit.

[2] Canon 949.

only first tonsure.[3]   Canon 2357 is concerned with lay persons, canon 2358 with minor clerics and canon 2359 with major clerics.   It would indeed be strange if clerics in first tonsure were excluded from an otherwise complete list.

Canon 2358 seems to refer to religious as well as secular minor clerics.[4]   An argument contrary to this opinion may be drawn from canon 2359 which explicitly mentions both religious and secular major clerics.   It may be objected that if canon 2358 wished to include religious it would likewise explicitly have mentioned them.   However, the specific mention of religious in canon 2359 may be explained by the fact that previously in the Code any mention of clerics living in concubinage was concerned primarily with secular clerics.   Thus, canon 133, although by virtue of canon 592 applicable to religious, cannot be applied in its entirety to religious, since the religious while at home is bound by the law of the cloister.   Again, the procedure against secular clerics, as outlined in canons 2176-2181, can hardly be applied in its entirety to religious, for religious pastors are removable *ad nutum loci Ordinarii* after the notification of the superior.[5]   Hence, to clarify the penal legislation regarding clerics living in concubinage canon 2359 explicitly mentions religious as well as secular major clerics.   Moreover, by a minor cleric is understood a religious as well as a secular minor cleric.   Canon 2358 mentions only minor clerics.   In harmony with the principle *"ubi lex non distinguit, nec nos distinguere debemus"* [6] there is not only no need of any such distinction, but also no proper warrant for it.

A. The Delict

The wording of canon 2358 is rather peculiar.   It states that minor clerics guilty of some *delict* are to be punished.   By a delict in ecclesiastical law is understood an external and morally imputable violation of a law to which is added at least an indeterminate canon-

---

[3] Vermeersch-Creusen, *Epitome,* III, n. 560; Blat, *Commentarium Textus Codicis Iuris Canonici* (5 vols. in 7, Vol. VII, *De Delictis et Poenis,* Romae, 1924), p. 265.   (Hereafter cited *De Delictis et Poenis.*)

[4] Pejška, *Ius Canonicum Religiosorum,* p. 137.

[5] Canon 454, § 5.

[6] Cf. Wernz, *Ius Decretalium,* I, n. 131, I.

ical sanction.[7] Does a cleric, then, in order to be punished according to canon 2358, have to commit a crime against the sixth commandment which is already punished by some canonical penal sanction? Again, in order that a crime against the sixth commandment become a delict for minor clerics, is it sufficient that it be specified in law as a delict for another class? For example, according to canon 2359, clerics in sacred Orders, both secular and religious, are to be punished for various external violations of the sixth commandment. Consequently for them any external violation which is morally imputable is a delict. By virtue of the wording of canon 2358, does it become a delict also for minor clerics?

Obviously, in order that a minor cleric be punished according to this canon, it is not necessary that he commit a crime already specified in law as a delict for minor clerics, for the canon states that the cleric is to be punished according to the gravity of the fault in addition to the penalties enacted in canon 2357, if they too have application. Evidently, then, the crimes of canon 2357 are delicts also for minor clerics. Moreover, by reason of the general wording of canon 2358 it appears that a crime against the sixth commandment specified as a delict for any other class becomes a delict also for minor clerics. Hence, arguing from the third paragraph of canon 2359, one may conclude that any external sin committed against the sixth commandment by minor clerics is subject to punishment according to the gravity of the fault and, if the circumstances warrant it, even with the dismissal from the clerical state.[8] The sin does not have to be one of consummated lust; sins which moralists list under non-consummated lust are also included. However, the sin does have to be external and gravely sinful.[9]

B. *The Penalty*

There can be no doubt that the reduction of the minor cleric to the lay state as mentioned in canon 2358 is a penalty. But it is

---

[7] Canon 2195.

[8] Cf. Vermeersch-Creusen, *Epitome,* III, n. 560; Ciprotti, "De consummatione delictorum attento eorum elemento obiectivo"—*Apollinaris* (Romae, 1928—), IX (1936), pp. 413-414, footnote 1.

[9] Canon 2218, § 2; Coronata, *Institutiones,* IV, 23.

not a censure, since it is clear from canon 212 that once the cleric has receded from his contumacy he still has no right to be received back into the clerical state. If the penalty were a censure, then the cleric would have the right to receive absolution, which in this case would connote also the right of returning to the clerical state. The penalty is a vindictive penalty, tending directly to the expiation of the delict, so that its remission is not dependent on the cessation of contumacy.[10]

C. *Infliction of the Penalty* Per Sententiam Iudicialem

The punishment is evidently not a *latae sententiae* penalty, that is, one which is contracted immediately upon the commission of the delict, but rather a *ferendae sententiae* penalty, that is, one which must be inflicted by a judge or superior.[11] However, the case cannot be tried in a criminal process unless the delict is public.[12] By a public delict is understood one which is already divulged, or a delict which was perpetrated in such circumstances that one can and must acknowledge that it will easily be divulged.[13] Hence delicts which are occult are not considered the object of a criminal process. However, in relation to canon 2358, it must be remembered that even though it is only probable that a delict was committed, or even if through the legal agency of prescription the possibility of a penal action against a certainly committed delict is no longer granted, the superior has not only the right but also the duty not to promote a cleric whose fitness is not evident.[14]

Furthermore, if the ordinary, after weighing the circumstances, prudently judges that the cleric cannot, in consideration of the dignity of the clerical state, be promoted to sacred Orders, he may issue a decree of reduction to the lay state for that cleric.[15] Thus, if the commission of an occult delict against the sixth commandment

10 Canon 2286.
11 Canon 2217, § 1, 2°.
12 Canon 1933, § 1.
13 Canon 2197, 1°.
14 Canon 2222, § 2.
15 Canon 211, § 2.

came to the certain knowledge of the ordinary he could deal with the cleric according to the possible measure indicated in canon 211, § 2, but there is no question of a criminal process as long as the delict is not public.   Before the ordinary can proceed in accordance with the specification of canon 2358 the delict must be public.   The process is to be governed by the norms outlined for criminal judgments [16] and, if the circumstances warrant it, the cleric is to be punished with dismissal from the clerical state.

The terms used in the canon are mandatory, that is, the judge is ordinarily to inflict a penalty in proportion to the gravity of the fault.[17]   The dismissal from the clerical state is not the ordinary penalty for a crime against the sixth commandment.   Canon 2358, after stating that the cleric is to be punished according to the gravity of the fault, declares that he is to be punished *even with the dismissal from the clerical state if the circumstances of the delict warrant it*.   Hence the canon does not presume that any crime against the sixth commandment demands a dismissal from the clerical state, but only such a crime in which the aggravating circumstances, whether these regard the crime itself or the external fact of scandal, demand that the crime be punished more severely.   The ordinary, then, or the judge if the ordinary himself does not sit on the case, is granted a certain option of discretion inasmuch as it is left to his judgment to decide whether in a particular case the circumstances warrant dismissal.

The question will arise whether it is necessary that this penalty of the reduction to the lay state be inflicted by a collegiate tribunal of five judges.   Canon 1576, § 1, 2°, demands this collegiate tribunal for causes which are concerned with delicts which are punished by means of deposition, of perpetual deprivation of the ecclesiastical garb, and of degradation.   Does the penalty of the reduction of the cleric to the lay state imply the penalty of the perpetual deprivation of the ecclesiastical garb?

It does not seem that the penalty of the perpetual deprivation of the ecclesiastical garb is implied in the penalty of the reduction

---

[16] Canons 1933-1959.
[17] Canon 2223, § 3.

of the cleric to the lay state. According to canon 2305, § 1, the penalty of degradation contains the perpetual deprivation of the ecclesiastical garb. But the penalty of degradation is the most severe vindictive penalty that can be inflicted on clerics. This penalty can be inflicted only for the crimes stated in law, or when the cleric, already deposed and deprived of the clerical garb, continues to give grave scandal for a year. This penalty is never incurred *ipso facto;* it must always be inflicted. But if it be held that the penalty of the reduction of the cleric to the lay state implies the perpetual deprivation of the ecclesiastical garb, then the penalty of degradation and the penalty of the reduction of the cleric to the lay state are identical. If this be true then the assertion that degradation may be inflicted only for the crimes stated in law is not accurate. It could also be inflicted for crimes for which a reduction to the lay state is inflicted. Furthermore, the penalty of the reduction to the lay state may be incurred *ipso facto.* Nobody would hold the opinion that degradation may be incurred in this manner without a previous sentence.

Hence it appears that the penalty of degradation and the penalty of the reduction to the lay state are distinct penalties. It likewise appears that the penalty of the deprivation of the clerical garb is not implied in the penalty of the reduction of a cleric to the lay state. Consequently there seems to be no convincing reason to demand a collegiate tribunal of five judges for the infliction of the penalty of the reduction to the lay state.

Blat thinks that the penalty is inflicted by a decree of the ordinary in accordance with canon 211, § 2.[18] However, the wording of canon 2358 seems to postulate a criminal process in the course of which circumstances will be brought to light so that the judge can better decide what penalty is to be inflicted. Moreover, with some exceptions which are specifically indicated, the punishment of delicts according to the penal law presupposes a criminal process. For a fuller explanation, then, one may well consider the infliction of a penalty *per modum praecepti,* which is the method alternative to the infliction *per sententiam iudicialem.*

[18] *De Delictis et Poenis,* p. 265.

D. *Infliction of the Penalty* Per Modum Praecepti

If the penalty is declared or inflicted by a judicial sentence, the prescripts of the canons regarding the infliction of a judicial sentence are to be observed; but if a *latae* or *ferendae sententiae* penalty is enacted or inflicted *per modum praecepti,* it is ordinarily to be declared or imposed in writing or before two witnesses, and likewise the reasons for the penalty are normally to be indicated.[19] The penalties which the Code specifically permits to be enacted or inflicted *per modum praecepti* outside of a process are excommunication, suspension and interdict.[20] Penances and penal remedies can likewise be enacted or inflicted in this manner, but these are not strictly canonical penalties.[21] However, before a penalty may be imposed *per modum praecepti,* it is necessary that the crime be certain [22] and that a criminal action at court be not ruled out through the agency of legal prescription.[23]

The purpose of considering this manner of imposing a penalty is to decide whether other penalties, and especially the reduction of a cleric to the lay state, may be imposed in this way. The opinions of the canonists interpreting canons 2225 and 1933, § 4, are greatly at variance. It is necessary to consider these in some detail before one endeavor to arrive at a conclusion.

The first opinion states that only the penalties listed in canon 1933, § 4, (excommunication, suspension and interdict) can be imposed or declared *per modum praecepti,* and then only as long as they were constituted by a precept.[24] According to this interpreta-

---

[19] Canon 2225.

[20] Canon 1933, § 4.

[21] Canon 1933, § 4; Roberti, *De Delictis et Poenis* (Romae: Apud Aedes Facultatis Iuridicae ad S. Apollinaris, 1938), nn. 233-234.

[22] Canon 1933, § 4.

[23] Canon 2233, § 1; cf. Roberti, *op. cit.,* n. 257.

[24] Canon 2225: . . . si vero poena latae vel ferendae sententiae inflicta sit per modum praecepti particularis, scripto aut coram duobus testibus ordinarie declaretur vel irrogetur, indicatis poenae causis, salvo praescripto can. 2193. Cf. Noval, "De ratione corrigendi et puniendi sive in iudicio sive extra iure Codicis I. C."—*Ius Pontificium* (Romae, 1921—), II (1922), 156 ss.; Coronata, *Institutiones,* III, 378.

tion the words *"inflicta sit"* in canon 2225 are understood as *"statuta sit."* Thus canon 2225 not only gives the reason for so proceeding, but also limits canon 1933, § 4, inasmuch as it demands that the penalties enumerated in canon 1933, § 4, be previously established by a precept. From this interpretation it follows that occult delicts against the law cannot be punished with the aforesaid penalties unless particular precepts strengthening the laws preceded their violation, since for the application or declaration of any penalties constituted by law a judicial process is always necessary.

This interpretation is strict and well corresponds to the nature of penal laws. The process in which the greatest caution in administering justice is present should not be relinquished for the adoption of a less severe process unless such an option is explicitly granted. Now, according to this opinion it is at least doubtful that the use of this option is recognized in law. Therefore, pending the doubtful character of the rightful availability of this option, such option should not be invoked for use.

The objection to this opinion is that it is at variance with the practice of ecclesiastical curiae which indiscriminately apply *per modum praecepti* penalties other than those enumerated in canon 1933, § 4. Furthermore, the practical reason, namely, that it would be almost impossible to apply penalties in many cases if a process were required for the least disciplinary punishment, also militates against this opinion.[25]

The second opinion holds that the penalties enumerated in canon 1933, § 4, can always be declared or imposed *per modum praecepti*, whether they were constituted by a law or by a precept. Cappello seems to insinuate the currency of this opinion, but he himself does not hold it.[26] Mention of this opinion is included here to complete the enumeration of opinions. To this opinion Roberti objects that it seems strange that the grave penalties of canon 1933, § 4, can be indiscriminately applied *per modum praecepti*, while the lighter penalties constantly require a judicial process. Moreover, this is contrary to the common practice of ecclesiastical curiae, which re-

---

[25] Roberti, *De Delictis et Poenis*, n. 259.
[26] *De Censuris*, n. 76.

peatedly apply and declare especially the lighter penalties *per modum praecepti.*[27]

The third opinion states that the penalties listed in canon 1933, § 4, which are constituted by law can be imposed or declared *per modum praecepti;* moreover, any other penalties constituted by a precept after the fashion of law can be imposed or declared in this manner. Roberti cites certain authors as hinting at or leaning towards this opinion.[28] It is not clear that these authors hold this opinion. Again, the opinion is mentioned to complete the enumeration. This opinion, more so than the immediately preceding one, harmonizes with the practice of ecclesiastical curiae. However, it deviates from that practice inasmuch as ecclesiastical curiae do not hesitate to impose or declare *per modum praecepti* at least the minor penalties which are stated in the common law.[29]

The fourth opinion maintains that any penalties, whether they were constituted by a law or by a precept, can be imposed or declared *per modum praecepti,* with the exception of those cases in which a judicial process is absolutely required. According to this interpretation canon 2225 is considered as indiscriminately proposing two ways of imposing or declaring penalties: the judicial process and the administrative method *per modum praecepti.* In this interpretation the verb *"infligere"* as used in certain canons is considered to mean *"applicare,"*[30] and the phrase *"inflicta sit"* of canon 2225 is understood as *"infligatur,"* for this interpretation does not admit the necessity of the precept being previously constituted. This interpretation is in perfect agreement with the practice of ecclesiastical curiae and of the Roman Congregations, which often apply *per modum praecepti* the penalties stated in common law.[31]

The objections to this interpretation are drawn from the nat-

---

[27] Roberti, *De Delictis et Poenis,* n. 260.

[28] Roberti, *op. cit.,* n. 261. Cf., e. g., Chelodi, *Ius Poenale,* n. 25; Vermeersch-Creusen, *Epitome,* III, n. 415; Michiels, "De reservatione censurae latae sententiae praecepto particulari adnexae"—*Ephemerides Theologicae Lovanienses* (Brugis, 1924—), IV (1927), 191.

[29] Roberti, *loc. cit.*

[30] Cf. canons 2217, § 1; 2223, § 3, 2°; 2225, first part; 2233, § 2.

[31] Roberti, *De Delictis et Poenis,* n. 262; Cappello, "Irrogatio poenae per modum praecepti extra iudicium"—*Periodica,* XIX (1930), 36*-38*.

ural reason which always requires a judicial process for the infliction
of penalties, and from the indefinite limits of its potential application. However, Roberti answers that the necessity of the judicial
process is not absolute, and that the positive law can abstract from
it especially when there is question of minor transgressions, and when
at the same time there is an immediate necessity of providing for the
proper maintenance of public order.[32]

Furthermore, the limits of the application made possible in consequence of this interpretation are not indefinite. The limits are
fixed by the Code itself. Thus, the Code absolutely requires a
judicial process for the act of depriving an irremovable incumbent
of his benefice,[33] inasmuch as for this judgment a collegiate body of
three judges is necessary.[34] The Code likewise states that the penalties of deposition, of perpetual deprivation of the ecclesiastical dress
and of degradation can be imposed only in such cases in which the
law expressly allows it.[35] Moreover, to impose these penalties a
collegiate body of five judges is required.[36] Again, the penalties
constituted for delicts which are reserved to the competence of the
Holy Office must be inflicted or declared according to the proper
method of procedure of the Holy Office.[37] Furthermore, the sanc-
tions mentioned in canons 2143-2194 can be invoked through the
infliction of the corresponding penalties only in accordance with the
norms described in these canons. Finally, for the dismissal of religious the Code indicates exact and specific norms of procedure,
which alone, to the exclusion of others, are to be followed.[38] These
then are the limits which this interpretation must respect and
observe.

How do these interpretations affect the law regarding the penalty
of the reduction of the cleric to the lay state? Since the first and
second opinions limit the application of a penalty *per modum*

---

[32] Roberti, *loc. cit.*
[33] Canon 192, § 2.
[34] Canon 1576, § 1, 1°.
[35] Canons 2223, § 3; argument from 2304, § 1; 2305, § 2.
[36] Canon 1576, § 1, 2°.
[37] Canon 1555, § 1.
[38] Canons 649 ff.; 654 ff.

praecepti to the penalties enumerated in canon 1933, § 4, these opinions exclude the possibility of inflicting the reduction to the lay state in this manner. The third opinion permits the reduction to the lay state to be applied in this manner, but only if this penalty has been constituted by a precept after the fashion of a law. The fourth opinion allows the application of the reduction of the cleric to the lay state by means of extra-judicial action also then when the penalty of such a reduction is called for in the law itself apart from any preceptive ordinance.

How are these opinions to be evaluated? The first opinion is to be held until more cogent arguments are adduced to discard it. This opinion appears to follow more closely the principles for the interpretation of penal laws.[39] Roberti admits that this interpretation well corresponds to the nature of penal laws.[40] The objections brought against it have not sufficient weight to overthrow it. Thus, the objection is brought forth that this interpretation is at variance with the practice of ecclesiastical curiae and even with the practice of the Roman Congregations.[41] But it can be answered that according to the principles of interpretation the style and practice of the Roman Curia, together with other sources, present a norm when an express prescript of law is absent regarding a certain matter, unless this matter concerns the application of penalties.[42] It is quite obvious, indeed, that the question under consideration is concerned with the application of a penalty.

The objection is made that it seems strange that the more grave penalties (suspension, excommunication and interdict) may be applied *per modum praecepti* while the lighter penalties require a judicial process. *A fortiori,* this argument continues, the lighter penalties may be so applied if the same procedure for the graver penalties is not disallowed.[43] However, the legislator in his enumeration mentioned penances and penal remedies,[44] which in fact are

---

[39] Cf. canons 2219 and 19.
[40] *De Delictis et Poenis*, n. 259.
[41] Roberti, *op. cit.*, n. 262.
[42] Canon 20.
[43] Roberti, *loc. cit.*
[44] Canon 1933, § 4.

not canonical penalties at all. If the argument on the side of the objection were a valid one, it could very well be used to apply also to the inflicting of penances and penal remedies, even though they were left unmentioned. Yet the legislator explicitly mentioned these. The conclusion seems to be that what he did not mention he intended not to include.

Finally, the argument is adduced that the interpretation which requires a judicial process renders almost impossible the application of penalties in many cases.[45] This argument is valid if there is question of making a law, but not when there is question of interpreting a law already made, particularly when the interpretation concerns a penal law regarding which any extension in the interpretation must be avoided.[46] Moreover, the necessity of inflicting penalties other than those which are enumerated is not apparent. If some more difficult cases occur, the Code provides special norms for them.[47]

Until more cogent arguments are brought forth, then, or until an authentic declaration contrary to this opinion has been issued,[48] the opinion to be held is that only the penalties of excommunication, suspension and interdict, if they have been constituted by a precept, may be applied or declared *per modum praecepti*.

How does this interpretation apply to canon 2358? Since the penalty mentioned in this canon is the reduction of the cleric to the lay state, it seems evident that this penalty cannot be applied *per modum praecepti*. The form to be used in imposing or declaring a penalty *per modum praecepti* is either written, or oral in the presence of two witnesses.[49] The written form is called a decree.[50] Since canon 212, § 2, states that the local ordinary may reduce a minor cleric to the lay state by means of a decree, confusion may

---

[45] Roberti, *De Delictis et Poenis*, n. 259; Cappello, "Irrogatio poenae per modum praecepti extra iudicium"—*Periodica*, XIX (1930), 36*-38*.

[46] Coronata, *Institutiones*, III, 379.

[47] Coronata, *loc. cit.* Cf. canons 188; 454, § 5; 471, § 3; 595, § 3; 646; 653; 970; 2222, § 2; 2147-2194.

[48] The renowned canonist Roberti ardently hopes for an authentic declaration. Cf. *De Delictis et Poenis*, n. 262.

[49] Canon 2225; Roberti, *op. cit.*, n. 263.

[50] Roberti, *loc. cit.*

arise. It must be borne in mind that the decree, whether it imposes a penalty or simply provides an administrative measure, connotes an administrative and not a judicial mode of procedure. It is readily admitted that the local ordinary by means of a decree can, as an administrative measure, reduce to the lay state the cleric who has been guilty of a sin against the sixth commandment. But the contention here is that the ordinary cannot, by the administrative procedure of a decree, reduce such a cleric to the lay state by way of penalty. For this there is required a judicial process.

To summarize this treatise, it is held that the penalty of canon 2358, namely, the reduction of the cleric to the lay state, may be imposed only in judicial procedure. If the judicial procedure is not used, then the local ordinary, by virtue of canon 212, § 2, may reduce the cleric to the lay state by means of a decree. However, in this instance the reduction is not a penalty. It is an administrative measure.

Finally, it is necessary to mention the present-day practice of the Sacred Congregation of the Holy Office. To the competence of this Sacred Congregation are reserved delicts *"de crimine pessimo."* By such delicts the Sacred Congregation understands any obscene external acts which are gravely sinful, and which are in any way perpetrated or attempted by a cleric with persons of either sex if they have not yet reached the age of puberty, or also with animals; or any obscene external acts which are gravely sinful, and which are in any way perpetrated or attempted with a person of his own sex.[51] By virtue of this reservation it is the right of any of the faithful to denounce directly to the Holy Office those who have been guilty of such a crime. If the denunciation is made to the Sacred Congregation of the Council or to the Sacred Congregation of Religious, it is to be sent to the Holy Office. If the denunciation is made to the diocesan tribunal, then this tribunal can treat of and decide the matter, but the Holy Office must be informed of the denunciation.[52] The faithful possess the right of making a denunciation

---

[51] López, "Casus Conscientiae"—*Periodica*, XXVII (1938), 32-35; Iorio, *Theologia Moralis*, II, n. 286; Aertnys-Damen, *Theologia Moralis*, I, n. 626.

[52] López, *art. cit.*, p. 33.

in order that the repairing of the scandal or the counteracting of the evil may be provided for.[53]

It is to be noted that the Holy Office interprets broadly, rather than strictly, the acts which are denounced, since the common good of the faithful demands this interpretation. Hence, if there is denounced some external act which of itself if done with the right intention does not constitute a sin, for example a kiss or an embrace, but for which it is not evident that a just cause is present, the presumption is that the agent had a libidinous intention.

According to canon 2359, § 2, major clerics are to be punished with the penalties therein enumerated for the commission of sins against the sixth commandment if they are perpetrated with minors under the age of sixteen years. However, in regard to sins committed with persons of the other sex, the competence of the Holy Office seems to extend only to the cases which involve minors who have not yet attained the age of puberty, that is, to girls under the age of twelve years.[54]

The Holy Office in these cases proceeds in the same manner as in the case of the delict of solicitation. However, a very important difference must be kept in mind. In these cases *there is no positive obligation placed upon the faithful to denounce the cleric,* unless, of course, at the same time there was solicitation in confession. Nevertheless they always may, and sometimes through the dictate of the natural law even must, denounce such clerics.[55]

In the article of López reference is made to *clerics.* Hence it seems to include all clerics, although the case of conscience solved in the article is concerned only with a priest.[56] It is not perfectly clear, though, that the reservation extends to minor clerics. If a minor cleric is denounced to the Holy See, however, there is little doubt that the Holy Office will reduce him to the lay state.

---

[53] Canon 1935, § 1.

[54] López, *art. cit.,* p. 34.

[55] López, *art. cit.,* pp. 34-35.

[56] Iorio (*Theologia Moralis,* II, n. 286), in commenting on the reservation, refers to the delict as mentioned in canon 2358 as well as in canon 2359. He seems to understand the reservation as extending to all clerics.

ARTICLE 2. FOR A RELIGIOUS PROFESSION DECLARED NULL BECAUSE OF *Dolus*

The final instance of the reduction to the lay state as a penalty for minor clerics is mentioned in canon 2387. According to this canon a religious cleric whose religious profession has been declared null because of *dolus* perpetrated by him is to be expelled from the clerical state if he is in minor Orders.[57] The first impulse upon a perusal of this canon is to refer to canon 572, § 1, 4°, which demands for the validity of a religious profession that the profession be made without *dolus*. But immediately a difficulty is encountered, for it is not clear from canon 572 that the *dolus* of which the candidate for profession is the author suffices of itself to invalidate his religious profession.

A. Religious Profession Null Because of Dolus

By *dolus* is understood every artifice, fraud and machination used to circumvent, delude and deceive another.[58] According to canon 103 acts placed in consequence of *dolus* are valid unless the contrary is stated in law. Canon 542, 1°, expressly states that the *dolus* of which the superior is either the author or the victim invalidates the admission to the novitiate. But canon 572, § 1, 4°, is not so clearly worded that it evidently requires that the superior be not the victim of *dolus* if the religious profession is not to be invalid. The canon states that for the validity of the profession it must be emitted without *dolus*.[59] It is the unanimous opinion of the authors that this requisite refers at least to the candidate for profession, that is, that he be not the victim of the *dolus*. But does this also mean, as canon 542 evidently does, that *dolus* must likewise be absent in such manner that the superior is not the victim of the *dolus* of the candidate?

[57] Canon 2387: Religiosus clericus cuius professio ob admissum ab ipso dolum nulla fuerit declarata, si sit in minoribus ordinibus constitutus, e statu clericali abiiciatur. . . .

[58] D. (4.3) 2: . . . ipse [Labeo] sic definiit dolum malum esse omnem calliditatem fallaciam machinationem ad circumveniendum fallendum decipiendum alterum adhibitam. . . .

[59] Canon 572, § 1: Ad validitatem cuiusvis religiosae professionis requiritur ut: 4°. Professio sine vi aut metu gravi aut dolo emittatur.

Some authors think that the *dolus* of which the superior is the victim does invalidate the profession.[60] This opinion appears to be in solid harmony with canon 2387, which evidently postulates that a profession may be "declared" invalid because of *dolus*. Moreover, other authors, in commenting on canon 2387, refer to canon 572, § 1, 4°, and thus apparently embrace the opinion that the *dolus* of which the superior is the victim suffices to invalidate the profession.[61]

However, the majority of authors who comment on canon 572 maintain that the *dolus* of which the superior is the victim does not invalidate the profession.[62] They compare canon 542, which explicitly states that *dolus* on either side invalidates the admission to the novitiate, with canon 572, in which neither the superior nor the candidate are expressly mentioned, but in which it is simply stated that the profession must be emitted without *dolus*. Then they argue that *dolus* does not invalidate an act unless the law states the contrary.[63] In canon 572 a contrary statement of the law, insofar as the superior in the capacity of a victim of the *dolus* is concerned, is at least doubtful. Hence it must be concluded that the *dolus* of which the superior is the victim does not invalidate a religious pro-

---

[60] Wernz-Vidal, *Ius Canonicum*, III, 270; Oesterle, *Praelectiones Iuris Canonici*, I, 314; Beste, *Introductio in Codicem*, p. 383; Palombo, *De Dimissione Religiosorum*, p. 176; Craisson, *Manuale Totius Iuris Canonici*, n. 2694; Frey, *The Act of Religious Profession*, The Catholic University of America Canon Law Studies, n. 63 (Washington, D. C.: The Catholic University of America, 1931), p. 95.

[61] Augustine, *A Commentary*, VIII, 474; Pistocchi, *I Canoni Penali del Codice Ecclesiastico Esposti e Commentati* (Torino-Roma: Marietti, 1925), p. 313; Smith, *The Penal Law for Religious*, The Catholic University of America Canon Law Studies, n. 98 (Washington, D. C.: The Catholic University of America, 1935), p. 109.

[62] Schäfer, *De Religiosis*, p. 575, 4; Larraona, "Commentarium Codicis-Canon 542"—*CpRM*, XVII (1936), 12; Vermeersch-Creusen, *Epitome*, I, n. 673; Chelodi, *Ius de Personis*, p. 453; Coronata, *Institutiones*, I, 754; Cappello, *Summa Iuris Canonici in Usum Scholarum Concinnata* (3 vols., Vol. II, Romae: Apud Aedes Universitatis Gregorianae, 1930), II, 217; Goyeneche, "Consultatio" —*CpRM*, XVI (1935), 233-234; Gerster a Zeil, *Ius Religiosorum* (Taurini, 1935), pp. 107-108; and many others.

[63] Canon 103, § 2: Actus positi ex metu gravi et iniuste incussus vel ex dolo, valent, nisi aliud iure caveatur. . . .

fession, since even invalidating laws are not to be upheld in an objective doubt of law.[64]

Finally, a strong argument in favor of this opinion is drawn from canon 647. In this canon it is stated that sickness is not a sufficient cause for the dismissal of a religious in temporary vows unless the sickness was *dolose* concealed or dissimulated before profession. If the profession were rendered invalid by the *dolus* of which the superior is the victim, then there would be no need of a dismissal, since the invalidly professed cleric would not be a member of the institute.[65] Hence the conclusion is that canon 647 appears to regard a profession which a religious made by deceiving the superior regarding the state of his health as valid.[66]

Because of this argumentation the contention that the *dolus* of which the superior is the victim does not invalidate the profession appears to reflect the better opinion. However, in view of this opinion, how can canon 2387 ever be applied? It should be noted that canon 2387 does not have application when an act or contract is rescinded. An act placed in consequence of *dolus* may be rescinded according to the norms of canons 1684-1689.[67] But this is quite different from the declaration of the nullity of the profession according to the norms of canons 1679-1683. Canon 2387 refers to the declaration of nullity, and not to the rescission of the profession. The answer appears to be that a profession may be declared null because of the *dolus* of which the superior was the victim when such *dolus* was present at the time of the admission to the novitiate. By reason of this *dolus* the novitiate is invalid, and also the consequent profession.[68]

Again, the profession may be declared invalid because of *dolus* whenever the *dolus* of the candidate induces substantial error on the part of the superior. In such a case the profession is invalid *ipso iure*.[69] Such a case can occur when through the intervention of *dolus* there has been concealed the presence of an impediment which

[64] Canon 15.
[65] O'Neill, *The Dismissal of Religious in Temporary Vows*, pp. 138-139.
[66] Schäfer, *De Religiosis*, p. 580.
[67] Canon 103, § 2.
[68] Canons 542, 1°; 572, § 1, 3°.
[69] Canon 104.

of itself invalidates the profession. If by means of *dolus* the candidate for profession concealed his age, for instance, even though in admitting his lack of age he would have obtained a dispensation, then it seems that his profession may be declared null because of the *dolus* of the candidate. In this case, while the immediate cause of the invalidity of the profession is the lack of the required age, the remote cause is the *dolus* of the candidate, for if he had applied for a dispensation it would have been granted.

Again, if the candidate did not express true consent in his profession and this later came to light, then the profession can be declared invalid because of the *dolus* of the candidate. However, in any event, the cleric is not to be punished according to canon 2387 unless the profession is declared invalid in view of the *dolus* perpetrated by him. Hence in the last analysis the decision which declares the profession to have been invalid and concomitantly states the reason for this decision will indicate also the factor which determines whether a cleric may be punished according to canon 2387.

Vermeersch-Creusen [70] and Cappello [71] consider the case wherein the *dolus* was present at the time of the admission to the novitiate, so that the novitiate and the consequent profession were rendered invalid. In this case they think that, if the impediment which was concealed by *dolus* remains a cause for which the candidate will be expelled even at the end of the novitiate, then the profession will be declared invalid because of *dolus*. However, if in view of the sterling qualities of the candidate the impediment would have been dispensed had the truth been known, then they think that the profession will be declared null rather because of the invalidity of the novitiate than because of *dolus*. But, as they point out, the infliction of the penalty will depend on the motive alleged in the declaration of the nullity. It is of importance to note that these authors in their consideration of canon 2387 look back to canon 572, § 1, 4°. And in their commentary on canon 572 they maintain that *dolus* in this canon refers only to the *dolus* of which the candidate is the victim. Evidently, then, they invoke some distinction, but they do not expressly state what this distinction is.

[70] *Epitome*, III, n. 591.
[71] *De Censuris*, n. 528.

B. *The Declaration of Nullity*

In the pre-Code law the process for determining the validity of a religious profession was governed by the norms outlined in the Council of Trent,[72] and in the Constitution *"Si datam"* of Benedict XIV, issued on March 4, 1748.[73] After the Code this process is no longer demanded. The Code itself has not expressly indicated any specific norms for handling the process. If the process ever were to be instituted, it may be conducted according to the norms of canons 1993-1998, as enacted for the causes regarding the validity of sacred Orders or the obligations arising from sacred Orders.[74] Since a cause of this kind is definitely a cause regarding the status of a person, it appears that a double conformable sentence is necessary.[75] However, it seems that most of the cases of this kind will be handled by the Sacred Congregation of Religious. Finally, the declaration of nullity in any case must be evident either from the judicial sentence of a major superior in a clerical exempt institute, or from a decree of the Sacred Congregation of Religious.[76]

C. *The Penalty*

Some authors think that canon 2387 refers only to clerics who have invalidly made a perpetual religious profession.[77] They argue principally on the word *religiosus* of canon 2387. By a religious is understood one who takes vows in some religious institute.[78] When a novice takes vows for his first profession he is not a religious, nor does he become one by his invalid profession. Therefore the canon can refer only to a religious already professed who then makes an invalid profession of simple perpetual or of solemn vows. Furthermore, they say, it does not seem indicated to presume that the Church wishes to be so severe, unless the question revolves around a pro-

---

[72] Sess. XXV, *de regularibus,* c. 19.

[73] *Fontes,* n. 385.

[74] Schäfer, *De Religiosis,* p. 951.

[75] Cf. canons 1998, § 1; 1987; 1903.

[76] Schäfer, *loc. cit.*

[77] Cipollini (*De Censuris Latae Sententiae iuxta Codicem Iuris Canonici* [Taurini, 1925], pp. 211-212) mentions the opinion. He does not hold it.

[78] Canon 488, 7°.

fession through which the bond of the professed with the religious institute is fully complete, that is, a perpetual profession. Cappello, although adhering to the opposite interpretation, thinks that in view of the doubtful interpretation the milder opinion is to be followed in practice.[79]

However, this does not seem to be a tenable interpretation. If the word *religiosus* be taken so strictly, then a cleric whose admission into the novitiate and consequent professions, both temporary and perpetual, were invalid because of *dolu*s could not be punished at all according to canon 2387, since he is not and never was a religious. Moreover, if this argument were extended to its ultimate conclusion, then the question would arise whether canon 2387 could ever be applied. Thus, the temporary vows of a religious cease after three years unless the constitutions demand only an annual profession, or unless the religious is so young that at the termination of his triennial temporary vows he will not have the age required for perpetual profession.[80] However, in accordance with canon 34, § 3, 5°, the profession may be renewed at any time during the day on which the vows cease. But the cleric at the termination has already decided that he will make an invalid perpetual profession. Now, for all practical purposes this decision in regard to the vows is the same as a decision to leave the institute. Hence the cleric has ceased to be a religious, and is not subject to the penalty of canon 2387. This last argument is of course absurd. Yet, if too great emphasis be placed on the word *religiosus* it is readily possible to arrive at this conclusion.

Canon 2387 makes no distinction between temporary and perpetual profession. In harmony, then, with the principle *"ubi lex non distinguit nec nos distinguere debemus,"* [81] it is held that any cleric whose profession, whether temporary or perpetual, has been declared null because of *dolus* is subject to the penalty of canon 2387.[82] Again, it should be pointed out that according to a decision

---

[79] *De Censuris,* n. 528.

[80] Canon 574, § 1.

[81] Cf. Wernz, *Ius Decretalium,* I, n. 131, I.

[82] Coronata, *Institutiones,* IV, 632; Cipollini, *De Censuris Latae Sententiae iuxta Codicem Iuris Canonici,* pp. 211-212.

of the Pontifical Commission for the Interpretation of the Code on June 3, 1918, canon 2387 is applicable also to societies of clerics without vows inasfar as the members live a common life.[83]

Before the penalty can be inflicted the *dolus* must be perpetrated by the cleric himself. If anyone other than the cleric was the cause of the *dolus* then the cleric is not subject to the penalty, since canon 2387 clearly indicates that the cleric must commit the *dolus*.[84] Furthermore, the declaration of invalidity must be on the score of *dolus* before the penalty can be inflicted. If the profession is declared null for any other reason, even though at the same time it could have been declared null because of *dolus*, it does not seem that the penalty can be inflicted.

The penalty of the reduction of the cleric to the lay state is clearly a *ferendae sententiae* penalty. Furthermore, in accordance with the opinion sponsored in the previous article, it is held that the local ordinary cannot inflict the penalty by means of the administrative measure of a decree according to canon 211, § 2. For the infliction of the penalty a criminal process is required. The terms used in the canon are mandatory. Hence, once the declaration of nullity on the score of *dolus* is given, the penalty is to be inflicted.

[83] *AAS*, X (1918), 347; Bouscaren, *The Canon Law Digest*, I, 330.
[84] Cappello, *De Censuris*, n. 528.

CHAPTER VII

REDUCTION EFFECTED BY THE CLERIC
AND THE ORDINARY

It has been seen in the law prior to the Code that gradually the old discipline which forbade minor clerics to leave the clerical state was abandoned. The Code did not renew the older discipline, but clearly states the freedom of the minor cleric to leave the clerical state. Furthermore, it grants the local ordinary rather wide powers to remand a minor cleric to the lay state. The canon regarding these methods of reduction will now be considered.

Article 1. Voluntary Reduction of Secular Minor Clerics

In the enumeration of means in canon 211, § 2, for the return of a minor cleric to the lay state, it is specifically stated that the cleric may leave the clerical state of his own choice after advising the local ordinary of his decision.[1] Hence this article may well be divided into the consideration (1) of the decision of the minor cleric; and (2) of the notification of the ordinary of this decision.

A. The Decision of the Minor Cleric

In the treatment of the decision of the minor cleric to leave the clerical state the question of vocation immediately presents itself. Neither time nor space will permit, nor does the scope of this dissertation demand, that any attempt be made to decide the essential constituents of a vocation to the clerical state. However, it will be helpful to mention some opinions regarding vocation and to see how these may influence the decision of the cleric.

Cappello lists seven opinions concerning the nature of vocation, but it is of interest for the question under discussion to consider only

---

[1] Canon 211, § 2: Clericus minor ad statum laicalem regreditur . . . sua ipsius voluntate, praemonito loci Ordinario. . . .

a few of these.[2] According to one opinion vocation consists in a certain inclination towards the clerical state, which inclination is so attractive, so constant and so strong that it can come only from God. This opinion is no longer tenable since the Commission of Cardinals appointed to review the work *La vocation sacerdotale* of Canon Joseph Lahitton in 1912 decided that the sacerdotal vocation does not consist, at least necessarily and by ordinary norms, in a certain internal inspiration of the subject, or in an invitation from the Holy Spirit to embrace the priesthood.[3]

A second opinion considers the sacerdotal vocation when judged from the consequent will of God to be the call of the bishop; when judged from the antecedent will of God to be the fitness for the clerical state with the sincere intention of fulfilling its obligations.[4] This opinion excludes the notion of an internal vocation.

Finally, many authors, while granting that a sacerdotal vocation consists formally in the call of the bishop, nevertheless postulate the necessity of a divine call antecedent to the call of the bishop.[5] While they differ to a certain extent in their opinions concerning the elements of this internal vocation, it is sufficient here to note that they do demand an internal vocation. This opinion appears to be the best if there be taken into consideration the wording of the Code,[6] the testimony of tradition which these writers cite, and finally the Instruction of the Sacred Congregation of the Sacraments of December 27, 1930.[7]

Now, since first tonsure and Orders are to be conferred only on

---

[2] *De Sacra Ordinatione*, n. 363.

[3] *AAS*, IV (1912), 485.

[4] Vermeersch, *Theologia Moralis*, III, n. 688.

[5] Raus, *La Doctrine de S. Alphonse sur la Vocation et la Grace en regard de l'Enseignement de S. Thomas et des Prescriptions du Code* (Lyon-Paris, Emmanuel Vitte, 1926), pp. 30-37; Cappello, *De Sacra Ordinatione*, n. 363; Prümmer, *Manuale Theologiae Moralis secundum Principia S. Thomae Aquinatis* (8. ed., recognita a P. Dr. Engelberto M. Münch, 3 vols., Friburgi Brisgoviae, 1935-1936), III, n. 602; Noldin-Schmitt, *De Praeceptis Dei et Ecclesiae* (25. ed., Oeniponte: Typis et Sumptibus Fel. Rauch, 1938), n. 751; Iorio, *Theologia Moralis*, III, n. 936.

[6] Canon 1353.

[7] *AAS*, XXIII (1931), 120-127. Cf. especially § 1, n. 1; § 1, n. 3; § 3, n. 3.

those who have the intention of becoming priests, and regarding whom it may rightfully be conjectured that they will some day be worthy priests,[8] the presumption is that the minor cleric had a vocation, or at least thought that he had a vocation, when he received Orders.[9] Between the time of the reception of Orders and of the decision of the minor cleric to leave the clerical state something intervened to make the cleric change his mind. It may have been that the cleric decided that he did not have a vocation, that is, either that he lacked the necessary qualifications, or that he was not called by God. In this case the decision of the cleric is worthy of high praise both for his courage in the face perhaps of human respect and for his understanding of the sublime dignity of the priesthood which he was unwilling to enter upon unless he felt he was truly called. Or it may have been that the cleric was firmly convinced that he had a vocation, but that, after considering the demands and obligations of the priesthood, he was unwilling to take these upon himself, though he had the conviction that he could observe them.

The question then arises whether the cleric is free to desert his vocation by leaving the clerical state. So far as positive law is concerned the minor cleric is perfectly free to leave the clerical state. There is no hint of any restriction in canon 211; there is simply the statement that the cleric may return to the lay state of his own volition. Furthermore, the Code explicitly states that it is wrong to force anyone in any way or for any reason into the clerical state,[10] and this rule likewise holds with reference to any coercion in retaining a minor cleric in the clerical state.

In the internal forum the case is somewhat different. In the extremely rare cases wherein the cleric understands it to be the absolute will of God that he ascend to the priesthood he would sin gravely in deserting his vocation.[11] Again, in the event that the cleric is morally certain of his vocation, though it is only an invita-

---

[8] Canon 973, § 1.

[9] Instructio, § 1, n. 3: Episcopus . . . prae oculis habeat oportet . . . ne ad tonsuram et minores Ordines admittantur ii, qui . . . a Deo non sunt vocati.

[10] Canon 971.

[11] Many, *Praelectiones de Sacra Ordinatione* (Parisiis: Apud Letouzey et Ané, 1905), n. 82; Cappello, *De Sacra Ordinatione*, n. 379.

tion and not a command from God, he would sin lightly against charity towards himself by deserting that vocation, since he would deprive himself of particular helps of grace and might expose himself to the danger of damnation.[12]   Finally, in some rare instances the cleric may be obliged to follow his vocation by reason of some exterior motive not dissociated from vocation, for in that case the vocation is presumed to be present.   Thus, if a cleric received a benefice, he would be obliged to receive the Order demanded by that benefice, even the priesthood.[13]

However, as was seen previously, the minor cleric may leave the clerical state.   But by so doing he relinquishes his right to that benefice, since only clerics may obtain benefices.[14]   If he wants to retain the benefice, he must remain in the clerical state.   In this way the law may be said to oblige him indirectly.   Again, the necessity of the Church in particular circumstances, especially because of the fewness of priests, may demand that the cleric remain in the clerical state and receive the priesthood.   However, Cappello demands three conditions before this case is verified: (1) There must be a true spiritual and grave necessity; (2) this necessity must be such that it cannot be appropriately provided for in any other way; and (3) the cleric must feel that he really has a divine vocation. It need hardly be remarked that the instances in which these circumstances will all coincide are very infrequent.

Lastly, the cleric may be obliged by the precept of a superior to receive the priesthood, and in consequence of this precept not to leave the clerical state.   While the conditions which warrant such a precept would be the same as those just mentioned in relation to the necessity of the Church, the difference between the two cases would result from the fact that by the precept of the superior the cleric would be bound also in the external forum.   However, in view of the present-day discipline regarding the reception of Orders and the continuance of life in the clerical state, which demands that the cleric be entirely free in his choice, the only superior who can impose such a precept is the Supreme Pontiff, since he alone is be-

[12] Cappello, *loc. cit.*; Aertnys-Damen, *Theologia Moralis*, II, n. 583.
[13] Cappello, *ibid.*, n. 384.
[14] Canon 118.

yond all subjection to this positive law.[15]   It seems needless to insist that the instances in which a cleric would be obliged by some exterior motive to remain in the clerical state are extremely isolated. In ordinary cases, as far as the positive law of the Church is concerned, the minor cleric is absolutely free to leave the clerical state.

B. Notification of the Ordinary

Before the minor cleric leaves the clerical state it is required that he inform his proper local ordinary of his decision.[16]   Consequently it is evident that the minor cleric cannot licitly leave the clerical state until he has notified the local ordinary of his decision. However, it cannot be argued from this canon that the notification of the ordinary is necessary before the cleric can validly leave the clerical state.   The consent of the ordinary is by no means required. Furthermore, canon 211, § 2, gives entire freedom to the minor cleric to quit the clerical state in spite of the dissent and even in disregard of an explicit precept of the ordinary, since nowhere in law is the ordinary granted the power to impose such a precept.

On the contrary, the entire spirit of the Church in regard to the reception of Orders and the continuance in the clerical state is that coercion be entirely absent.   This is evident not only from the Code,[17] but also from the Instruction of the Sacred Congregation of the Sacraments, in accordance with which the cleric must sign a document that he is receiving first tonsure and the minor Orders of his own free will.[18]   If there be taken into consideration the law of canon 211, § 2, which grants the cleric entire freedom, and the Instruction just mentioned together with the present discipline of the Church in which unwillingness to receive major Orders practically implies unwillingness to remain in the clerical state, it must be concluded that coercion is entirely to be avoided both as regards the minor cleric receiving major Orders and as regards his continuance in the clerical state.

When a cleric does decide to quit his state of life it seems suffi-

---

[15] Cappello, *De Sacra Ordinatione*, n. 385.

[16] Canon 211, § 2.

[17] Canon 971.

[18] *Instructio*, § 2, n. 1—*AAS*, XXIII (1931), 122.

cient that he notify the seminary officials, whose duty it will then be
to notify the proper ordinary of the cleric. It does not seem essential that the cleric personally inform the ordinary, since no consent
of the latter is necessary; the cleric may furnish this information
mediately through the seminary officials. In practice the latter
method will perhaps be more feasible, although in accordance with
the law it is to be noted that the ordinary should be informed before
the cleric deserts the clerical state.

Again, it should be pointed out that the obligation to notify the
ordinary rests primarily on the cleric. This obligation may be trans-
ferred to the seminary officials for its execution only if they are willing to accept it, or if the cleric knows from practice that this is the
procedure. Finally, in the notification of the ordinary it is not
necessary that any reasons be given for the decision of the cleric,
though to do this is perhaps the better practice. The reason that
the cleric has decided that he has no vocation is certainly sufficient
to effect his withdrawal from the clerical state.

ARTICLE 2. REDUCTION BY DECREE OF THE ORDINARY

The last method, as listed by the Code, of reducing a minor cleric
to the lay state is that which is achieved by means of a decree of
the local ordinary issued for a just cause. The just cause is present
if the ordinary, after considering all the facts and circumstances,
prudently judges in view of the dignity of the clerical state that
the cleric should not be promoted to sacred Orders.[19]

A. *The Ordinary*

The decree which reduces the minor cleric to the lay state is to
be issued by the local ordinary. Canon 198 enumerates in detail all
who are embraced under the term *"Ordinarius."* In the second paragraph of the same canon it is indicated that all comprehended in the
term *"Ordinarius"* are comprehended also in the phrase *"Ordinarius*

---

[19] Canon 211, § 2: Clericus minor ad statum laicalem regreditur . . . eiusdem
(loci) Ordinarii decreto iusta de causa lato, si nempe Ordinarius, omnibus per-
pensis, prudenter iudicaverit clericum non posse cum decore status clericalis ad
ordines sacros promoveri.

loci" with the exception of religious major superiors.[20]   Consequently, since canon 211 explicitly mentions the local ordinary, it is evident that the canon is considering only secular minor clerics to the exclusion of religious minor clerics.

The local ordinary competent to reduce the minor cleric is the proper ordinary of that cleric, the ordinary in whose diocese the cleric was incardinated through first tonsure.   Since any other local ordinary cannot incardinate a cleric if the proper ordinary is unwilling to relinquish his cleric,[21] *a fortiori* it is beyond the power of another ordinary to reduce to the lay state a cleric who is incardinated in another diocese.   The only exception would be the case in which a cleric committed a delict against the sixth commandment in the diocese of another ordinary.   Then, if the adjuncts warrant it, the cleric is to be reduced to the lay state [22] and the competent forum becomes the place where the delict was committed.[23]

The case will occur in which a minor cleric studying in a seminary outside his diocese is dismissed from the seminary for one of the reasons outlined in canon 1371.[24]   What is the juridical status of this cleric?   There is no indication in law that the cleric, by the fact of his dismissal, is reduced to the lay state.   Consequently, though the reasons for dismissal from a seminary and the reasons for the reduction to the lay state are somewhat parallel, the reduc-

---

[20] Canon 198, § 1: In iure nomine *Ordinarii* intelliguntur, nisi qui expresse excipiatur, praeter Romanum Pontificem, pro suo quisque territorio Episcopus residentialis, Abbas vel Praelatus *nullius* eorumque Vicarius Generalis, Administrator, Vicarius et Praefectus Apostolicus, itemque ii qui praedictis deficientibus interim ex iuris praescripto aut ex probatis constitutionibus succedunt in regimine, pro suis vero subditis Superiores maiores in religionibus clericalibus exemptis.

§ 2: Nomine autem *Ordinarii loci* seu *locorum* veniunt omnes recensiti, exceptis Superioribus religiosis.

[21] Canons 112-114.

[22] Canon 2358.

[23] Canon 1566, § 1; cf. Coronata, *Institutiones,* III, 17-18.

[24] Canon 1371: E seminario dimittantur dyscoli, incorrigibiles, seditiosi, ii qui ob mores atque indolem ad statum ecclesiasticum idonei non videantur; itemque, qui in studiis adeo parum proficiant ut spes non affulgeat eos sufficientem doctrinam fore assecuturos; praesertim vero statim dimittantur qui forte contra bonos mores aut fidem deliquerint.

tion to the lay state, as a deprivation of rights with reference to which the law demands a strict interpretation,[25] is not considered a result of the dismissal from a seminary.

Furthermore, though the ordinary of the place where the seminary is located judges that this cleric cannot be promoted to sacred Orders, it is by no means apparent that he can reduce this cleric to the lay state. It would indeed be strange if the ordinary of a diocese other than that in which the cleric is incardinated could reduce the cleric to the lay state, thereby depriving the proper ordinary of a cleric. Consequently the proper ordinary of the cleric, to the exclusion of other ordinaries, has the right to reduce the cleric if he judges that the cleric cannot be promoted to sacred Orders.

The proper ordinary may judge it fitting to delegate with the power to reduce the cleric to the lay state the superiors of the seminary who dismiss the cleric. Since the power to reduce the cleric is annexed by law to the office of the ordinary it is ordinary power.[26] Whoever has ordinary power may delegate it in whole or in part unless the contrary is stated in law.[27] In the law nothing is stated which restricts the delegation of the power to reduce clerics to the lay state. Therefore it appears that this power can be delegated. However, since it is according to the judgment of the proper ordinary that the decree of reduction is to be issued, it appears that this ordinary should previously learn from the seminary officials what norms they use to dismiss a cleric. If these norms in his judgment are sufficient to indicate the advisability of simultaneously reducing the cleric to the lay state, he may delegate this power to them.

The ordinary may use either method, that is, he may himself reduce the cleric, or he may delegate to others the power to do so. But it does seem that some provision should be made for the reduction, unless the ordinary intends to have the cleric continue his studies elsewhere. Otherwise the cleric, though according to law he is still attached to his diocese, for all practical purposes would acquire a nondescript status much like that of a vagrant cleric. Thus there

[25] Canon 19.
[26] Canon 197, § 1.
[27] Canon 199, § 1.

would be occasioned a situation which runs contrary to the spirit of the Code.[28]

B. The Just Cause

Since the causes for which a minor cleric may be reduced to the lay state are so many and so manifold, the Code prefers to leave the question of the just cause to the judgment of the ordinary. The Code simply furnishes a general norm. According to canon 211, § 2, a just cause is present when the ordinary, after considering all the facts and circumstances, prudently judges that in view of the dignity of the clerical state the cleric should not be promoted to sacred Orders. From causes which are judged sufficient in somewhat parallel cases it is possible to a certain extent to particularize this general norm. However, it is not contended here that the causes which will be mentioned constitute an exhaustive enumeration.

The causes which are sufficient for a dismissal from a seminary likewise are just causes for the reduction of the minor cleric to the lay state. This is evident from the general norm of canon 1371, which treats of causes sufficient for dismissal from a seminary. The canon states that the seminarians who, because of character and temperament, do not seem fitted for the ecclesiastical state are to be dismissed. More specifically the canon mentions that students who are stubborn, incorrigible or seditious are to be dismissed. Again, those who progress so little in their studies that there appears no hope that they will attain sufficient learning are to be dismissed. Finally, and especially so, those seminarians who fail against faith or morals are to be dismissed.

The ordinary will be assisted in his decision by a perusal of the canons which treat of irregularities,[29] of simple impediments [30] and of the requisites for a licit ordination.[31] As a rule these matters will be settled before the candidate receives minor Orders, but through some mistake they may have been overlooked, or an irregularity or also an impediment may arise after the candidate has received these

[28] Cf. canon 111, § 1.
[29] Canons 984; 985.
[30] Canon 987.
[31] Canon 974.

Orders. Again, the norms outlined on December 27, 1930, by the Sacred Congregation of the Sacraments for the testing of seminarians before their promotion to Orders will be of great assistance to the ordinary in making his decision. The model questionnaires given in the appendix of the Instruction for the inquisition of the pastor of the cleric, and the interrogation of other approved persons, will be of particular help to the ordinary, not only as guides for these interrogations, but also as norms in accordance with which he may reach his decision that the cleric is not to be promoted to higher Orders and, as a result, is to be reduced to the lay state.[32]

Finally, it should be pointed out that the ordinary is not easily to be judged too severe if he decides to reduce the cleric to the lay state. The Sacred Congregation, in its Instruction, recalls to the mind of the ordinary the recommendation of St. Paul to Timothy, "Do not lay hands hastily upon anyone, and do not be a partner in other men's sins." [33] Moreover, the encyclical on the priesthood issued by the late renowned Holy Father, Pius XI, indicates the need for unyielding stringency in demanding from the candidate for Holy Orders positive evidence of holiness.[34]

C. The Decree

By a decree is understood an administrative mode of procedure in contradistinction to the judicial process with its definitive sentence, which is the climax of the judicial mode of procedure. The decree may be employed to provide an administrative measure or, in certain limited cases, to impose a penalty. However, as was seen previously, the decree cannot be used to impose the reduction of the cleric to the lay state in the nature of a penalty.[35] Hence the decree contemplated in canon 211 always provides for the reduction of the cleric to the lay state as an administrative measure.

The Church is unwilling that this administrative procedure be used indiscriminately to impose penalties. Consequently the cases in which this mode of procedure may be used to inflict a penalty are

[32] *AAS,* XXIII (1931), 128-129.
[33] *AAS,* XXIII (1931), 120.
[34] *AAS,* XXVIII (1936), 5-53; cf. especially pp. 42-44.
[35] Cf. *supra,* pp. 95-101.

exhaustively enumerated.[36]   Nevertheless, in her ardent wish that none but worthy candidates approach the priesthood, the Church has provided the ordinary with the wide power of canon 211, § 2. With this power the ordinary may reduce to the lay state not only those who fail grievously, but also those whom he judges not to be suitable for the sacerdotal life. But, in the use of this power the ordinary does not impose a penalty. By this administrative procedure he provides by means of an administrative measure for the reduction of the cleric to the lay state.

Against this decree of the ordinary the cleric has no appeal. However, he may always have recourse to the Holy See. This recourse does not suspend the effects of the decree. But, if the recourse is favorably answered, the cleric will be restored to his former state. Still, in view of the power granted the ordinary by canon 211, it seems clear that the cases in which the decision of the ordinary will be overruled are extremely rare. Nevertheless, in a case of manifest injustice there is no doubt that the Holy See will provide for the rights of the cleric.

[36] Canon 1933, § 4.

CHAPTER VIII

THE REDUCTION OF MAJOR CLERICS

BEFORE consideration will be given to the reduction of major clerics to the lay state it should again be emphasized that this reduction does not theologically imply any change of status. In other words, the character of Holy Orders received in the conferral of the priesthood or of the diaconate, and, according to some, also of the subdiaconate, remains untouched. In the sight of God, as far as the Sacrament of Holy Orders is concerned, the cleric who has been reduced to the lay state still remains a cleric. The reduction spoken of here is simply of the nature of an external, canonical or juridical reduction. In the eyes of the law and for legal effects the cleric is now a layman.

The Code explicitly indicates three methods for the reduction of a major cleric to the lay state. The major cleric may be reduced by means of a rescript of the Holy See, in virtue of a decree or sentence according to the norm of canon 214, and by way of the penalty of degradation.[1] To these three another method not excluded by the Code may be added. This method consists in the granting of a dispensation for marriage to a major cleric. The reasons for this will be seen later. It is now necessary to examine each method. It is thought preferable to postpone until last the consideration of canon 214, since that will require a more detailed study.

ARTICLE 1. REDUCTION BY A RESCRIPT OF THE HOLY SEE

The sole reference in the entire Code to the method of reduction by means of a rescript of the Holy See is made in canon 211, § 1. This canon simply states that a major cleric may be reduced to the lay state by means of a rescript of the Holy See.[2] The commentary

---

[1] Canon 211, § 1.

[2] Canon 211, § 1: Etsi sacra ordinatio, semel valide recepta, nunquam irrita fiat, clericus tamen maior ad statum laicalem redigitur rescripto Sanctae Sedis. . . .

of the authors likewise is extremely concise. Most of the authors content themselves with a restatement of the canon. In a close study of this kind, however, it is necessary to go into more detail. Consequently it is proposed to consider the rescript itself, the Congregations which are competent to issue the rescript, the effect of the rescript when it is granted for deacons and subdeacons and, finally, its effect when it is granted for bishops and priests.

A. The Rescript

A rescript is the response of a prelate of the Church given in writing in answer to a petition. Rescripts, considered from the standpoint of the subject matter, are divided into rescripts of justice, rescripts of favor and rescripts of a mixed character. Rescripts of justice pertain to legal suits and the administration of justice, as exemplified in the appointment of judges, the explanation of obscurities in the law, and so forth. Rescripts of favor grant benefits or execute provisions which in no way pertain to judicial contentions, as exemplified in the grant of dispensations, of privileges, of indulgences, and so forth. Rescripts of a mixed character contain provisions which implement both the administration of justice and the granting of favors, the latter being unconnected with judicial affairs. In relation to the law, rescripts are either contrary to, conformed to, or outside of the scope of the law. Finally, considered according to their form, rescripts are granted *in forma gratiosa,* when there is no requirement of any intermediary for the execution of the rescript, and *in forma commissoria,* when there is a requirement of such an intermediary.[3]

The rescript by means of which a major cleric is reduced to the lay state is a rescript of favor. It is not concerned with legal suits or judgments. It runs counter to the law. It contains a dispensation from some or all of the obligations of the clerical state. It may be issued *in forma gratiosa* or *in forma commissoria.* The latter form is the one more frequently used. In this case the ordinary is usually named as the executor of the rescript.

[3] O'Neill, *Papal Rescripts of Favor,* The Catholic University of America Canon Law Studies, n. 57 (Washington, D. C.: The Catholic University of America, 1930), pp. 1-3.

B. The Competent Authorities of the Roman Curia

As a rule the reduction of the cleric to the lay state will pertain to the external forum. The authorities of the Roman Curia competent to issue the rescript of reduction are for secular clerics the Sacred Congregation of the Sacraments [4] and the Sacred Congregation of the Council; [5] for religious clerics the Sacred Congregation of the Sacraments [6] and the Sacred Congregation of Religious.[7] Moreover, in cases which are reserved to the Holy Office this Supreme Congregation will issue the rescript of reduction to the lay state.[8] Finally, in certain cases, which however are not at all frequent, there may exist a sufficient reason for effecting the reduction as a matter pertaining to the internal forum. In such instances the authority competent to grant the reduction is the Tribunal of the Sacred Penitentiary.[9]

C. The Cases of Deacons and Subdeacons

An outstanding feature in the discipline of the Church regarding the reception of Holy Orders is the emphasis placed on the freedom of the candidate. Thus there is the explicit statement of the Code that it is wrong to force anyone in any way or for any reason to embrace the clerical state.[10] Again, a cleric who is unwilling to receive higher Orders may not be constrained by the bishop to receive them.[11] Finally, before the reception of first tonsure and the minor Orders as well as before the reception of each of the major Orders students for the secular clergy,[12] and before their temporary profession and their

[4] Canon 249, § 3. Cf. Coronata, *Institutiones,* I, 360.

[5] Canon 250, § 1. Cf. Haring ("Zurückversetzung in den Laienstand"— *Theologisch-praktische Quartalschrift* [Linz, 1832—], LXXXVI [1933], 816), who cites such a rescript from the Sacred Congregation of the Council. (Hereafter the listed periodical will be cited as *TPQ.*)

[6] Canon 249, § 3.

[7] Canon 251, § 3. Cf. Coronata, *Institutiones,* I, 360.

[8] López, "De reconciliatione sacerdotis, qui matrimonium attentare praesumpsit"—*Periodica,* XXVI (1937), 505.

[9] Canon 258, § 1.

[10] Canon 971.

[11] Canon 973, § 2.

[12] S. C. de Sacr., *Instructio ad Rmos locorum Ordinarios de scrutinio alumnorum peragendo antequam ad ordines promoveantur,* 27 dec. 1930, § 2, n. 1;

reception of the subdiaconate the students for the religious clergy,[13] must present a signed statement that they are proceeding in this matter with full personal liberty.

On the other hand, the Church is extremely solicitous that only worthy candidates be promoted to sacred Orders. Thus the Code states that the bishop shall not confer sacred Orders on anyone unless from positive arguments he is morally certain of the canonical fitness of the candidate.[14] The Instruction of the Sacred Congregation of the Sacraments recalls to the mind of the bishop the words of St. Paul, "Do not lay hands hastily upon anyone, and do not be a partner in other men's sins." [15] The entire spirit of the law and the corresponding documents emanating from the Holy See breathe forth the intense desire of the Church for a clergy worthy of following in the footsteps of the Master.

However, in spite of all the precautions that are taken, it sometimes happens that a cleric is ordained a deacon or a subdeacon and is afterwards unwilling to advance to the priesthood. In this connection the Instruction of the Sacred Congregation of the Sacraments declares that if, before a person is ordained to the diaconate or the priesthood, the bishop knows for certain, either from the admission of the candidate or from other sources, that he really has no vocation, the bishop shall not fail to have recourse to the Holy See, candidly and fully stating the situation, that is, the reasons which produce a grave doubt regarding the fitness of the candidate to bear worthily and faithfully still greater burdens.[16]

Hence, when a deacon or a subdeacon decides that he has no vocation and therefore is unwilling to advance to the priesthood, or when a bishop prudently judges that he cannot promote a deacon or a sub-

---

§ 3, n. 1—*AAS,* XXIII (1931), 122, 125. The instruction in its entirety is contained on pp. 120-129.

[13] S. C. de Rel., *Instructio ad supremos religionum et societatum clericalium moderatores: de formatione clericali et religiosa alumnorum ad sacerdotium vocatorum, deque scrutinio ante ordinum susceptionem peragendo,* 1 dec. 1931, nn. 14-17—*AAS,* XXIV (1932), 79-80. The instruction in its entirety is contained on pp. 74-81.

[14] Canon 973, § 3.

[15] I Tim., V. 22.

[16] *Instructio,* § 3, n. 3—*AAS,* XXIII (1931), 126.

deacon to higher Orders, recourse should be made to the Sacred Congregation of the Sacraments. In the event that the cleric is a religious and wishes to be dispensed from his vows, it appears that this recourse should be made to the Sacred Congregation of Religious. In such a case a petition may be made for the reduction of the deacon or the subdeacon to the lay state. This petition should be made by the cleric himself, but likewise the petition should be accompanied with the approval of the ordinary. The Holy See, taking into consideration the great obligations of a cleric in major Orders together with the solicitude of the Church for the welfare of souls, will probably grant in the rescript the reduction to the lay state along with a dispensation from all the obligations, including celibacy and the divine office, and in the case of a religious a dispensation from the vows.[17] However, the customary procedure of the Curia in such cases seems to be to include in the rescript the phrase *"sine spe readmissionis ad statum clericalem,"* thereby indicating the reluctance of the Holy See to re-admit the beneficiary of the dispensation to the clerical state.

D. The Cases of Bishops and Priests

The reduction of a major cleric to the lay state may or may not entail a dispensation from the obligation of celibacy. Thus, the Code states that when a major cleric has been reduced to the lay state he is still obliged by the law of celibacy, exception being made for those clerics who were ordained through grave fear.[18] On the other hand, it has just been seen that a deacon or a subdeacon may receive the dispensation by means of a rescript of the Holy See. History has presented an instance in which a bishop was granted a reduction to the lay state, but was not freed from the obligation of celibacy. This case occurred in 1802. The bishop was Charles Talleyrand (1754-1838), Bishop of Autun in France (1788-1791).[19] In the present discipline likewise a bishop may be reduced to the lay state by means of an apostolic rescript if the circumstances warrant such a

---

[17] Cappello, *De Sacra Ordinatione*, n. 381.
[18] Canon 213.
[19] Roskovány, *Coelibatus et Breviarium*, Tom. III, Mon. 1970.

course. It does not seem that a bishop will ever be given permission to marry.

There have been cases in the past in which priests were granted a reduction to the lay state along with a dispensation from the obligation of celibacy. Instances frequently cited are those of the priests in England in 1554 after the religious upheaval, when Pope Julius III (1550-1555) granted his Legate the power to dispense major secular clerics who were already invalidly married,[20] and of the priests in France in 1801 after the French Revolution, when Pope Pius VII (1800-1833) gave his Legate the same faculty.[21] However, it should be indicated that this granted dispensation was valid only for priests who had already invalidly married, in regard only to the woman whom the priest had thus married, and only for the period of her lifetime. After the death of his wife the priest was forbidden to re-marry. Furthermore, in a dispensation granted to a French priest in 1802 it was stated that any sin against the sixth commandment committed by this priest was also a sacrilege.[22]

Again, Benedict IX (1032-1044) permitted a religious priest to marry in order to propagate the family of Aragon which was threatened with extinction.[23] Gasparri (1852-1934) appears to raise some question about the practice of granting to a priest a dispensation for marriage in a case in which no scandal could arise in consequence of the dispensation, inasmuch as the sacerdotal condition of the man is wholly unknown to all, even to his so-called wife, in the place where he is now residing and no memory of him remains at all in the faraway place where he received his ordination. Regarding such an unusual situation Gasparri simply stated that he did not know whether the Sacred Penitentiary had ever denied this dispensation when it was sought.[24] Cappello testifies that in such an extremely rare situation the dispensation was sometimes given. However, as a further

---

[20] Roskovány, *op. cit.,* Tom. II, Mon. 1333.

[21] Roskovány, *op. cit.,* Tom. III, Mon. 1969.

[22] Roskovány, *op. cit.,* Tom. III, Mon. 1970.

[23] Gasparri, *Tractatus Canonicus de Matrimonio* (ed. nova, 2 vols., Romae: Typis Polyglottis Vaticanis, 1932), I, 373. (Hereafter cited as *De Matrimonio.*)

[24] Gasparri, *De Martrimonio,* I, 373, footnote 1.

consideration for the granting of the dispensation he points to the consideration that a separation was impossible or extremely difficult under the given circumstances.[25]

Finally, a dispensation is sometimes given when a priest, on the score of the grave fear or constraint under which he received his ordination, impugns the obligations which arise in consequence of the ordination. If in such a case full proof of the grave fear or constraint is lacking, but there still remains some grave doubt that the cleric actually contracted the obligations, then the Sacred Congregation of the Sacraments may ask the Holy Father to grant a dispensation from celibacy. When such a dispensation is granted, certain conditions may be demanded of the cleric, for instance, that he dwell in a place where his former condition is not known.[26] In any case in which a dispensation from celibacy is given by the Holy See the cleric is always reduced to the lay state.

Ordinarily, however, when a priest is reduced to the lay state there is no dispensation from celibacy. The reasons which may impel a priest to seek such a reduction are manifold. It may be that he has developed such a distaste for the priestly life that he feels incapable of remaining therein and fulfilling his priestly duties. Again, he may have developed such an aversion for this manner of life that, if he has not already illicitly abandoned it, he is ready and anxious to do so at the first possible moment. Possibly the hardships of religious life have occasioned a priest's apostasy from the religious and clerical life, even though he continues to observe his obligation of celibacy. Or, again, a priest may unfortunately have become so habitually addicted to drink that as a result of it much grave scandal will continuously impend.

Oftentimes in such cases there is no well-founded hope that the priest will ever return to the correct practice of his sacerdotal vocation. Yet, if he were reduced to the lay state, the consideration thereby accorded to him might well enable him as an ordinary layman to lead a respectable life. In such cases the Holy See is by no

---

[25] *De Sacramentis*, III, n. 442, footnote 39.

[26] Fuchs, "Erpresster Zutritt zu den höheren Weihen und Zölibatspflicht des Klerikers"—*Archiv für katholisches Kirchenrecht* (Innsbruck, 1857-1861; Mainz, 1862—), XCVI (1939), 25-26. (Hereafter cited as *AKKR*.)

means reluctant to grant a reduction to the lay state. Indeed, in such cases charity often urges that the priest be informed of the possibility of obtaining this reduction and correspondingly be advised to apply for it. Along with the reduction to the lay state he will be relieved of many of his onerous obligations. With his obligations lessened and mitigated he will in turn be mercifully delivered from many occasions of sin.

E. *Priest Attempting Marriage*

Special consideration must now be given to the case of a priest who attempts to contract marriage. According to the Code major clerics who presume to contract marriage, even only civilly, incur a *latae sententiae* excommunication simply reserved to the Holy See; moreover clerics, if they are admonished and do not amend within the time fixed by the ordinary according to the circumstances, are to be degraded.[27] Furthermore, major clerics in committing such a delict contract an irregularity.[28] Here, however, the consideration is concerned only with priests. If a deacon or a subdeacon unfortunately offended in this matter, the Holy See will without much difficulty grant a dispensation from celibacy and effect the reduction of the cleric to the lay state. However, with priests the policy of the Holy See is quite different. Two cases call for consideration: the case of a priest who has attempted marriage, but now wishes to observe continence the while it remains morally impossible for him to separate from the woman, and the case of a priest who has attempted marriage, but is now repentant and wishes to return to the priestly life.

In regard to canon 2388, § 1, the decree of the Sacred Penitentiary on April 18, 1936, must be taken into consideration. This decree concerned itself with the case of a priest who has attempted marriage, but because of this and other grave reasons cannot put an end to his cohabitation under the same roof with his accomplice. However, having become repentant and promising absolute and perpetual continence forever, he now wishes for the quiet of his own conscience

[27] Canon 2388, § 1.
[28] Canon 985, 3°.

and that of his accomplice to be readmitted to the Sacraments after the manner of a layman. The decree states that the absolution from the excommunication and the consequent admission to the Sacraments in this case can be granted only by the Sacred Penitentiary, which observes a special form of procedure attended with specific safeguards and conditions as prescribed by the Pope. Moreover, if this absolution was granted to a priest because of his danger of death, then the obligation of recourse to the Sacred Penitentiary, as canon 2252 prescribes it in the case of absolution from censures reserved *specialissimo modo* to the Holy See, is in effect.[29]

After the publication of this decree some authors pointed out that the faculties granted in canon 2254 were no longer applicable in such instances.[30] Other authors, however, thought that the decree did not eliminate the possible use of canon 2254.[31] This latter opinion occasioned a declaration of the Sacred Penitentiary on May 4, 1937. According to this declaration the decree is to be understood as precluding the use, except in danger of death, of any faculty, whether granted by canon 2254, or by privilege, or by any other right, and the absolution is reserved to the Sacred Penitentiary alone.[32]

Hence the case wherein a priest has attempted marriage and cannot forsake his cohabitation under the same roof with his accomplice must be referred to the Sacred Penitentiary for absolution from the excommunication. The Sacred Penitentiary demands that there be certitude that perfect chastity will be observed and that all scandal will be effectively removed.[33] Then the Sacred Penitentiary will grant the absolution and bestow permission for the reception of the Sacraments after the manner in which laymen receive them. In

---

[29] S. Paenit., decr. *Absolutio sacerdotum ab excommunicatione, ob attentatum etiam civile tantum matrimonium, et actu cum muliere caste conviventium eorumque admissio ad participationem sacramentorum more laicorum Sacrae Paenitentiae Apostolicae exculsive reservatur*—*AAS*, XXVIII (1936), 242-243.

[30] Cf., e. g., Rossi, "S. Poenit. Apos., Decretum 18 Aprilis, 1936—Annotationes,"—*Apollinaris*, IX (1936), 587-588.

[31] Cf., e. g., Beijersbergen, "Decretum 18 Aprilis, 1936—Annotationes"—*Periodica*, XXV (1936), 202.

[32] *AAS*, XXIX (1937), 283-284.

[33] López, "De reconciliatione sacerdotis, qui matrimonium attentare praesumpsit"—*Periodica*, XXVI (1937), 503.

such a case, however, if degradation has not preceded, there is no doubt that the Sacred Penitentiary will demand that the cleric be reduced to the lay state, and will accordingly issue a rescript to effect this reduction. In regard to the absolution it should be noted that the priest may conduct himself as one who has been absolved in the external forum, according to the norm of canon 2251, unless the rescript of the Sacred Penitentiary states the contrary.[34]

The second case is concerned with a priest who has attempted marriage, but later, fully repentant, wishes to return to his priestly ministry. In this instance there is question not only of the absolution from the excommunication, but also of a dispensation from the irregularity incurred according to canon 985, 3°. According to the present-day practice the dispensation from the irregularity and the absolution from the censure in the external forum are reserved to the Holy Office.[35] When a priest who has attempted marriage has recourse to the Holy Office, then, if from previous information received from the ordinary it appears that he is truly penitent, the Holy Office will grant him absolution from the excommunication with the faculty of receiving the Sacraments after the manner of laymen. Here it appears that, if the cleric has not been degraded according to canon 2388, § 1, the Holy Office will demand that he be reduced to the lay state, and will grant the rescript of reduction. This rescript will most likely accompany the rescript which grants the absolution from the excommunication in the external forum. Reduction to the lay state seems to be understood as a necessary condition for the granting of the absolution. This is what seems to be implied in the permission to receive the Sacraments *more laicorum*. Moreover, it will be noted that with the granting of the absolution there is not associated any grant of dispensation from the irregularity.

If after a long period of probation the priest has persevered in his necessitated resolution, the Holy Office, after consulting the ordinary, will grant a dispensation from the irregularity, but only with a view to the celebration of Mass, and with certain definitely specified safeguards according to the circumstances. Here, then,

---

[34] López, *art. cit.*, p. 505.
[35] López, *art. cit.*, p. 504.

there is evidently a return of the priest to the clerical state. In such a case, however, there is always demanded the testimony of the ordinary that the priest has showed signs of true repentance proved by a long period of trial. It is also demanded that a real separation and departure from the accomplice have occurred. Finally, the Holy Office demands that, if there has been a civil marriage, there must be a civil divorce or separation whenever the civil laws allow it. Lopez points out that added difficulties usually arise in the external forum if children have been born of the marriage. For, beyond the difficulty of providing for the sustenance and education of the children, there is the grave difficulty of obviating the scandal which would be so apt to arise from the association of the priest with the children born of a sacrilegious union. In the light of this consideration there is not much hope that a dispensation from the irregularity will be granted in such a case.[36]

ARTICLE 2. REDUCTION BY WAY OF THE PENALTY OF DEGRADATION

Probably the best-known and most ancient form of the reduction of clerics to the lay state is that which is effected by way of the penalty of degradation. This method of reduction is mentioned in canon 211, § 1.[37] Canon 2305, § 1, expressly states that degradation includes deposition, the perpetual deprivation of the ecclesiastical garb, and the reduction of the cleric to the lay state. Degradation can be inflicted only for a delict mentioned in the law, or if the cleric, already deposed and deprived of the right to wear the ecclesiastical garb, continues to give grave scandal for a year. The degradation may be verbal, also called edictal. It is effected simply by means of the condemnatory sentence itself, so that all the judicial effects are present immediately upon the passing of the sentence, without the need of its further execution. The other form of degradation, as

[36] López, *art. cit.*, pp. 504-505. Cf. also in regard to these cases Moriarty, *The Extraordinary Absolution from Censures*, The Catholic University of America Canon Law Studies, n. 113 (Washington, D. C.: The Catholic University of America, 1938), pp. 279-290.

[37] Canon 211, § 1: Etsi sacra ordinatio, semel valide recepta, nunquam irrita fiat, clericus tamen maior ad statum laicalem redigitur . . . poena degradationis.

contrasted to verbal, is real. In this form the solemnities prescribed
in the Roman Pontifical are observed.[38]

This penalty is the most severe vindictive penalty which can be
inflicted upon clerics. Because of the severity of this penalty judicial causes concerned with delicts which call for degradation are
reserved to a tribunal of five judges.[39] Furthermore, the penalty is
always of a *ferendae sententiae* character. There is no crime mentioned in law which causes degradation simply by the fact of its
commission.

The reduction of the cleric to the lay state is a constituent element of the inflicted penalty of degradation. While the other elements which constitute degradation are penalties in their own right,
nowhere in the Code is the reduction of a major cleric to the lay
state mentioned as a distinct penalty. However, it is used as a
penalty for minor clerics. Furthermore, the reduction to the lay
state connotes the specific difference between the penalty of degradation and the penalty of the perpetual deprivation of the right
to wear the ecclesiastical garb.[40]

According to the law of the Code the sole method of reducing a
major cleric to the lay state by way of penalty is that which employs
the penalty of degradation.[41] The Pope, however, is not bound by
the procedure of the Code. Consequently, on June 30, 1938, Pius XI,
as Prefect of the Sacred Congregation of Seminaries and Universities
declared that the priest Ladislaus Ereminas was reduced to the lay
state by way of penalty. This priest, even though he had been
expelled from several ecclesiastical institutions at the command of
the Sacred Congregation of Seminaries and Universities, dared to

[38] Canon 2305, § 1. Degradatio in se continet depositionem, perpetuam
privationem habitus ecclesiastici et reductionem clerici ad statum laicalem.

§ 2. Haec poena ferri solummodo potest propter delictum in iure expressum,
aut si clericus, iam depositus et habitu clericali privatus, grave adhuc scandalum
per annum praebere pergat.

§ 3. Alia est *verbalis* seu *edictalis,* quae sola sententia irrogatur, ita tamen
ut omnes suos effectus iuridicos statim habeat sine ulla executione; alia *realis,*
si serventur solemnia praescripta in Pontificali Romano.

[39] Canon 1576, § 1, 2°.

[40] Canons 2304; 2305.

[41] Findlay, *Deposition and Degradation of Clerics,* p. 210.

receive the sacred Order of the priesthood fraudulently with falsified documents. Wherefore the Pope, at the request of all the bishops of Lithuania, ordered that this priest be reduced to the lay state as a penalty, and that by the present decree he be declared to have been so reduced.[42] There is no indication in the decree that the form of a verbal degradation was employed. It appears that the Pope was acting over and above the law. However, this fact furnishes no argument that lesser dignitaries may likewise act in this manner. This power is not given to them anywhere in the Code. If a major cleric is to be reduced to the lay state by way of penalty, then in conformity with the law the penalty of degradation must be employed.

The Code is quite explicit in determining the instances in which the penalty of degradation is to be inflicted. If the cleric has been deposed and deprived of the ecclesiastical garb and continues to give grave scandal for a year he may be degraded.[43] The grave scandal must be given for a year from the infliction of the penalty of the deprivation of the clerical garb.[44] The year is to be computed according to the norms of canon 34, § 3, 1°-3°. The present instance underlying the use of the penalty of degradation is delineated in more generic terms than the other cases. With the exception of this rather generically delineated case the Code defines quite clearly and specifies quite precisely the delicts and the circumstances in which the penalty of degradation may be employed.

All apostates from the Christian faith and all heretics and schismatics alike incur *ipso facto* an excommunication which is reserved to the Holy See in a special manner. Unless they repent after an admonition, they are to be deprived of any benefice, dignity, pension, office or other position they have or hold in the Church, they are to be declared infamous, and clerics, after the admonition has been repeated in vain, are to be deposed. Finally, if they have enrolled in or publicly belonged to a non-Catholic sect they are *ipso facto* infamous and, with the prescription of canon 188, 4°, duly observed, offending clerics are to be degraded if the warning issued to

---

[42] *AAS*, XXX (1938), 274.

[43] Canon 2305, § 2.

[44] Findlay, *Deposition and Degradation of Clerics*, pp. 223-224.

them has gone unheeded and by the same token has proved useless and futile.[45]

Clerics who lay violent hands on the person of the Roman Pontiff automatically contract an excommunication which is reserved to the Holy See in a most special manner. Furthermore such clerics are by that very fact *excommunicati vitandi, ipso iure* infamous and subject to degradation by way of a *ferendae sententiae* penalty.[46] Likewise any cleric guilty of culpable homicide is to be degraded.[47]

Any priest who commits the crime of solicitation is to be suspended from the celebration of Mass and from the hearing of sacramental confessions, or even, in line with the gravity of the delict, to be declared disqualified for the hearing of confessions, to be deprived of all benefices, of all dignities, of the active and passive vote, or also to be declared disqualified for these, and in more serious cases to be subjected to degradation.[48] Similarly any confessor who indirectly violates the sacramental seal of confession is held liable to the penalties enumerated in canon 2368, § 1.[49] As was just seen, listed among these penalties is degradation.

Finally, any major cleric who presumes to contract a marriage, even only a civil marriage, incurs automatically an excommunication simply reserved to the Holy See. If, however, after an admonition, he does not repent within the time designated by the ordinary according to the diversity of circumstances, then, with the prescription of canon 188, 5°, duly observed, he is to be degraded.[50]

The penalty of degradation may in and of itself be applied also to minor clerics.[51] But in view of the greater facility granted by the Code for the reduction of minor clerics to the lay state, this penalty is not enumerated among the methods listed for the reduction of minor clerics to the lay state.

[45] Canon 2314, §§ 1-2.

[46] Canon 2343, § 1.

[47] Canon 2354, § 1.

[48] Canon 2368, § 1.

[49] Canon 2369, § 1.

[50] Canon 2388, § 1. Cf. also *supra,* pp. 128-131, where the same matter is treated in a somewhat different approach.

[51] Maroto, *Institutiones,* I, 880; Findlay, *Deposition and Degradation of Clerics,* p. 209.

ARTICLE 3. REDUCTION BY A DISPENSATION FOR MARRIAGE

Major Orders constitute a diriment impediment to marriage. Consequently no subdeacon, deacon, priest or bishop, unless ordained through grave fear, can validly contract marriage without a dispensation from the law of celibacy.[52] Nevertheless it sometimes happens that subdeacons or deacons do attempt marriage or live in concubinage with women. In certain ominous circumstances, the Church, in her mercy and zeal for souls, allows local ordinaries or, if these cannot be reached, even priests to dispense deacons or subdeacons from the impediment of sacred Orders. In danger of death of one of the parties living in such a condition—be it the cleric or be it his partner in sin—local ordinaries for the peace of conscience of the parties may dispense the deacon or subdeacon from the impediment of sacred Orders after taking care to obviate all impending scandal and, if there be need also of a dispensation from the impediment of mixed religion or of disparity of cult, to demand beforehand the requisite *cautiones*.[53]

Canon 1043 mentions other impediments for which a dispensation may be granted. It lists also an additional reason for the granting of the dispensation, namely, the legitimation of the children. Cappello thinks that the opinion which states that the contemplated legitimation furnishes a sufficient reason even when the case is concerned with a deacon or a subdeacon is solidly probable.[54] However, it is difficult to see how this reason may be adduced in view of the doctrine expressed in canons 1051 and 1116. These canons explicitly exclude the possibility of legitimation, either through the subsequent marriage, or in consequence of the granted dispensation preliminary to the marriage, for any child which was conceived or born as the evil fruit of a sacrilegious act.[55] In such a case the juridical effect

---

[52] Cf. canon 1072.

[53] Canon 1043.

[54] *De Sacramentis*, III, n. 231, d.

[55] Canon 1051.—Per dispensationem super impedimento dirimente concessam sive ex potestate ordinaria, sive ex potestate delegata per indultum generale, non vero per rescriptum in casibus particularibus, conceditur quoque eo ipso legitimatio prolis, si qua ex iis cum quibus dispensatur iam nata vel concepta fuerit, excepta tamen adulterina et sacrilega.

of legitimated status would have to be obtained through a rescript from the Holy See, for nowhere does the Code under any conditions extend to ordinaries or anyone else the faculty to legitimate children whose conception or birth connotes at the same time the sin of sacrilege committed by their parents.

In the same circumstances in which the local ordinary has the faculty to dispense, but only when the local ordinary cannot be reached, the pastor, the priest who is present at a marriage contracted according to the simpler form as allowed by the ruling of canon 1098, 2°, and likewise the confessor, have the faculty to grant a dispensation. The confessor, however, must use his faculty in the act of sacramental confession. Furthermore, the effect of his granted dispensation will be of avail solely for the internal forum.[56]

Local ordinaries, under the same conditions and with the same precautions, also enjoy the faculty to dispense if the impediment is discovered when everything is ready for the marriage and the marriage cannot be postponed without probable danger of grave harm until a dispensation is obtained from the Holy See.[57] This faculty obtains also for the convalidation of the marriage if the same danger is present in delay and time does not permit recourse to the Holy See.[58] Finally, in the same circumstances, the pastor, the priest who is present at a marriage contracted in accordance with the norm of canon 1098, 2°, and also the confessor, have the same faculty, but only in occult cases in which not even the local ordinary may be reached, or in which if he can be reached, there is danger of the violation of the seal of secrecy.[59]

Is a deacon or a subdeacon who obtains a dispensation in this fashion reduced to the lay state? There is no explicit mention of such a reduction in the Code. Yet nobody would deny that it is the mind and practice of the Church never to grant a dispensation from

---

Canon 1116.—Per subsequens parentum matrimonium sive verum sive putativum, sive noviter contractum sive convalidatum, etiam non consummatum, legitima efficitur proles, dummodo parentes habiles exstiterint ad matrimonium inter se contrahendum tempore conceptionis, vel praegnationis, vel nativitatis.

[56] Canon 1044.
[57] Canon 1045, § 1.
[58] Canon 1045, § 2.
[59] Canon 1045, § 3.

celibacy apart from a reduction to the lay state. Therefore Maroto (1875-1937) strongly championed the opinion that the cleric who receives such a dispensation is reduced *ipso iure* to the lay state. For this opinion he adduces certain definite reasons. From the history of law in the Latin Church it is evident that the co-existence of the clerical state and marriage is much more repugnant for those in major Orders than for those in minor Orders. Yet the present law decrees a reduction *ipso iure* to the lay state for those in minor Orders when they marry. Hence, from the analogy which is inherent in laws of a similar character it seems a legitimate conclusion that this same reduction be acknowledged with reference to those who are in major Orders, even though the Code does not mention such a reduction the while it is treating of an exceptional case.

Again, canon 213, § 2, states that a cleric in major Orders who has been reduced to the lay state is still bound by the obligation of celibacy. From this there is seen the close connection between sacred Orders and celibacy, so that not even a juridical reduction to the lay state destroys this connection unless a dispensation of the Holy See is added. *A fortiori,* then, it may be argued, a major cleric who has been dispensed from celibacy ought by that very fact, and for the more cogent reason that is present, to be considered as reduced to the lay state.

Finally, the practice of the Holy See, and especially that of the Holy Office, is to reduce to the lay state major clerics who in any way are dispensed from celibacy. This manner of procedure on the part of the Roman Curiae constitutes an assured rule of action which ought to be followed by those who either *ab homine* or *a iure* receive a commission to dispense from celibacy.[60]

Oesterle does not agree with this opinion. To his mind the case contemplated by Maroto does not fall within the purview of canon 211, § 1. Rather, the explicit wording of this canon directly bars its inclusion. According to canon 213, § 2, a major cleric who has been reduced to the lay state still retains the obligation of celibacy. But this obligation can surely no longer be urged for the cleric who has received a dispensation for marriage in virtue of the faculties granted in canons 1043-1045. Hence the absence of the obligation cannot

---

[60] Maroto, *Institutiones,* I, 878-880.

lead one to conclude that a reduction to lay status has been effected. For the dispensed major cleric Oesterle prefers to apply the ruling of canon 132, § 3, which quite apart from the consideration of a reduction to the lay state simply forbids the exercise of Orders. Finally, in line with the ruling of canon 2388, § 1, Oesterle points out that major clerics who have contracted a marriage without obtaining an apostolic dispensation must in consequence of that fact still be degraded if the ordinary's warning goes unheeded within the time which he has opportunely set for the cleric's repentance of his wrongful act.[61]

In reply to Oesterle's opinion it should be stated that the case contemplated in canons 1043-1045 is an altogether exceptional one. The normal procedure is first to effect the reduction of the cleric to the lay state, and then, if the Holy See sees fit, to grant the dispensation from celibacy. But in the case here considered the dispensation from celibacy comes first. Since the case is of an altogether exceptional character, it is indeed not contemplated in the assertion of canon 213, § 2, namely, that a major cleric when reduced to the lay state still retains his obligation of celibacy. Canon 213 prescinds entirely from the notion of a dispensation from celibacy. If Oesterle's interpretation of canon 213 be valid, then a deacon or subdeacon dispensed from the obligation of celibacy according to canons 1043-1045 can never be reduced to the lay state. For, no matter whether the reduction is effected by a rescript of the Holy See or by the penalty of degradation, the cleric still would not be reduced to the lay state, for the reason that he does not retain his obligation of celibacy. And according to canon 213 in the interpretation of Oesterle, a major cleric who is reduced to the lay state always retains his obligation of celibacy, unless he is the cleric contemplated in canon 214, or unless he was dispensed from celibacy after his reduction to the lay state. Hence it appears that the argument of Oesterle is not very strong.

As Maroto has indicated, the assertion of canon 213, § 2, illustrates very well the close connection between sacred Orders and celibacy.[62] The complete severance of the bond can come only from

---

[61] *Praelectiones Iuris Canonici,* I, 115.
[62] *Institutiones,* I, 879.

one side, that is, from the side of celibacy, and then only by means of apostolic dispensation.[63] Once the bond is broken, then it seems to be the mind of the Church, in the light of her consistent and unvarying practice, to lend added effect to her abhorrence for that fact by removing the cleric as far as possible from his former status. This is done by means of the reduction of the cleric to the lay state.[64]

ARTICLE 4. REDUCTION OF CLERICS ORDAINED UNDER DURESS OF GRAVE FEAR

In canon 214 there appears for the first time a positive enactment regarding a case of reduction which the Church has recognized for centuries. The canon states that a cleric who has been forced in consequence of grave fear to receive sacred Orders, and who did not afterwards, when the fear had been removed, ratify that ordination, not even tacitly by exercising his Orders and by wishing at the same time to subject himself to the clerical obligations by such an act, may be reduced to the lay state by the sentence of a judge with the effect that no obligation of celibacy or of the canonical hours remains, provided of course that the coercion and the lack of ratification have been legitimately proved. The coercion and the lack of ratification must be proved according to the norms outlined in canons 1993-1998.[65]

At the outset it should be made clear that it is not the purpose of this dissertation to consider at any great length the process outlined in canons 1993-1998. However, it is practically impossible to

---

[63] The case of clerics ordained under duress of grave fear is here left out of consideration. In that case the bond does not actually exist.

[64] Cf. also Wernz-Vidal, *Ius Canonicum*, II, n. 394; Coronata, *Institutiones*, I, 361.

[65] Canon 214, § 1. Clericus qui metu gravi coactus ordinem sacrum recepit nec postea, remoto metu, eandem ordinationem ratam habuit saltem tacite per ordinis exercitium, volens tamen per talem actum obligationibus clericalibus se subiicere, ad statum laicalem, legitime probata coactione et ratihabitionis defectu, sententia iudicis redigatur, sine ullis coelibatus ac horarum canonicarum obligationibus.

§ 2. Coactio autem et defectus ratihabitionis probari debent ad normam can. 1993-1998.

comment on canon 214 without some reference to these canons. Hence these canons will not be entirely overlooked, but they will be considered only insofar as they have reference to canon 214. Any detailed commentary on canons 1993-1998 would require a special dissertation.

The consideration of canon 214 readily concerns itself (1) with the grave fear or coercion through which the cleric is ordained, and (2) with the lack of ratification of the ordination. Each of these will be considered in turn. First of all, though, it may be stated that, while the procedure which is mentioned in canon 214 could be used by clerics in minor Orders or in first tonsure, still in view of the liberty which is granted to the minor cleric through canon 211, § 2, namely, to leave the clerical state, it is evident that all cases of this kind will concern a cleric who is in major Orders. Hence any mention of a cleric in the rest of this article is to be understood as denoting a cleric in major Orders.

A. *Ordination Through Coercion or Under Duress of Grave Fear*

Before the question of an ordination received through coercion or under duress of grave fear is given any fuller consideration, there should be recalled the definitions of coercion and of grave fear, and there should be indicated also the various types of fear which may influence the reception of Orders. With these definitions clearly fixed in one's mind, one will then the better be able to consider how the reception of Orders is affected by the factors of coercion and grave fear. For the primary decision must be made whether the ordination itself is affected by coercion or grave fear, or whether only the obligations arising from the ordination are thus affected. This is clear from canon 1993, which indicates that the causes regarding ordination may concern either the obligations contracted in consequence of the ordination, or the validity of the ordination itself.

1. Coercion and Grave Fear

The classical definition of coercion or violence is given by Paulus (early third century) as "the impetus of a greater thing to which resistance cannot be offered." [66] From this definition it is quite evi-

[66] Vis est maioris rei impetus, cui resisti non potest.—D. (4.2) 2.

dent that an act performed under coercion is not a *voluntarium*, that is, there is no free consent of the will. Hence the Code expressly states that an act which a person performs in consequence of an extrinsic force which he cannot resist is to be considered invalid.[67] Canon 214 makes no explicit mention of coercion. However, *a fortiori*, everyone will grant that, if the influence of grave fear releases a cleric from the obligations of his ordination, then coercion also effects the same release.

Fear is well defined as "the trepidation of the mind in view of a danger either imminent or future." [68] In relation to its cause fear is divided into fear from within (*metus ab intrinseco*) and fear from without (*metus ab extrinseco*). Fear from within is usually understood as fear which arises either from some cause internal to the person or from some external necessary cause. For instance, sickness would be a cause internal to the person; an earthquake or storm would be an external necessary cause. Fear from without is the fear which arises from an external free cause, a human agent. For instance, the threatening of death by some person would be an external cause, and thus would produce in its victim a fear from without.[69]

In relation to the manner in which fear is inflicted fear is divided into fear which is justly inflicted and fear which is unjustly inflicted. Fear is justly inflicted when the threatened evil is just both in itself and in the manner in which it is inflicted. For example, the threat of court action by a father against his daughter's suitor who has promised marriage but who will neither fulfill his promise nor repair the damage constitutes a fear which is justly inflicted. Fear is unjustly inflicted when the threatened evil either in itself (*quoad substantiam*) or in the manner in which it is inflicted (*quoad modum*) is unjust. For example, the threat of a father to shoot a man unless the latter marries the daughter to whom a promise of marriage was

---

[67] Canon 103, § 1.

[68] Metus est instantis vel futuri periculi mentis trepidatio.—D. (4.2) 1.

[69] Cf., e. g., Vermeersch, "De metu qui, saltem ex lege positiva, excusat ab obligationibus vitiato consensu susceptis, praecipue de metu ab intrinseco vel extrinseco"—*Periodica*, XVII (1928), 138*-144*; Aertnys-Damen, *Theologia Moralis*, I, n. 35.

never made constitutes a fear which is unjust in itself. The threat of a father to take private revenge upon a man unless he marries the daughter to whom he has promised marriage constitutes a fear which is unjust in the manner in which it is inflicted.[70]

In respect to its quantity or degree, fear may be divided into grave fear and light fear. Light fear is fear which is induced by the apprehension of some slight evil, or also by the apprehension of even a grave evil as long as the apprehension arises from a cause whose existence or influence remains in the realm of the improbable. Grave fear is fear which is induced from the apprehension of a grave evil which is truly probable. Fear is absolutely grave when the fear is such as would influence even resolute men. For instance, the fear of death is absolutely grave if it arises from a cause which is truly probable. Fear is relatively grave when the fear which is light in itself is grave in relation to the subject in view of the timorous temperament, the tender age, the feminine sex, the fragile health or some other such influencing factor peculiar to the subject.[71]

Special consideration must be given to reverential fear. By this fear is understood the fear of a child towards its parents, of a wife towards her husband, of a subject towards his superior. This fear, light in itself, can often become grave when it is accompanied with blows, with threats or with the apprehension of some dreaded evil, for example, the hatred of the parents or their wounded sensibilities over a protracted period of time.[72]

2. Coercion and Grave Fear As Affecting Ordination

The question of the effect of coercion in reference to the obligations arising from ordination does not present much difficulty. If a man is physically forced to submit to the ordination, then his will remains opposed to the ordination. Consequently the ordination it-

---

[70] Cf. McCoy, *Force and Fear in Relation to Delictual Imputability and Penal Responsibility,* The Catholic University of America Canon Law Studies, n. 200 (Washington, D. C.: The Catholic University of America Press, 1944), pp. 80-81.

[71] Aertnys-Damen, *loc. cit.;* Marc-Gestermann-Raus, *Institutiones Morales,* I, n. 285.

[72] Aertnys-Damen, *loc. cit.*

self is invalid, and there can be no question of the effective contracting of the obligations. Ordinarily it should not be difficult to prove the presence of the coercion, for when a subject is forced the fact of coercion readily stands out as something quite evident to the onlooker.

The question of the effect of grave fear can present considerable difficulty. Ordinarily grave fear gives rise to a *voluntarium simpliciter* and an *involuntarium secundum quid*. Thus, a man who is obliged through grave fear to receive ordination really chooses to be ordained, though of course he would not choose to receive ordination if the grave fear were not influencing him. In some cases grave fear may be so strong a factor as to preclude the use of reason on the part of the acting subject. In such a case the ordination itself will be invalid, since the man has no free exercise of the will with which he can accept the reception of Orders. Usually, however, grave fear does not take away the use of reason. In consequence of this the will remains fundamentally free in the acceptance of the ordination. Hence the ordination is valid. Still the clear statement of canon 214 indicates that the cleric contracts no obligations from his ordination.

Among the species of fear, slight fear may be immediately discounted in relation to ordination. The law makes no provision with reference to slight fear in canon 214. As a rule slight fear will not influence a man to seek ordination. The fear must be grave as judged by absolute norms, or grave at least in relation to the subject.

It will be noted that canon 214 makes no reference to the manner in which the fear is inflicted. Consequently it is the opinion of some authors that even a justly inflicted fear is comprehended within the extension of fear as contemplated in the canon. An argument may be advanced for this position.

Canon 214 makes no distinction between fear justly inflicted and fear unjustly inflicted, whereas canons 1087 and 185 definitely state that the fear as contemplated in these canons must be unjustly inflicted. Hence in harmony with the principle, *ubi lex non distinguit nec nos distinguere debemus* [73] it must reasonably be concluded that canon 214 is not restricted in its scope simply to a fear which is unjustly inflicted.

[73] Cf. Wernz, *Ius Decretalium*, I, n. 131, I.

Again, the purpose of the law is to grant clerics who are ordained against their will the opportunity to regain their liberty. It is immaterial whether the fear was sustained from within or inflicted from without. Hence it is likewise indifferent whether the fear was inflicted justly or unjustly.

However, the argument thus proposed does not seem to reflect the correct doctrine. It does not seem that any author could deny that canon 214 crystallizes the discipline of the pre-Code law. It is true that the pre-Code law did not contain any explicit statement to the same effect as canon 214. Nevertheless the juridical reasoning of the authors together with the practice of the Roman Curia evolved substantially the discipline which regarded only an unjustly inflicted fear as a factor which militated against the willingness to receive Orders, or against the free acceptance of the obligations connected with the reception of Orders. This doctrine formed the basis for the enactment which is now contained in canon 214. Now, even if it could be questioned that canon 214 reflects the earlier discipline, the very fact that the consideration is involved in doubt argues, according to a firmly acknowledged legal principle,[74] that no departure is to be made from the interpretation current in the earlier law or discipline. To say that the doubt revolves around the question either of variance or of agreement between the previous discipline and the present law connotes but a twofold approach to stating one and the same fundamental issue. Hence canon 214 must be interpreted in the light of the earlier jurisprudence. In turn, like the earlier jurisprudence, it contemplates only the unjustly inflicted fear.

Again, canon 1307 declares that a vow made under the duress of grave and unjust fear is *ipso iure* null. According to a solidly tenable opinion the vow of celibacy is taken in the reception of sacred Orders. From this, in turn, it would follow that, if the vow is to be considered null and void, then the fear which canon 214 contemplates must be a fear which has been inflicted unjustly. Moreover, the use of the words *coactus* and *coactio* in canon 214 seems to indicate that the fear is unjustly inflicted from without by a free agent. For in

[74] Canon 6, 4°.

ecclesiastical law the use of these terms is usually understood in this way.[75]

Finally, in view of canon 971, which states that it is wrong (*nefas*) to force anyone in any way or for any reason to receive ordination, it appears that any fear brought to bear on the subject in order to compel him to receive Orders is unjust.[76]

To this it may be objected that already in this dissertation it has been shown that the Supreme Pontiff can give the cleric a precept to receive ordination. Likewise a cleric as the incumbent of a benefice may be put under obligation to receive higher Orders or else forfeit his benefice.[77] Now, although as the supreme lawgiver the Roman Pontiff is above all purely ecclesiastical legislation, yet he could not enforce his precept if the applied coercion were in itself something intrinsically unjust. If, then, the Roman Pontiff can issue a coercive precept calling for the reception of Orders, such action can be justified solely on the score that canon 971 reflects a purely ecclesiastical law. Conversely, if the fulfillment of the coercive precept were accomplished by a cleric who is unwilling to accept the obligations which derive from his ordination, then such a cleric, once he has furnished conclusive proof of that unwillingness, would have to be dispensed from the said obligations.[78]

For the case in which the cleric is obliged either to receive higher Orders or else to forfeit his benefice it may be answered that he willingly accepted the benefice, knowing the obligations which would arise from his incumbency in the benefice. It can hardly be said that he was compelled by means of fear to receive the higher Orders, since it was of his own free will that he accepted the benefice together with the resulting obligations.[79] Consequently any fear which would arise in such a case would be fear from within, namely, the apprehension of the cleric lest he be obliged to earn a living by

---

[75] Oesterle, "Die Zurückversetzung der Kleriker in den Laienstand nach dem neuen Rechte"—*TPQ*, LXXIV (1921), 505-506.

[76] Gasparri, *De Matrimonio*, I, 368-369; Cappello, *De Sacra Ordinatione*, n. 437.

[77] Cf. *supra*, pp. 113-114.

[78] Cappello, *De Sacra Ordinatione*, n. 385.

[79] Cappello, *op. cit.*, n. 383.

manual labor in the fields or in some manner equally repugnant to him.

From the postulation that the fear be inflicted unjustly it is evident that it must likewise proceed from without (*ab extrinseco*). It is impossible to conceive of an unjust fear from within or from an external necessary cause. One cannot be unjust towards oneself, nor can an inanimate agent ever be conceived as unjust. The very conception of injustice postulates moral imputability.

The fear must be so inflicted that the subject is forced to choose ordination in order to be freed from the fear. Otherwise the cleric cannot be said to receive ordination under the duress of grave fear. It is this particular condition which is contemplated in canon 214.[80]

Before giving consideration to the question of the ratification of the obligations concomitant with the reception of Orders one may well indicate some of the causes which are more frequently alleged than others for the non-contracting of the clerical obligations, and then endeavor to arrive at a solution. First of all there is the case of the seminarian who is in the seminary during wartime. He feels that he does not wish to be ordained. Yet, if he leaves the seminary he will be inducted into military service. Consequently he proceeds with the reception of Orders even to the priesthood. When the war is over he protests against his clerical obligations on the score that he was ordained in view of the grave fear of being inducted into military service. What is the status of this cleric?

The fear of being inducted into military service ordinarily does not constitute grave fear. It would be ridiculous to assert that the majority, or even a good-sized minority, of the men inducted into military service experience the impact of grave fear in connection with their induction. It is true that the fear of death does constitute a grave fear. Yet this fear is, as a rule, rather remote when a man is inducted into the military, and consequently has no great influence upon his actions. In an individual case grave fear is perhaps present. But this fear cannot be said to be unjustly in-

---

[80] S. R. R., *Onerum Sacrae Ordinationis,* 16 apr. 1928, *coram R. P. D. Iosepho Florczak, Ponente,* Dec. XIII, n. 2, *in fine— Sacrae Romanae Rotae Decisiones seu Sententiae* (ab anno 1909), (Romae: Typis Vaticanis, 1912—), XX (1928), 129. Hereafter this collection of the Rota decisions will be cited *S. R. R. Dec.*

flicted. In the presumption that the war is just, a presumption which the ordinary citizen can hardly overthrow, the country has a right to induct its citizens for its protection. Finally, neither the Church nor the State compels the cleric to receive ordination. Immunity from military service is simply a privilege of the clerical state, which the cleric loses when he leaves that state. Consequently it does not seem that this fear can be alleged as a reason for the non-contracting of the clerical obligations.[81]

Sometimes a cleric protests that he was ordained in consequence of the grave fear that he would otherwise be obliged to lead a life of drudgery, for instance, by working at menial tasks. A similar case was proposed by Vidal (1867-1938) as proof against the assertion of Cappello that all fear in relation to ordination is unjust.[82] In the case as proposed the cleric was thinking of leaving the clerical state. His father recalled to his mind the modest circumstances in which the family lived, and pointed out that the cleric would likewise be obliged to live poorly and to earn his living laboriously, since the father had not the means to enable the cleric to continue his studies and thus gain civil honors. Cappello agrees that in this case the proposition of the father was very just, both as regards the substance and as regards the manner in which it was proposed. But, he contends, there is no fear in the case, and certainly not a fear inflicted from without.[83]

In such a case it is true that absolute grave fear is not present. Nevertheless, in an individual case the possibility of relative grave fear cannot be ruled out. However, as both Cappello and Vidal agree, in such a case the fear does not arise from without. The father in the case used no coercion whatsoever. He simply pointed to external circumstances. These circumstances cannot, however, be regarded as a cause which inflicted grave fear unjustly.

The Sacred Congregation of the Sacraments in its Instruction of December 27, 1930, indicated causes commonly alleged by clerics who assert that they were invalidly ordained, or at least that they did not contract the clerical obligations. Some of these reasons are in-

---

[81] Haring, "Laiserung nach can. 214"—*TPQ*, LXXVII (1924), 338.

[82] Wernz-Vidal, *Ius Canonicum*, V, n. 286, footnote 52.

[83] *De Sacramentis*, III, n. 438, footnote 30.

trinsic to the subject, such as the desire to enjoy the clerical life, which in wide circles may be conceived of as an easy life, or the desire to win honors, to make money, to escape (and this is nowadays the reason most commonly alleged) manual labor, lest they be forced to dig or work in the fields with their parents and brothers, the desire to enjoy the clerical privileges, especially the exemption from military service or from the secular courts, or the desire to attain to a higher social position through the clerical state.[84]

In respect to all these causes it may simply be stated that any fear which is present is certainly not unjustly inflicted from without. Hence it must be concluded that in such circumstances clerics have contracted the clerical obligations. However, the Instruction seems to insinuate that the Sacred Congregation at least considered these cases. The explanation may be that in an individual case there is the possibility that the cleric was not validly ordained, either because there was a deliberate defect of intention, or because his mind was so disturbed that there is doubt whether the use of reason was present. But if in these cases it be presumed that the cleric was validly ordained, there can be little if any doubt that he contracted the clerical obligations. Whether in an individual case and by reason of peculiar circumstances the Sacred Congregation will request a dispensation from the Holy Father it is difficult to say. The possibility is present, but it seems quite remote.

The Sacred Congregation of the Sacraments likewise indicated the extrinsic reason which may be called the classical reason in these cases. This reason is the absolutely grave fear or also the relatively grave fear as exemplified in reverential fear. It does not seem necessary to make any digression with reference to reverential fear. This fear will be judged according to the general norms already indicated. Hence it must be established that the fear was grave and that it was inflicted from without. Again, it must be proved that the fear was directed toward the achieving of the ordination. If the fear was inflicted from without and was directed toward the achieving of the ordination it cannot be other than a fear unjustly inflicted.

Lastly it should be pointed out that, if a cleric has been promoted to minor Orders in consequence of grave fear, but afterwards freely

[84] *AAS*, XXIII (1931), 121.

receives the subdiaconate, he is bound by the obligations of celibacy and the divine office. Again, if a cleric is ordained to the sub-diaconate freely, but later receives the diaconate and the priesthood through grave fear, he is likewise bound by these obligations. Never-theless, if in this latter case the cleric proves the moral coercion for the reception of the diaconate and the priesthood, he may ask for a dispensation from the obligations of celibacy and the divine office. If the dispensation is granted, the cleric will of course be reduced to the lay state.[85] If a cleric receives the subdiaconate in consequence of grave fear, but afterwards freely receives the diaconate and the priesthood, he is likewise bound by the obligations of celibacy and the divine office. In this case the free reception of the diaconate and the priesthood indicates a ratification of the subdiaconate. But if there is grave doubt whether the fear has ceased, the Sacred Con-gregation of the Sacraments will probably consider the case leniently and accordingly will petition the Roman Pontiff for a dispensation from these obligations.

Finally, mention must be made of the Instruction of the Sacred Congregation of the Sacraments on December 27, 1930, regarding secular clerics,[86] and the Instruction of the Sacred Congregation of Religious on December 1, 1931, regarding religious clerics.[87] Accord-ing to the Instruction of the Sacred Congregation of the Sacraments candidates for the secular priesthood must present a sworn declara-tion that they are proceeding to major Orders with full liberty. This declaration is to be demanded of them before each of the major Orders.[88]

Similarly the Instruction of the Sacred Congregation of Religious requires that religious candidates for the subdiaconate bring for-ward a sworn declaration that they are proceeding of their own free will and with full liberty. If the candidate is a member of a re-ligious institute of solemn vows then this declaration is to be made before the candidate pronounces his solemn vows.[89]

---

[85] Cappello, *De Sacra Ordinatione*, n. 359, 5.
[86] *AAS*, XXIII (1931), 120-129.
[87] *AAS*, XXIV (1932), 74-81.
[88] *AAS*, XXIII (1931), 125.
[89] *AAS*, XXIV (1932), 80-81.

In the event that a cleric ordained after the time of these In-structions impugns the obligations arising from his ordination it must be objected to him that he had previously sworn that he was proceeding with full liberty. Likewise those who were present at the pre-ordination examination of this cleric and who allowed him to proceed to ordination are to be questioned regarding his freedom at the time of ordination.[90]

B. Ratification of the Ordination

The ratification of an ordination may be either express or tacit. If the ratification is to be express it is required that the influence of the fear has been removed. It is likewise postulated that the re-cipient of the ordination realizes that he was ordained in con-sequence of grave fear inflicted on him, and that as a result he did not then effectively contract the clerical obligations which the law ordinarily couples with the reception of Orders. In the absence of certain knowledge on these points the recipient of Orders must at least be in serious doubt regarding them. He must also be aware of the fact that he can impugn the binding power of the obligations normally deriving from the ordination, and that with properly estab-lished proof of his non-ratification he can be declared free of the clerical obligations. Given these conditions, the ratification is ex-press when the cleric freely manifests his preference to continue in the clerical life and to assume the obligations as binding for him. The ratification is tacit when upon the removal of the fear the cleric exercises the Order he has received, thereby intending to subject himself to the clerical obligations.[91] The removal of the fear must necessarily take place before the ratification can be effective. If the fear were still influencing the cleric, the ratification would by no means be free. The same grave fear would stand in the way of the contracting of the obligations through the act of ratification as stood in the way of the contracting of the obligations in the earlier act of ordination.

It is an important feature in the ratification that the cleric must

[90] *AAS*, XXIII (1931), 485.
[91] Canon 214, § 1.

perceive at least in a confused manner that he has not contracted the clerical obligations.[92] In other words, the cleric must desire by his exercise of Orders to subject himself to the clerical obligations before there is any ratification. The mere fact that the cleric has exercised his Orders does not necessarily indicate a ratification. The perception, at least confusedly, that he has not contracted the obligations, and the later will to subject himself to them, are essential for the ratification.

Ratification is not presumed while the case to try the nullity is pending; but when the case has been judicially decided either by a sentence adverse to the declaration of nullity, or by failure to appeal, or by the conclusion of the proceedings on appeal, then the presumption of ratification arises if the cleric either freely and willingly resumes the exercise of his Orders, or continues to exercise them without trying to acquire his liberty, when he could acquire it without difficulty from the fact that there are no obstacles or inconveniences. But this presumption, too, can be overcome by contrary indications or proofs which show clearly that, notwithstanding a certain appearance of the facts and circumstances, the will to ratify was by no means present.[93] Practically a ratification can hardly be proved with full certainty in the face of a contrary assertion of the cleric. Therefore the lack of ratification is easily admitted, and must in fact be admitted in cases of this kind.[94]

C. The Reduction to the Lay State

After it has been legitimately proved that the cleric was ordained in consequence of grave fear and did not afterwards ratify that ordination, he may be reduced to the lay state by means of a sentence of a judge, no obligations of celibacy and of the divine office remaining for him. The coercion and the lack of ratification are to

[92] S. C. de Sacr. decr. (Regulae servandae in processibus super nullitate sacrae ordinationis vel onerum sacris ordinibus inhaerentium a Sacra Congregatione de disciplina Sacramentorum editae), 9 iun. 1931, n. 65—*AAS*, XXIII (1931), 471. Cf. S. R. R., *Sacrae Ordinationis*, 1 aug. 1928, *coram R. P. D. Francisco Parillo, Ponente,* Dec. XXXVIII, n. 6—*S. R. R. Dec.* XX (1928), 350.

[93] S. C. de Sacr., decr. 9 iun. 1931, nn. 66-67—*AAS,* XXIII (1931), 471.

[94] Cappello, *De Sacra Ordinatione,* n. 699.

be proved according to the norms of canons 1993-1998.[95]   It will be noticed that canon 214 makes no explicit mention of the possibility for effecting this reduction by means of a decree.   Yet canon 211, which enumerates the various methods of reducing a cleric to the lay state, specifically mentions a decree in relation to canon 214. Since canon 214 points out that the coercion and the lack of ratification are to be proved according to the norms of canons 1993-1998, and among these canons canon 1993, § 3, explicitly mentions the method of reduction by means of a decree, it is evident that canon 211 is pointing actually to these later canons, but mediately through canon 214.

In the cases wherein the obligations arising from ordination are impugned on the score of grave fear which attended the ordination, the introductory *libellus* is sent to the Sacred Congregation of the Sacraments.   This Sacred Congregation then decides whether the case is to be handled in a judiciary or in a disciplinary manner.[96] If the judiciary process is to be used, the Sacred Congregation sends the case to the tribunal of the diocese proper to the cleric at the time of his ordination.[97]   Before the cleric can be declared free of his obligations two conformable sentences are required.[98]   If the sentences are not conformable, then the case is sent to the Holy See. If it is to be handled in a judiciary manner, it will be considered in the third instance by the Sacred Roman Rota.   Once the case has received two conformable and favorable decisions, the cleric is *ipso facto* free, in both the internal and the external forum, from the clerical obligations, and accordingly is reduced to the lay state.

If the Sacred Congregation of the Sacraments decides that the case is to be handled in a disciplinary manner, then the Sacred Congregation itself will decide the question after an informative process has been conducted by the tribunal of the competent curia.[99]   In this event the curia will proceed according to the Instruction of June 9, 1931, of the Sacred Congregation of the Sacraments.   Once

[95] Canon 214, § 2.
[96] Canon 1993, § 1.
[97] Canon 1993, § 2.
[98] Canon 1998, § 1.
[99] Canon 1993, § 3.

the informative process has been concluded, the acts together with the written opinion of the bishop are to be sent to the Sacred Congregation. In the Congregation the defender of the bond will make his animadversions. Then three consultors of the Congregation will examine the acts and the animadversions, and thereupon will write their opinion regarding the validity or the nullity of the obligations. If the opinion holds for the nullity of the obligations, then the opinion of the defender of the bond will again be sought to discover whether he agrees or disagrees, whether the proofs seem to him to need corroboration, and whether in consequence a supplement to the acts should be demanded.[100] Then the definite decision of the Sacred Congregation is issued. If the decision is favorable to the cleric, then he is *eo ipso* free from the clerical obligations and reduced to the lay state.

D. Dispensation from the Obligations

It has already been seen that the discipline of the Holy See with regard to deacons and subdeacons in their clerical obligations is somewhat mitigated in comparison with the pre-Code law. Nowadays, if a deacon or subdeacon is unwilling to ascend to higher Orders, or protests against his clerical obligations on the score of force or fear attending his ordination, the Holy See will most likely grant a dispensation from the obligations when equitable causes support such a grant.

When a priest protests that he has not contracted the obligations in view of the grave fear which attended his ordination, the possibility of a dispensation is not utterly excluded. Thus, if the grave fear and the lack of ratification really seem to be proved, but there are still some lingering doubts, then the Holy See may see fit to grant a dispensation from these obligations. In one case of this kind which had gone through two instances, in both of which it was held that the complaint was not fully justified, the cleric sought redress with the Sacred Congregation of the Sacraments. The Sacred Congregation decided that the asserted coercion was sufficiently perceived from the acts and testimonies, but that there were still some

---

[100] Cappello, *De Sacra Ordinatione*, n. 720.

obstacles to complete proof. In view of these circumstances the Holy Father deigned to grant to the priest, after an absolution from the censures, a dispensation *ad cautelam* from all the obligations of the ordination.[101]

Again, the case may be one in which the presence of the requisites demanded by canon 214 has remained doubtful, but special reasons seem to call for a milder treatment of the cleric. In a case of this kind three questions were proposed in the Sacred Congregation: (1) whether the nullity of the ordination is evident, and, if not: (2) whether at least it is evident that there was grave fear and a lack of ratification, so that in accordance with canon 214 the cleric should be reduced to the lay state without any obligation of celibacy and the divine office, and, if not: (3) whether, while there is grave doubt about the validity of the ordination, or about the presence of grave fear and the lack of ratification, with other reasons also claiming consideration, a suggestion is to be made to the Holy Father for a dispensation from the obligations of the ordination.[102] In regard to these questions it may be stated that it is the practice of the Sacred Congregation to consider them in each case. As Cappello points out, the cleric will be favored in a case of doubt.[103] Nevertheless, as the third question plainly indicates, there must be a *grave* doubt.

In one such instance it was decided that it was not evident that the ordination was invalid, or that there was no contracting of the obligations, but that there was a grave doubt. Correspondingly the Holy Father graciously granted to the cleric a dispensation from the obligations. However, before the ordinary informed the cleric of the decision and executed it, he had to inform the cleric that he

[101] Fuchs, "Erpresster Zutritt zu den höheren Weihen und Zölibatspflicht des Klerikers"—*AKKR*, XCVI (1939), 25-26, footnote 2.

[102] I°. An constet de nullitate S. Ordinationis in casu; et quatenus Negative:

II°. An saltem constet de gravi metu et de ratihabitionis defectu, ut, ad normam can. 214, actor redigendus sit ad statum laicalem sine ullis coelibatus et horarum canonicarum obligationibus; et quatenus Negative:

III°. An exstante gravi dubio de validitate S. Ordinationis, vel de gravi metu, et de ratihabitionis defectu, aliisque concurrentibus causis, consilium praestandum sit SSᵐᵒ pro dispensatione ab oneribus S. Ordinationis in casu.— Fuchs, *loc. cit.*

[103] *De Sacra Ordinatione*, n. 359.

was forbidden, under pain of excommunication to be imposed according to the norm of law by a decree of the ordinary, to visit or dwell in those regions where his previous status was known and where the knowledge of it could beget scandal. The cleric was obliged especially to depart from his place of birth. To attain this end the ordinary had to demand a written declaration, strengthened with an oath, which was to be preserved along with the acts of the case. Furthermore, the cleric was to be gravely admonished to receive frequently the Sacraments of Penance and the Holy Eucharist, and to be an example to others by his probity and uprightness of life. Moreover, if the cleric wished to contract marriage within the Church, all solemnity was to be avoided. The marriage was to be contracted secretly in the presence only of the pastor and two confidential witnesses. Again, he was to lead a simple and unpretending life, not undertaking any offices which entailed the furnishing of any pledges or the giving of any guarantees. He was to remember that he was incapable of assuming any ecclesiastical office or also of exercising any of the ecclesiastically authorized acts enumerated in canon 2256, § 2. Finally, if any of the faithful should wonder about the dispensation which had been granted, then the ordinary was to take care to inform them in a fitting manner about the reasons justifiably supporting the disposition of the case.[104]

Some perplexity may arise from the diversity of the treatment accorded to the clerics in the two instances. In the first case the cleric received no instructions qualifying his liberty; in the second case the cleric was straitened with various restrictions. However, it must be remembered that the first case concerned a cleric whose grave fear and lack of ratification were all but established. It was only because of some obstacles to the achievement of full proof that the Holy See resorted to the granting of a dispensation *ad cautelam*. In this case the cleric seemed to have a right to freedom. The second case was quite different. There the grave fear and the absence of ratification were not so well established, but there were present, also, certain reasons which called for a mild treatment of the cleric. Hence, in that instance there was clearly a dispensation, a true favor, so that certain restrictions could be imposed over and above any pro-

---

[104] Fuchs, *loc. cit.*

visions in the law. These restrictions served as safeguards against the danger of scandal.

In view of the possibility of a dispensation, then, one readily perceives the reason why these cases should be handled for the most part in an administrative manner by the Sacred Congregation. In a judicial process it is the duty of the tribunal to render a judgment according to the norm of law, that is, the nullity is either evident or not evident. It is not the part of the tribunal to recommend to the Holy See the granting of a dispensation. However, it is well within the authority of the Sacred Congregation of the Sacraments, proceeding as it does in an administrative manner and upon confirming the previous decision, to consider the case on the score of equity. Then it can recommend to the Holy Father the feasibility of the granting of a dispensation.

E. Ignorance Regarding the Obligation of Celibacy

In canon 214 no provision is made with reference to ignorance of the obligation of celibacy on the part of the cleric. Yet it could happen that a cleric is ordained though he be ignorant of what the obligation of celibacy entails. It may be objected that this case can hardly be imagined nowadays in view of the Instruction of the Sacred Congregation of the Sacraments on December 27, 1930, regarding secular clerics,[105] and the Instruction of the Sacred Congregation of Religious on December 1, 1931, regarding religious clerics.[106] Both of these Instructions require the candidate for major Orders to take an oath that he is fully cognizant of the obligations which flow from sacred Orders, and that he is fully aware of what the obligation of celibacy entails. Certainly this sworn declaration makes it extremely difficult for the cleric to prove his ignorance. Yet it does not entirely eliminate the possibility, although it surely does exclude the probability, of a cleric being so ordained. Again, the question of the status of a cleric who deliberately decides to exclude the obligation of celibacy in his ordination will arise. While it must be admitted by all that these cases are quite rare, still, in view of the possibility, it is necessary to consider them.

[105] *AAS*, XXIII (1931), 120-129.
[106] *AAS*, XXIV (1932), 74-81.

There is another case of ignorance which the authors once considered, but which is hardly practical today. This is the instance wherein the cleric is unaware that the obligation of celibacy is annexed to major Orders. St. Alphonsus (1696-1787) considered the question and decided that, if the cleric was invincibly ignorant of this obligation, he was not bound, since in that case the Church would not intend to oblige the cleric. The case would be different, he pointed out, if the ignorance were culpable, or if the cleric received Orders with the general intention of assuming the same obligations that the other clerics assumed in receiving Orders.[107] In view of the present-day discipline the case of even a culpable ignorance regarding the existence of an obligation of celibacy barely remains within the pale of possibility.

However, the case in which the cleric is ignorant of what the obligation of celibacy entails is somewhat different. Despite his sworn statement to the contrary, the cleric may still lack sufficient knowledge to make the assumed obligation of celibacy strictly binding for him. In view of his incomplete knowledge the cleric may have taken his oath in good faith. He may have understood the obligation of clerical celibacy as implying no more for him than a simple prohibition of marriage. Is such an imperfect knowledge a sufficient knowledge of what the obligation of celibacy entails? Of its nature the observance of celibacy implies the fulfillment of a negative duty. But knowledge of the negative duty is gained through the comprehension of its opposite which is prohibited. Hence, to know the object of celibacy one needs to know the object of marriage. Consequently an understanding of the object of celibacy is made possible through an understanding of the object of marriage. If a cleric was without knowledge of the object of marriage, then he would also lack the requisite knowledge of the object of celibacy. This lack of knowledge would preclude celibacy from becoming a binding obligation when accepted by the cleric. For an obligation is not assumed as truly binding when one is in substantial error regarding the nature of the thing promised.

If a cleric were so ignorant or mistaken about the object of marriage that his ignorance or error would preclude the possible

---

[107] St. Alphonsus, *Theologia Moralis*, Lib. VI, n. 809.

contraction of a valid marriage, then such ignorance or error would likewise preclude celibacy from becoming a binding obligation. It is true that the knowledge postulated for the contraction of a valid marriage does not have to be a very detailed knowledge. But if the object of marriage is not known even *in confuso,* then the contraction of a valid marriage becomes impossible.[108]   Under such circumstances of ignorance or error it also becomes impossible to accept celibacy as a binding obligation, for it would be assumed in the nature of a thing which, if not altogether unknown, would stand appraised with substantial error. No strict obligation could ensue as long as either of these factors was truly present.

To prove in the external forum the presence of such ignorance or error is extremely difficult. Hence in such cases the cleric would probably be obliged in the external forum to observe celibacy, though in the forum of conscience he would be free of that obligation. The condition of a cleric in such a case of conflict between the external and the internal forum will be considered more at length in a later article.

Finally, what is the condition of a cleric who deliberately intends not to contract the obligation of celibacy when he freely receives ordination? Such a cleric certainly does contract the obligation of celibacy. The law of the Church states that clerics in major Orders cannot marry and are bound by the obligation of observing chastity.[109] The law makes an explicit exception for clerics who are ordained under duress of grave fear and who do not afterwards ratify their ordination. Likewise it may be safely asserted that the law does not intend, even if it could, to oblige clerics who are invincibly ignorant of or in substantial error regarding the nature of the obligation of celibacy. But nowhere in law is it stated, nor would anyone ever assert, that a cleric by his mere contrary intention could exclude entirely the obligation of celibacy from his valid ordination. Such a doctrine would open the road to scandalous abuses and might even, in time, endanger the very law of celibacy. Hence it must reasonably be maintained that a cleric who deliberately intends to exclude the

[108] Cappello, *De Sacramentis,* III, n. 582.
[109] Canon 132, § 1.

obligation of celibacy when he is validly ordained actually contracts this obligation in spite of his intention.[110]

F. Canon 214 in Relation to Canon 1072

Canon 1072 states that when clerics in sacred Orders undertake to contract a marriage they attempt it invalidly.[111] Canon 214 declares that clerics who have been ordained in consequence of grave fear and who have not afterwards ratified their ordination may be reduced to the lay state without any obligations of celibacy and the divine office remaining incumbent upon them. A comparison of these two canons gives rise to some perplexity. How is canon 214 to be understood in relation to canon 1072?

A possible interpretation of these canons may be made from an analogy with the civil law action of *querela nullitatis*. In the civil laws of some nations certain juridical acts are void from the very beginning. Nevertheless they beget juridical effects as long as they are not impugned. Once they are impugned, however, they may be annulled. In such a case the acts are considered as null from the very outset, and the juridical effects of them are likewise annulled.

In applying this action to canon 214 the result would be the following. The contraction of the clerical obligations of celibacy and the divine office is null from the very beginning. Nevertheless the diriment impediment of sacred Orders remains until the declaration of nullity is rendered. Once the declaration is given, however, the diriment impediment automatically ceases. The decision in the case is essentially of a confirmatory nature, but in its effect it is of a constitutive nature. The decision confirms the non-contraction of the clerical obligations; but by the cessation of the diriment impediment it likewise constitutes the cleric's freedom to marry.

The *querela nullitatis* is recognized only in the formal law of the Code, that is, as a legal means against a sentence which is null.[112] It is not recognized in the material law of the Code, that is, it may

---

[110] St. Alphonsus, *Theologia Moralis,* Lib. VI, n. 809, 2; Cappello, *De Sacra Ordinatione,* n. 600.

[111] Canon 1072.—Invalide matrimonium attentant clerici in sacris ordinibus constituti.

[112] Canons 1892-1897.

not be used against the juridical act itself.[113] This interpretation of
canon 214 is not held by any of the authors. It is mentioned here in
order to enumerate all possible solutions.

The difference of opinion among the authors today regards the
nature of the decision which is rendered according to canon 214.
According to one interpretation the decision referred to in canon 214
has a constitutive effect. In other words, the decision establishes
the cleric as free from his obligation of celibacy, an obligation to
which he was subject prior to the decision. In this opinion the decision is a necessary condition for the valid marriage of the cleric.[114]
Arendt (1852-1937) seemed to consider the decision as a dispensation.[115] Whether it be considered a dispensation or an essential condition for the valid contraction of marriage does not make
much difference. In either case the marriage is invalid before the
decision, but there may be a valid contraction thereafter.

The other opinion considers the decision rendered according to the
norm of canon 214 as having a confirmatory effect. In this opinion
the cleric is entirely free from the obligation of celibacy prior to
the decision. The sentence or decree merely confirms or recognizes
in the external forum what was previously existent in the internal
forum or the forum of conscience.[116]

---

[113] Cf. Fuchs, "Erpresster Zutritt zu den höheren Weihen und Zölibatspflicht
des Klerikers"—*AKKR,* XCVI (1939), 4-5, footnote 1.

[114] Cf. Eichmann, *Lehrbuch des Kirchenrechts* (4. ed., 2 vols.: Paderborn,
1934), I, 205; von Kienitz, *Der kirchliche Weiheprozess* (Freiburg, 1934), p. 24;
Linneborn, *Grundriss des Eherechts nach dem Codex Iuris Canonici* (4. und 5.
Aufl., Paderborn: Ferdinand Schöningh, 1933), p. 246, as cited by Fuchs, *art.
cit.—AKKR,* XCVI (1939), 22, footnote 1.

[115] . . . quoties iuridice demonstratum fuerit votum invalide fuisse emissum,
in casu particulari sententia iudicis decernatur legi ecclesiasticae coelibatus esse
dispensatione derogandum . . .—Arendt, "Quomodo concordare debeant can.
214 et 1072?"—*Ius Pontificium,* VIII (1928), p. 68. The article in its entirety
is contained on pp. 63-77; 168-173.

[116] Maroto, *Institutiones,* I, 462; Wernz-Vidal, *Ius Canonicum,* V, n. 285;
Gasparri, *De Matrimonio,* I, 368; Cappello, *De Sacra Ordinatione,* n. 360;
Coronata, *Institutiones,* I, 232; Vermeersch-Creusen, *Epitome,* II, n. 347;
Roberti, *De Processibus* (2 vols., Romae: Apud Aedes Facultatis Iuridicae ad
S. Apollinaris, 1926), I, 286; Iorio, *Theologia Moralis,* III, n. 1199; Prümmer,
Theologia Moralis, III, n. 814; Merkelbach, *Summa,* III, n. 890; also Michiels,

Arendt, defending the contention that a dispensation is required before the cleric is freed of his obligations, frames his arguments in this manner. The obligation of celibacy arises from a twofold source, that is, from the positive law of the Church and from the vow of celibacy implicitly taken in the reception of sacred Orders. If a cleric is ordained in consequence of grave fear, the vow is invalid in consequence of the natural law itself. But it does not by any means follow that the positive law of the Church, which annexes the obligation of celibacy to a valid ordination, is likewise devoid of its effect. Consequently, though the cleric thus ordained does not take the vow of celibacy, celibacy is still demanded of him by the positive law of the Church.[117]

A comparison may be instituted between marriage and sacred ordination. If a man knows with certainty of the death of his wife, though he cannot furnish conclusive proof of it, his consequent marriage is valid in the internal forum, for in this forum the validity or invalidity depends upon the objective status of the matter. But in the external forum the marriage is presumed invalid, for in the external forum the recognition of validity depends on the demonstration which is offered in proof of the objective status. In an ordination received under the constraint of grave fear the matter is quite different. In this case the incapacity for marriage is determined by the ecclesiastical law. The condition upon which the incapacity in both the internal and the external forum depends is not something objective which as a factor is distinct and separate from the ecclesiastical law; that condition is the very law itself. The incapacity for marriage arises solely from the law. Hence, as long as the law is in effect, the incapacity is present, arising initially in the external forum and then by consequence in the internal forum. When the law ceases to be operative, then likewise the incapacity

Principia Generalia de Personis in Ecclesia (Lublin, 1932), 522; and others cited by Fuchs, *loc. cit.*

[117] Ipsa [inhabilitas ad nuptias ineundas] resultat simul ex lege ecclesiastica coelibatus, ac firmatur iure divino hypothetico voti solemnis implicite in s. ordinatione nuncupati . . . si contigerit votum hoc esse invalidum, nequaquam inde sequitur eo ipso cessasse legem ecclesiasticam coelibatus et perfectae castitatis . . . Arendt, *art. cit.—Ius Pontificium*, VIII (1928), p. 67.

for marriage ceases in both the internal and the external forum. Hence, when a cleric is ordained under the constraint of grave fear, he does not take the *vow* of celibacy, but the *law* of celibacy obliges him until he is released from that law by a dispensation.[118]

As has been seen, the majority of the authors does not agree with this solution. They point out that, according to canon 1994, § 2, only a cleric who thinks he has *not contracted* the obligations annexed to Orders can ask for a *declaration of the nullity* of these obligations.[119] Hence the Code itself definitely presumes that the cleric can be validly ordained without contracting the clerical obligations. Furthermore, it is the object of the process to obtain a declaration of nullity of the obligations, not a dispensation from existing obligations. A declaration of nullity does not render null and void the binding power of obligations which do exist. It simply grants recognition in the external forum for the nullity of the obligations which in the internal forum were already regarded as non-existing.

Again, according to canon 1998 two conformable and favorable sentences are required before the cleric is free of his obligations. The lodging of an appeal in these cases is governed by the norms established for the making of an appeal in marriage cases. From this canon it appears that such cases are cases regarding the status of a person. But such cases never become *res iudicatae*.[120] Hence the sentence in the case is purely of a confirmatory nature, that is, the sentence confirms what was previously established in the internal forum.

---

[118] "Si itaque inhabilitas ad nuptias ineundas simul oritur in ordinato in sacris tum ex lege ecclesiastica *per se solum* spectata, tum ex iure divino hypothetico voti solemnis quod ecclesia precepit implicite saltem annecti susceptioni subdiaconatus; dum votum ex metu gravi iniuste incusso emissum, iure naturali destuitur vi obligandi ideoque ex se inhabilitatem non inducit; simul tandem nedum in foro externo tantum, sed etiam in foro interno lex ecclesiastica prosequitur eandem urgere inhabilitatem, non obstante invaliditate voti; ideoque donec lex non fuerit vel abrogata vel particulari dispensatione a Pontifice derogata."—Arendt, *art. cit.—Ius Pontificium*, VIII (1928), p. 70.

[119] Canon 1994, § 2.—Solus clericus, qui existimet se ex sacra ordinatione obligationes ordini adnexas non contraxisse, potest declarationem nullitatis onerum petere.

[120] Canon 1903.

In regard to the question of Orders von Kienitz restricts the comprehension of cases which consider the status of persons exclusively to the cases which regard the validity of the Orders received. He points out that the reason such causes do not become *res iudicatae* is that sentences issued on the validity of a Sacrament as a matter of course are always issued *salvo iure divino*.[121]   But it may be answered that the institute of religious profession, which admittedly comes under the processes regarding the status of persons is clearly of ecclesiastical law, and even a solemn profession may be dispensed from.   Hence it must be admitted that cases regarding the status of persons do not simply comprise cases wherein the divine law is concerned.   Among these cases must be listed the cases regarding the obligations arising from sacred Orders.   The Code includes these causes under the title of causes against sacred ordination.   The object of the cause is to decide whether the cleric has contracted the obligation of celibacy.   If he has not contracted the obligation, then he will be reduced to the lay state.   Hence the cause clearly is concerned with the status of a person.   Since such causes do come under the classification of causes regarding the status of a person, they never become *res iudicatae,* for their solution is dependent, not upon the judgment of the tribunal, but rather upon the objective status of the person.[122]

The Decree of the Sacred Congregation of the Sacraments on June 9, 1931, certainly indicates the opinion that causes regarding the obligations attached to ordination merely confirm what is already established in the internal forum.[123]   In several places the Decree refers to the nullity of the obligations.[124]   The mind of the Sacred Congregation is clearly indicated in the preface to the Decree.   The purpose of the Decree, according to this preface, is that local ordinaries may proceed more safely and expeditiously in the preliminary drawing up of causes regarding the nullity of the sacred Orders re-

---

[121] *Der kirchliche Weiheprozess,* p. 126-ff., as cited by Fuchs, "Erpresster Zutritt zu den höheren Weihen und Zölibatspflicht des Klerikers"—*AKKR,* XCVI (1939), 16-17.

[122] Fuchs, *loc. cit.*

[123] *AAS,* XXIII (1931), 457-473.

[124] Decretum, nn. 12, 65, 70, § 2.—*AAS,* XXIII (1931), 460, 471, 472.

ceived or the non-binding effect of obligations encompassed in the ordination. From the use of the word *nullitas* it is evident that the cleric is considered never to have incurred the obligations.[125]

In respect to the opinion of Arendt it may be remarked that the law does not seem to support his contention. The law refers to a declaration of nullity of the obligation of celibacy, and of course also of the impediment of sacred Orders. Arendt thinks it implies a dispensation from celibacy, and consequently also of the impediment of sacred Orders, which in his opinion arises from the twofold foundation of the vow of celibacy and the ecclesiastical law of celibacy. Yet he does not explain the use of the word *nullitas* in the Code.[126]

Arendt was primarily concerned with the appropriateness of his opinion. But this too can be called into question. In the supposition that a cleric who has been ordained under duress of grave fear and who has not afterwards ratified that ordination enters marriage, which opinion is the more appropriate? Obviously before the case is submitted to the ecclesiastical authorities in order that they may decide whether or not the cleric actually was ordained under duress of grave fear, the scandal is the same no matter which opinion is held. But in the opinion of Arendt the marriage is invalid regardless of the fact that the other conditions requisite for a valid marriage were present. In the other opinion the marriage is valid, provided that the other conditions requisite for a valid marriage were also present. Hence, when the case is submitted to ecclesiastical authorities, it will be be far easier to contend with the factor of scandal when the marriage is recognized as valid from the very outset, than when the marriage is declared invalid. Consequently in such a case the opinion of Arendt is less appropriate.

It may be objected that in such a case the contracting of a valid marriage would be impossible for the cleric, even if he had not contracted the clerical obligations. However, it may be answered that the contracting of a valid marriage would indeed be difficult, but not impossible. Since the reception of the subdiaconate must be en-

---

[125] Fuchs, *art. cit.*, 18-19; Cappello, *De Sacra Ordinatione*, n. 360.
[126] Cf. canon 1994, § 2.

tered in the baptismal register,[127] and the baptismal certificate is inspected before the marriage, there is the difficulty that no priest would assist at the marriage. However, the cleric might obtain a false baptismal certificate, or the priest might be careless in establishing the free state, and in this case the marriage would be valid although the means are not lawful. Again, the cleric might retire to an isolated place where a priest cannot be obtained without grave inconvenience, and where it is prudently foreseen that this state of affairs will continue for a month. Then in accordance with canon 1098 he could marry in the presence of witnesses alone, and the marriage would be valid.[128]

Finally, in the solution of the difficulty as to whether or not the cleric ordained under duress of grave fear contracts the clerical obligations there is a question for the moral theologians. The question is: Has the Church the power to place the extraordinary burden of celibacy upon a person who does not willingly accept it? The question is not going to be approached from the standpoint of moral theology here. But it certainly is a question which must be kept in mind by the authors interpreting canon 214.[129] The authors who state the cleric is not free from the clerical obligation of celibacy before a decision is made by the Church authorities must for themselves answer this question in the affirmative. The authors who hold that the cleric does not contract this obligation need not answer the question at all, for with them the question cannot logically arise.

---

[127] Canons 1011; 470, § 2.

[128] Cf. Fuchs, "Erpresster Zutritt zu den höheren Weihen und Zölibatspflicht des Klerikers"—*AKKR,* XCVI (1939), 27-29.

[129] Cf. Fuchs, *art. cit.—AKKR,* XCVI (1939), 29.

CHAPTER IX

EFFECTS OF REDUCTION AND THE RETURN TO THE CLERICAL STATE

ARTICLE 1. THE EFFECTS OF REDUCTION

ALL who are reduced or who return to lay status from the clerical state by that very fact lose their offices, benefices, clerical rights and privileges, and are forbidden to go about in the clerical dress and to wear the tonsure. But a major cleric who has returned to the lay state is bound by the obligation of celibacy, with the provision of course that the special ruling of canon 214 retains its force.[1]

It will be noticed that canon 213 speaks of those who are reduced or who return to the lay state. The present dissertation has not concerned itself to any considerable extent with the distinction between a reduction to the lay state and a return to the lay state. In the practical order the distinction does not imply any difference. The terminology of the Code itself does not indicate any marked difference. Thus canon 211, § 2, states that minor clerics return to the lay state *ipso facto* for the reasons mentioned in law. But among these reasons are the dismissal of a minor religious cleric in temporary vows [2] and the dismissal of a minor religious cleric in perpetual vows.[3] In both of these cases the canons themselves state that the cleric is reduced to the lay state. Again, canon 211, § 1, mentions the various methods by means of which a major cleric is reduced to the lay state. But canon 212, § 2, refers to any major cleric who has returned to the lay state, and thus it appears that this canon refers to any major cleric who in any manner has been reduced or who has returned to the lay state. Hence there seems to be no need to search for a subtle distinction in the law.

---

[1] Canon 213, § 1. Omnes qui e clericali statu ad laicalem legitime redacti aut regressi sunt, eo ipso amittunt officia, beneficia, iura ac privilegia clericalia et vetantur in habitu ecclesiastico incedere ac tonsuram deferre.

§ 2. Clericus tamen maior obligatione coelibatus tenetur, salvo praescripto can. 214.

[2] Canon 648.

[3] Canon 669, § 2.

When a cleric is reduced to the lay state he loses any office or benefice which up to that time he possessed. This prescription of canon 213 is in harmony with the statement of canon 118, namely, that only clerics can obtain the power of Orders or of jurisdiction or also the possession of benefices or of ecclesiastical pensions.

The reduction to the lay state entails also the loss of the clerical rights and privileges. This prescription agrees perfectly with canon 123, which states that the cleric cannot renounce the clerical privileges, but that he loses them if he is reduced to the lay state.

Finally, by reason of his reduction to the lay state, the cleric is forbidden to go about in ecclesiastical garb and to wear the tonsure. This prescription is similar to the declaration of canon 683, which states that it is not licit for laymen to wear the clerical garb, unless they are students in a seminary, or unless they aspire to Orders under the vigilance and instruction of a pious priest, or finally, unless as laymen they have part in some ecclesiastical ministrations either in or outside of the church at which their services are rightfully engaged.

These effects of the reduction of a cleric to the lay state are in no wise to be considered penalties. They are merely administrative measures arising from the fact that these clerics are, in the eyes of the Church and for legal effects, laymen.

Since in the eyes of the Church and for legal effects a cleric who has been reduced to the lay state is a layman, it follows that such a cleric is no longer bound by the clerical obligations enumerated in canons 124-144.[4] However, in regard to major clerics the law makes an exception. Major clerics are still bound by the law of celibacy, unless they were ordained under constraint of grave fear and did not afterwards ratify their ordination, as canon 214 points out. It need hardly be remarked that when a major cleric has been dispensed from his obligation of celibacy by means of a rescript of the Holy See, or in the extraordinary case contemplated in canons 1043-1045, he is no longer obliged to observe celibacy.

Some authors maintain that when a cleric has been reduced to the lay state, at least if the reduction is effected through the penalty of degradation, he is still obliged to recite the divine office.[5] How-

[4] Chelodi, *Ius de Personis*, n. 124; Wernz-Vidal, *Ius Canonicum*, II, n. 395.

[5] Vermeersch-Creusen, *Epitome*, III, n. 499; Raus, *Institutiones Canonicae*, n. 462.

ever, this obligation does not seem to bind him. Canon 135 explicitly excepts from this obligation the clerics who are mentioned in canons 213-214.[6] Among the clerics mentioned in canon 213 must be included the degraded clerics, for they too have been reduced from the clerical to the lay state. Consequently it must be concluded that even degraded clerics as well as clerics who have been reduced to the lay state in any other manner are not obliged to recite the divine office.[7]

Moreover, the cleric who has been reduced to the lay state may receive the Sacraments after the manner of laymen. He is not permitted to dispense the Sacraments, except in altogether extraordinary circumstances. But the reduction to the lay state, even though it be imposed as a penalty, does not preclude his reception of the Sacraments. Finally there is no intrinsic reduction to the lay state. The character of Holy Orders imprinted upon the soul of an ordained cleric is not touched by the juridical reduction to the lay state. This is a point which must be emphasized. The reduction is simply an ecclesiastical measure to indicate that the cleric, in the eyes of the Church and for legal effects, is now a layman.

ARTICLE 2. THE RETURN TO THE CLERICAL STATE

Any cleric in minor Orders who has returned to the lay state for any cause requires the permission of the ordinary of the diocese into which he was incardinated through his ordination before he can return to the clerical state. This permission is not to be granted except after a diligent examination into the life and morals of the cleric, and after a period of trial which is suitable in the judgment of the ordinary.[8]

[6] Canon 135.—Clerici in maioribus ordinibus constituti, exceptis iis de quibus in can. 213-214, tenentur obligatione quotidie horas canonicas integre recitandi. . . .

[7] Findlay, *Deposition and Degradation of Clerics*, pp. 214-217; Augustine, *A Commentary*, VIII, 262, note 19; Chelodi, *Ius Poenale*, n. 53; Beste, *Introductio in Codicem*, p. 930.

[8] Canon 212, § 1. Qui in minoribus ordinibus constitutus ad statum laicalem quavis de causa regressus est, ut inter clericos denuo admittatur, requiritur licentia Ordinarii dioecesis cui incardinatus fuit per ordinationem, non concedenda nisi post diligens examen super vita et moribus, et congruum, iudicio ipsius Ordinarii, experimentum.

From canon 212, § 1, it is evident that in respect to the permission necessary for a return to the clerical state no distinction is made among minor clerics who returned to the lay state of their own accord, minor clerics who were reduced to the lay state by a decree of the ordinary, and minor clerics who were reduced by way of penalty. However, in conformity with the law regulating the dispensation from vindictive penalties, it appears that the cleric must first be dispensed if he was reduced to the lay state by way of penalty. The remission of a penalty by way of dispensation may be granted only by the one who as an ordinary enacted or inflicted the penalty, by his successor, by his superior, or finally by one to whom this power is conceded.[9]

Hence, if a minor cleric were reduced to the lay state because of some delict in matters of the sixth commandment and committed by him in the diocese of another ordinary, then he would have to be dispensed by the ordinary who inflicted the penalty. It is clear that such a dispensation will be given only with the permission of the ordinary of the diocese in which the cleric was incardinated by ordination. Both the dispensation and the permission are necessary for the erstwhile cleric to return to the clerical state. If either were refused, the cleric could not again be admitted to the clerical state.

If the erstwhile cleric has been reduced to the lay state by way of a penalty incurred *ipso facto,* or by way of a penalty inflicted by the ordinary of the diocese in which he was incardinated through ordination, then this ordinary has the power to dispense from this penalty.[10] This dispensation will probably be included in the permission granted for the cleric to return to the clerical state. Finally, if the cleric has returned to the lay state of his own accord, or if he has been reduced to lay status by means of a decree of the ordinary, it is sufficient that he obtain the permission of the ordinary in whose diocese he was incardinated through ordination in order to return to the clerical state.

In canon 212 no explicit mention is made of minor religious clerics who have been reduced to the lay state. If the minor religious cleric

[9] Canon 2236, § 1.
[10] Canon 2237.

was reduced by way of penalty, it is of course necessary to obtain a dispensation from the one who inflicted the penalty, his successor, his superior, or finally the one to whom this power has been delegated, before he can return to the clerical state. If the penalty was a *latae sententiae* penalty it may be dispensed by a major superior in a clerical exempt institute; by the local ordinary in a clerical non-exempt or lay institute. The case would occur, for instance, if a minor religious cleric in perpetual vows volunteered for military service.

Is the permission of the local ordinary or of the major superior in a clerical exempt institute necessary before the religious ex-cleric can return to the clerical state? The case would occur, for instance, if a minor religious cleric in perpetual vows was dismissed from his institute. In such a case the one dismissed remains a religious, unless the constitutions of the institute or an indult of the Holy See state the contrary, but he is reduced to the lay state.[11] From an analogy of law it appears that such a permission is necessary.[12] If the religious is in a clerical exempt institute, it appears that the major superior is competent to grant this permission. If the religious is in a non-exempt clerical or lay institute, it seems that the ordinary competent to grant the return to the clerical state is the ordinary who had the right to ordain the man, namely, the bishop of the diocese in whose territory is situated the religious house to which the man belongs.[13]

The ordinary is not to grant the permission to return to the clerical state until he has diligently examined into the life and morals of the ex-cleric and the ex-cleric has successfully passed through the period of trial which the ordinary deems sufficient and suitable. The examination into the life and morals of the ex-cleric may be made in conformity with the suggested questionnaire appended to the Instruction of the Sacred Congregation of the Sacraments as issued on December 27, 1930, for the examination of the life and morals of clerics

---

[11] Canon 669, §§ 1-2.

[12] Canon 20.

[13] Canons 964, 1°, 2°, 4°; 965. Cf. O'Leary, *Religious Dismissed after Perpetual Profession,* pp. 116-117.

during the time they have spent on vacation.[14]   However, the ordinary is not obliged to follow any definite procedure.   Again, the determination of the length and of the nature of the period of trial is left entirely to the judgment of the ordinary.

A major cleric who has returned to the lay state needs the permission of the Holy See in order to return to the clerical state.[15]   If the reduction to the lay state was effected through the penalty of degradation, then the permission to return to the clerical state will have to include a dispensation from the penalty.   Ordinarily the Holy See is reluctant to grant permission for the return of such a major ex-cleric to the clerical state.

If a deacon or a subdeacon was reduced to the lay state by means of an apostolic rescript with a dispensation from celibacy, the case would be very extraordinary in which he would be permitted to return to the clerical state.   The practice of the Roman Curia today seems to be to insert in the rescript which grants the reduction the phrase *"sine spe readmissionis ad statum clericalem."*   In the case of a priest who upon an attempted marriage has been reduced to lay status by means of an apostolic rescript, the Supreme Congregation of the Holy Office may grant him a return to the clerical state after a long period of repentance.[16]

In regard to the admission of an ex-religious to a seminary, or of an ex-seminarian to a religious institute, the Sacred Congregation of Religious and the Sacred Congregation of Seminaries and Universities issued a joint decree on July 25, 1941.   According to this decree, before a person who has belonged by any title to a religious institute may be admitted to a seminary, the ordinary must have recourse to the Sacred Congregation of Seminaries and Universities, which, after all that the case requires has been done, will inform the ordinary of its judgment in the case.   Likewise, before a person who for any reason has quit the seminary may be enrolled in a religious institute, the religious superior must have recourse to the Sacred Con-

[14] *AAS,* XXIII (1931), 128-129.

[15] Canon 212, § 2.—Clericus vero maior qui ad statum laicalem rediit, ut inter clericos denuo admittatur, indiget Sanctae Sedis licentia.

[16] López, "De reconciliatione sacerdotis qui matrimonium attentare praesumpsit"—*Periodica,* XXVI (1937), 505.

gregation of Religious, which, after all that the case requires has been done, will inform the superior of its judgment in the case.[17]

Hence, if an ex-religious who was a cleric wishes to return to the clerical state and enter a seminary, the ordinary must have recourse to the Sacred Congregation of Seminaries and Universities. If an ex-seminarian who was a cleric wishes to return to the clerical state and enter a religious institute, the religious superior must have recourse to the Sacred Congregation of Religious.

Moreover, those who are bound or were bound by the bond of religious profession are without a previous dispensation invalidly admitted to the novitiate.[18] Again, major clerics are without the consultation of their ordinary illicitly admitted to the novitiate.[19] Hence any such cleric who wishes to return to the clerical state and to enter a novitiate must abide by these laws.

Finally, there is no re-ordination upon the return to the clerical state, not even for those who had received only first tonsure. The wearing of the tonsure is resumed in those regions where it is of obligation for clerics, but there is no re-ordination. The Orders which are of a sacramental nature cannot be taken away. The Orders which are of merely ecclesiastical institution can be taken away, but the law explicitly states that it is not an effect of the reduction of a cleric to the lay state that his Orders are taken away.[20] Hence any re-ordination must be avoided as contrary to the law of the Church.

---

[17] *AAS*, XXXIII (1941), 371; *The Clergy Review*, XXI (1941), 364; Bouscaren, *The Canon Law Digest*, II, 426.

[18] Canon 542, 1°.

[19] Canon 542, 2°.

[20] Canon 211, § 1.

CONCLUSIONS

As a result of this study the following conclusions are offered:

1. A minor cleric who marries falls from the clerical state whether the marriage be valid or invalid, with the exception of the minor cleric whose marriage is invalid because of force or fear inflicted on him (p. 50), and of the minor cleric whose marriage is invalid because of lack of consent on the part of him or his contemplated partner. This exception does not hold when the validity of the consent is vitiated; it holds only when the consent is absolutely absent. (Pp. 51-55.)

2. The departure of a religious minor cleric, whether in temporary or in perpetual vows, from the religious institute for any reason other than dismissal does not cause the reduction of this cleric to the lay state. (Pp. 79-83, 87-88.)

3. If the minor cleric is to be reduced to the lay state as a penalty for a delict, then this penalty must be inflicted in a true judicial process. (Pp. 95-101.)

4. The *dolus* on the part of the candidate for religious profession, as referred to in canon 2387, is to be understood as a substantial *dolus*. (Pp. 103-106.)

5. The decree of the local ordinary by means of which the cleric is reduced to the lay state always provides for the reduction as an administrative measure. Such a decree may never be used for the infliction of the reduction as a penalty. (Pp. 95-104, 119-120.)

6. The dispensation from the impediment of sacred Orders granted to a deacon or a subdeacon in accordance with the faculties granted in canons 1043-1045 effects the reduction of the deacon or the subdeacon to the lay state. (Pp. 135-139.)

7. By the grave fear which canon 214 contemplates is understood grave fear which is unjustly inflicted from without and which is directed toward the ordination as a goal to be achieved. (Pp. 142-146.)

8. A cleric who is in invincible ignorance or in substantial error regarding the nature of the obligation of celibacy does not contract that obligation when he is ordained. (Pp. 156-159.)

9. A cleric who is ordained under duress of grave fear and who does not afterwards ratify that ordination does not contract the obligation of celibacy, and in consequence is not impeded from marriage by the diriment impediment of sacred Orders. (Pp. 159-164.)

10. A minor cleric who has been reduced to the lay state by way of penalty needs a dispensation from this penalty as well as the permission of the ordinary of the diocese into which he was incardinated through his ordination before he can return to the clerical state. (Pp. 169-170.)

BIBLIOGRAPHY

SOURCES

Acta Apostolicae Sedis, Commentarium Officiale, Romae, 1909-1929; Civitate Vaticana, 1929—

Acta et Decreta Concilii Plenarii Baltimorensis III, A. D. MDCCCLXXXIV, Baltimorae, 1886.

Acta Sanctae Sedis, 41 vols., Romae, 1865-1908.

Bouscaren, T. Lincoln, *The Canon Law Digest,* 2 vols., Milwaukee: Bruce, 1934-1943.

Canones et Decreta Sacrosancti et Oecumenici Concilii Tridentini, Parisiis, 1832.

Codex Iuris Canonici Pii X Pontificis Maximi iussu digestus Benedicti XV auctoritate promulgatus, Romae: Typis Polyglottis Vaticanis, 1917.

Codicis Iuris Canonici Fontes cura Eﬁi Card. Gasparri Editi, 9 vols., Romae (postea Civitate Vaticana): Typis Polyglottis Vaticanis, 1923-1939. (Vols. VII, VIII et IX cura et studio Eﬁi Card. Serédi.)

Corpus Iuris Canonici, editio Lipsiensis secunda post Aemilii Ludovici Richteri curas ad librorum manu scriptorum et editionis Romanae fidem recognovit et adnotatione critica instruxit Aemilius Friedberg, Lipsiae, 1879-1881.

Corpus Iuris Civilis, Vol. I, *Institutiones*—recognovit P. Krueger; Vol. II, *Codex Iustinianus*—recognovit et retractavit P. Krueger; Vol. III, *Novellae Constitutiones*—R. Schoell; opus Schoelli morte interceptum absolvit G. Kroll, Berolini: apud Weidmannos, 1928-1929.

———, *Digesta Iustiniani Augusti*—recognoverunt et ediderunt P. Bonfante, C. Fadda, C. Ferrini, S. Riccobono, V. Scialoia, Mediolani: Società Editrice Libraria, 1931.

Decisiones Sacrae Rotae Romanae coram bon: mem: Reverendissimo Iacobo Emerix, Romae, 1701.

Decretum Gratiani Emendatum et Notationibus Illustratum una cum glossis, Romae, 1582.

Decretales D. Gregorii Papae IX, una cum glossis restitutae, Romae, 1582.

Jaffé, Philippus, *Regesta Pontificum Romanorum, ab condita ecclesia ad annum post Christum natum 1198,* 2. ed., correctam et auctam auspiciis Gulielmi Wattenbach curaverunt S. Loewenfeld, F. Kaltenbrunner, P. Ewald, 2 vols. in 1, Lipsiae, 1885-1888.

Pallottini, Salvator, *Collectio Omnium Conclusionum et Resolutionum Quae in Causis Propositis apud Sacram Congregationem Cardinalium S. Concilii Tridentini Interpretum Prodierunt ab eius Institutione Anno MCLXIV ad MDCCCLX, Distinctis Titulis Alphabetico Ordine per Materias Digestas,* 18 vols., Romae, 1868-1895.

Potthast, Augustus, *Regesta Pontificum Romanorum inde ab A. post Christum natum 1198 ad A. 1804,* 2 vols., Berolini, 1874-1875.

175

S. Romanae Rotae Decisiones seu Sententiae (ab anno 1909), Romae, Typis Vaticanis, 1912—

Schroeder, H., *Canons and Decrees of the Council of Trent*, St. Louis: Herder, 1941.

Thesaurus Resolutionum Sacrae Congregationis Concilii, 167 vols., Romae, 1718-1908.

REFERENCE WORKS

Aertnys-Damen, *Theologia Moralis*, 13. ed., 2 vols., Taurini-Romae: Marietti, 1939.

Aichner, Simon, *Compendium Iuris Ecclesiastici*, 6. ed., Brixinae, 1887.

Alphonsus Liguori, St., *Theologia Moralis*, ed. L. Gaudé, 4 vols., Romae, 1905-1912.

Andreae, Ioannes, *In Quinque Decretalium Libros Novella Commentaria*, 4 vols., Venetiis, 1581.

———, *In Sextum Librum Novella Commentaria*, Venetiis, 1581.

Augustine, Charles, *A Commentary on the New Code of Canon Law*, 8 vols. Vol. II, *Clergy and Hierarchy*, 5. ed., 1928; Vol. VIII, *Penal Code*, 2. ed., 1924.

Ayrinhac, H. A., *General Legislation in the New Code of Canon Law*, New York: Longmans, 1933.

Ayrinhac, H. A.-Lydon, P. J., *Penal Legislation in the New Code of Canon Law*, revised edition, New York: Benziger, 1936.

Barbosa, Augustinus, *Collectanea Doctorum tam Veterum quam Recentiorum in Ius Pontificium Universum*, 2 vols., Lugduni, 1716.

Barrett, John D. M., *A Comparative Study of the Councils of Baltimore and the Code of Canon Law*, The Catholic University of America Canon Law Studies, n. 83, Washington, D. C.: The Catholic University of America, 1932.

Benedictus XIV, *De Synodo Dioecesana*, Prati, 1844.

Beste, Udalricus, *Introductio in Codicem*, Collegeville, Minn.: St. John's Abbey Press, 1938.

Blat, Albertus, *Commentarium Textus Codicis Iuris Canonici*, 5 vols. in 6, 1921-1927; Lib. II, *Ius de Religiosis*, 3. ed., 1938; Lib. V, *De Delictis et Poenis*, Romae: Apud "Angelicum."

Cappello, Felix, *Summa Iuris Canonici in Usum Scholarum Concinnata*, 3 vols., Vol. II, Romae: Apud Aedes Universitatis Gregorianae, 1930.

———, *Tractatus Canonico-Moralis de Censuris*, 3. ed., Romae: Marietti, 1933.

———, *Tractatus Canonico-Moralis de Sacramentis*, 3 vols. in 6, Romae: Marietti, 1932-1939. Vol. II, Pars III, *De Sacra Ordinatione*, 1935; Vol. III, Partes I et II, *De Matrimonio*, 4. ed., 1939.

Chelodi, Ioannes, *Ius de Personis iuxta Codicem Iuris Canonici*, ed. altera a Sac. Ernesto Bertagnolli recognita et aucta, Tridenti: Libr. Edit. Tridentum, 1927.

————, *Ius Poenale et Ordo Procedendi in Iudiciis Criminalibus iuxta Codicem Iuris Canonici*, 4. ed., recognita et aucta a Virgilio Dalpiaz, Tridenti: Ardesi, 1935.

Cipollini, Albertus, *De Censuris Latae Sententiae iuxta Codicem Iuris Canonici*, Taurini: Marietti, 1925.

Coronata, Mathaeus, Conte a, *Institutiones Iuris Canonici*, 5 vols., Vols. I-II, 2. ed., 1939; Vols. III-V, 1933-1936, Taurini: Marietti.

Cocchi, Guidus, *Commentarium in Codicem Iuris Canonici*, 5 vols. in 8, Lib. II, *De Personis*, Taurinorum Augustae: Marietti, 1922.

Craisson, D., *Manuale Totius Iuris Canonici*, 6. ed., 4 vols., Pictavii, 1880.

Creusen, Joseph-Garesché, Edward-Ellis, Adam, *Religious Men and Women in the Code*, 3. English ed., Milwaukee: Bruce, 1940.

De Luca, I. B., *Theatrum Veritatis et Iustitiae*, 16 vols. in 5, Venetiis, 1734.

De Meester, Alphonsus, *Iuris Canonici et Iuris Canonico-civilis Compendium*, nova ed., 3 vols. in 4, Brugis: Desclée, 1921-1928.

De Smet, Aloysius, *Tractatus Theologico-Canonicus de Sponsalibus et Matrimonio*, 4. ed., Brugis, 1927.

Devoti, Ioannes, *Institutionum Canonicarum Libri IV*, 3 vols., Romae, 1825.

Engel, Ludovicus, *Collegium Universi Iuris Canonici*, Salisburgi, 1726.

Fagnanus, Prosper, *Commentaria in Quinque Libros Decretalium*, 4 vols., Venetiis, 1697.

Fanfani, Ludovicus, *De Iure Religiosorum ad normam Codicis Iuris Canonici*, 2. ed., Taurini-Romae: Marietti, 1925.

Ferraris, Lucius, *Prompta Bibliotheca, Canonica, Iuridica, Moralis, Theologica necnon Ascetica, Polemica, Rubricistica, Historica*, 8 vols., Parisiis, 1860-1863.

Findlay, Stephen, *Canonical Norms Governing the Deposition and Degradation of Clerics*, The Catholic University of America Canon Law Studies, n. 130, Washington, D. C.: The Catholic University of America Press, 1941.

Frey, Wolfgang, *The Act of Religious Profession*, The Catholic University of America Canon Law Studies, n. 63, Washington, D. C.: The Catholic University of America, 1931.

Gasparri, Petrus, *Tractatus Canonicus de Matrimonio*, ed. nova, 2 vols., Romae: Typis Polyglottis Vaticanis, 1932.

Gerster a Zeil, Thomas Villanova, *Ius Religiosorum in Compendium Redactum Pro Iuvenibus Religiosis*, Taurini: Marietti, 1935.

Giraldi, Ubaldus, *Expositio Iuris Pontificii iuxta Recentiorem Ecclesiae Disciplinam*, 3 vols. in 2, Romae, 1769.

Grassis, Carolus de, *Tractatus de Effectibus Clericatus*, Venetiis, 1674.

Guilfoyle, Merlin Joseph, *Custom*, The Catholic University of America Canon Law Studies, n. 105, Washington, D. C.: The Catholic University of America, 1937.

Hostiensis (Henricus de Segusio), *Commentaria in V Libros Decretalium*, 3 vols., Venetiis, 1581.

————, *Summa Aurea*, Venetiis, 1586.

Iorio, Thomas A., *Theologia Moralis iuxta Methodum Compendii Ioannis P. Gury et Raphaelis Tummulo,* 6. ed., 3 vols., Neapoli: D'Auria, 1938-1939.

Lega, Michaelis, *De Delictis et Poenis,* 2. ed., Romae, 1910.

Many, S., *Praelectiones de Sacra Ordinatione,* Parisiis, 1905.

Marc, Clement-Gestermann, Fr. X.-Raus, J. B., *Institutiones Morales Alphonsianae,* 19. ed., 2 vols., Lugduni: Emmanuel Vitte, 1933-1934.

Maroto Philippus, *Institutiones Iuris Canonici,* 2 vols., Romae, 1919-1921. Vol. I, 3. ed., Romae: Apud Commentarium pro Religiosis, 1921.

Merkelbach, Benedictus Henricus, *Summa Theologiae Moralis ad Mentem D. Thomae et ad Normam Iuris Novi,* 3. ed., 3 vols., Parisiis: Desclée de Brouwer, 1938-1939.

Moeder, John M., *The Proper Bishop for Ordination and Dimissorial Letters,* The Catholic University of America Canon Law Studies, n. 95, Washington, D. C.: The Catholic University of America, 1935.

Moriarty, Francis E., *The Extraordinary Absolution from Censures,* The Catholic University of America Canon Law Studies, n. 113, Washington, D. C.: The Catholic University of America, 1938.

Noldin, H.-Schmitt, A., *Summa Theologiae Moralis,* 3 vols., Oeniponte: Typis et Sumptibus Fel. Rauch, 1938-1940. Vol. I, 27. ed., 1940; Vol. II, 25. ed., 1938; Vol. III, 26. ed., 1940.

Oesterle, Gerardus, *Praelectiones Iuris Canonici,* Vol. I, Romae, in Collegio S. Anselmi, 1931.

Ojetti, B., *Commentarium in Codicem Iuris Canonici,* 4 vols., Romae: Apud Aedes Universitatis Gregorianae, 1927-1931.

O'Leary, Charles G., *Religious Dismissed after Perpetual Profession,* The Catholic University of America Canon Law Studies, n. 184, Washington, D. C.: The Catholic University of America Press, 1943.

O'Neill, Francis J., *The Dismissal of Religious in Temporary Vows,* The Catholic University of America Canon Law Studies, n. 166, Washington, D. C.: The Catholic University of America Press, 1942.

O'Neill, William H., *Papal Rescripts of Favor,* The Catholic University of America Canon Law Studies, n. 57, Washington, D. C.: The Catholic University of America, 1930.

Palombo, Josephus, *De Dimissione Religiosorum,* Taurini-Romae: Marietti, 1931.

Panormitanus (Nicolaus de Tudeschis), *Commentaria in Quinque Libros Decretalium,* 5 vols. in 7, Venetiis, 1588.

Pejška, Joseph, *Ius Canonicum Religiosorum,* 3. ed., Friburgi Brisgoviae: Herder, 1927.

Piontek, Cyril, *De Indulto Exclaustrationis necnon Saecularizationis,* The Catholic University of America Canon Law Studies, n. 29, Washington, D. C.: The Catholic University of America, 1925.

Pistocchi, Mario, *I Canoni Penali del Codice Ecclesiastico Esposti e Commentati,* Torino-Roma: Marietti, 1925.

Prümmer, Dominicus, *Manuale Iuris Ecclesiastici,* Friburgi Brisgoviae, 1909.

————, *Manuale Iuris Canonici in Usum Scholarum,* 5. ed., Friburgi Brisgoviae: Herder, 1927.

————, *Manuale Theologiae Moralis secundum Principia S. Thomae Aquinatis,* 8. ed., recognita a P. Dr. Engelberto M. Münch, 3 vols., Friburgi Brisgoviae, 1935-1936.

Raymundus de Penaforte, St., *Summa,* ed. nova, Veronae, 1744.

Raus, J. B., *Institutiones Canonicae,* ed. altera, Lugduni-Parisiis: Typis Emmanuelis Vitte, 1931.

————, *La Doctrine de S. Alphonse sur la Vocation et la Grace en regard de l'enseignement de S. Thomas et des Prescriptions du Code,* Lyon-Paris: Emmanuel Vitte, 1926.

Reiffenstuel, Anacletus, *Ius Canonicum Universum,* 5 vols. in 3, Maceratae, 1760.

Roskovány, Augustinus, *Coelibatus et Breviarium, duo gravissima clericorum officia e monumentis omnium saeculorum demonstrata,* 13 vols., Vols. 1-5, Pestini, 1861; Vols. 6-13, Nitriae, 1877-1888.

Santi, Franciscus-Leitner, Martinus, *Praelectiones Iuris Canonici,* 4. ed., 5 vols. in 2, Ratisbonae, 1903-1905.

Schäfer, Timotheus, *Compendium de Religiosis ad Normam Codicis Iuris Canonici,* 3. ed., Romae: S. A. L. E. R., 1940.

Schmalzgrueber, Franciscus, *Ius Ecclesiasticum Universum,* 5 vols. in 3, Neapoli, 1738.

Schroeder, H., *Disciplinary Decrees of the General Councils,* St. Louis: Herder, 1937.

Sipos, Stephanus, *Enchiridion Iuris Canonici,* Pécs: Ex Typographia "Haladás R. T.," 1926.

Soglia, Ioannes, *Institutiones Iuris Publici et Privati Ecclesiastici,* 10. ed., 2 vols., Boscoduci, 1853.

Smith, Mariner, *The Penal Law for Religious,* The Catholic University of America Canon Law Studies, n. 98, Washington, D. C.: The Catholic University of America, 1935.

Suarez, Franciscus, *Opera Omnia,* 28 vols., Parisiis, 1856-1861.

Tanquerey, A., *Synopsis Theologiae Dogmaticae,* 3 vols., Vol. III, 23. ed., quam recognovit J. B. Bord, Parisiis-Tornaci-Romae, 1934.

Toso, Albertus, *Ad Codicem Iuris Canonici Commentaria Minora,* 5 vols. in 2, Romae: Marietti, 1921-1927.

Tymczak, Adolphus, *Quaestiones Disputatae de Ordine,* Premisliae (Polonia), 1936.

Van Espen, Zegerus, *Ius Ecclesiasticum Universum,* 5 vols. in 2, Lovanii, 1729.

Vermeersch, Arthurus, *Theologiae Moralis Principia, Responsa, Concilia,* ed. altera, 3 vols., Brugis: Charles Beyaert, 1926-1928.

Vermeersch, Arthurus-Creusen, Josephus, *Epitome Iuris Canonici,* 3. ed., 3 vols., Mechliniae-Romae: Dessain, 1927-1928.

Wernz, Franciscus, *Ius Decretalium,* 2. ed., 6 vols., Romae et Prati, 1906-1913.

Wernz, Franciscus-Vidal, Petrus, *Ius Canonicum ad Codicis Normam Exactum,*
7 tomes in 8 vols., Tom. II, *Ius de Personis,* 2. ed., 1928; Tom. III, *De
Religiosis,* 1933, Romae: Apud Aedes Universitatis Gregorianae.

Articles

Arendt, G., "Quomodo concordare debeant can. 214 et 1072?"—*Ius Pontificium,*
VIII (1928), 63-77; 168-173.

Beijersbergen, H., "Decretum 18 Aprilis, 1936—Annotationes"—*Periodica,* XXV
(1936), 199-203.

Cappello, "Irrogatio poenae per modum praecepti extra iudicium"—*Periodica,*
XIX (1930), 36*-38*.

Ciprotti, "De consummatione delictorum attento eorum elemento obiectivo"—
Apollinaris, IX (1936), 413-414.

Ellis, A., "De religiosi minoristae saecularizati incardinatione"—*"Periodica,* XXV
(1936), 53*-55*.

Fuchs, V., "Erpresster Zutritt zu den höheren Weihen und Zölibatspflicht des
Klerikers"—*AKKR,* XCVI (1939), 3-30.

Goyeneche, S., "Consultatio"—*CpR,* IV (1923), 146-147.

———, "Consultatio"—*CpRM,* XVI (1935), 233-234.

———, "Consultatio"—*CpRM,* XIX (1938), 163-164.

Haring, J., "Laiserung nach can. 214"—*TPQ,* LXXVII (1924), 338.

———, "Zurückversetzung in den Laienstand"—*TPQ,* LXXXVI (1933), 816.

Larraona, Arcadius, "Commentarium Codicis — Canon 542" — *CpRM,* XVII
(1936), 8-19.

López, Ulpianus, "Casus Conscientiae"—*Periodica,* XXVII (1938), 32-35.

———, "De reconciliatione sacerdotis, qui matrimonium attentare praesumpsit"
—*Periodica,* XXVI (1937), 501-506.

Michiels, Gommarus, "De reservatione censurae latae sententiae praecepto particulari adnexae"—*ETL,* IV (1927), 180-194; 613-619.

Noval, I., "De ratione corrigendi et puniendi sive in iudicio sive extra iure
Codicis I. C."—*Ius Pontificium,* II (1922), 147-156; III (1923), 36-40;
204-210.

Oesterle, G., "De domicilio religiosorum"—*CpR,* V (1924), 167-168.

———, "Die Zurückversetzunz der Kleriker in den Laienstand nach dem neuen
Rechte"—*TPQ,* LXXIV (1921), 500-512.

Rossi, Joseph, "S. Poenitentiaria Apostolica, Decretum 18 Aprilis, 1936—Annotationes"—*Apollinaris,* IX (1936), 587-588.

Schaaf, Valentine, "Episcopus proprius ordinationis religiosorum"—*ER,* XC
(1934), 491-509.

Tabera, A., "De dimissione religiosorum"—*CpR,* XI (1930), 277-285; 411-420;
XII (1931), 140-148; 369-375; XIV (1933), 53-59; 266-274.

Vermeersch, Arthurus, "De metu qui, saltem ex lege positiva, excusat ab obligationibus vitiato consensu susceptis, praecipue de metu ab intrinseco vel
extrinseco"—*Periodica,* XVII (1928), 138*-144*.

PERIODICALS

American Ecclesiastical Review, The, Philadelphia, 1889-1943; Washington, 1944—

Apollinaris, Romae, 1928—

Commentarium pro Religiosis (later 1935 *Commentarium pro Religiosis et Missionariis*), Romae, 1920—

Ephemerides Theologicae Lovanienses, Brugis, 1924—

Ius Pontificium, Romae, 1921—

Periodica de Re Canonica et Morali utili praesertim Religiosis et Missionariis, Brugis, 1905—

Theologisch-praktische Quartalschrift, Linz, 1832—

ABBREVIATIONS

AAS—Acta Apostolicae Sedis.
AKKR—Archiv für katholisches Kirchenrecht.
ASS—Acta Sanctae Sedis.
D.—Digestum (Iustinianum).
ER—Ecclesiastical Review.
ETL—Ephemerides Theologicae Lovanienses.
Fontes—Codicis Iuris Canonici Fontes.
Periodica—Periodica de Re Canonica et Morali.
TPQ—Theologisch-praktische Quartalschrift.

ALPHABETICAL INDEX

Benefice, minor cleric with a,
    after Council of Trent, 22
    after const. *"Cum Sacrosanctam,"* 23
    after const. *"Apos. Sedis,"* 23
    according to contrary custom, 23
    after Code, 49

Cause,
    for decree of reduction, 118
    vs. ordination itself, 142, 143
    vs. obligations of ordination, 152, 153.
Celibacy, 15, 30, 36
    ignorance of, 156
Character of Holy Orders, 1, 41
    as regards major Orders, 2, 41
    as regards minor Orders, 2, 42
Cleric, definition of, 43
Clerical state, 44
Consent, matrimonial, 52
    absence of as regards reduction, 54, 55

Decision,
    of minor cleric to leave clerical state, 110, 112, 113
Declaration of Nullity,
    of clerical obligations, 162, 163
    of profession, 107
Decree, of ordinary as means of reduction, 119, 120
    necessity of just cause for, 118
    competent ordinary for, 116, 117
    not to be used for penalty, 100, 101, 119, 120
Degradation, actual as cause of reduction,
    before Council of Trent, 8
    after Council of Trent, 21

after Code, 131, 132, 133, 134
verbal,
    as identified with deposition before Council of Trent, 7, 8
    as distinct after Council of Trent, 20, 21
    as cause of reduction after Code, 131, 132, 133, 134
Delict, vs. sixth commandment,
    as cause of reduction, 89
    as understood in canon 2358, 90, 91
    as *crimen pessimum,* 101, 102
    in religious profession, 103
    nature of delict, 106
    may be punished with reduction, 108
Deposition, not a cause of reduction,
    before Council of Trent, 7, 8
    after Council of Trent, 21
Dismissal of religious,
    in temporary vows, 70, 71, 72
    causes reduction of minor cleric, 71
    ordained before entrance into religion, 76, 77, 78, 79
    in perpetual vows, 85, 86
    causes reduction of minor cleric, 86
Dispensation,
    from clerical obligations, 30, 125, 127, 132
    from irregularity, 130
    from religious vows, 82, 87
    from penalty of reduction, 169, 171
    for marriage of major cleric, 138, 139
Divine Office, 37, 167, 168
Dolus,
    definition, 103
    invalidating profession, 105, 106

185

BIOGRAPHICAL NOTE

FRANCIS PATRICK SWEENEY was born on November 21, 1915, in Boston, Massachusetts. After completing his elementary education in the parochial school of Our Lady of Perpetual Help, Roxbury, Massachusetts, he entered St. Mary's College, the Juvenate of the Redemptorist Fathers at North East, Pennsylvania, in August, 1929. On August 1, 1935, he received the habit of the Congregation of the Most Holy Redeemer at Ilchester, Maryland, and made his religious profession on August 2nd of the following year. His seminary course was made at the Redemptorist House of Studies, Mount St. Alphonsus, Esopus, New York, where he was ordained to the priesthood on June 22, 1941. In September of 1942 he entered the Catholic University of America to pursue a graduate course of studies in the School of Canon Law. He received his Baccalaureate in Canon Law in May, 1943, and his Licentiate in Canon Law in May, 1944.

CANON LAW STUDIES *

1. FRERIKS, REV. CELESTINE A., C.PP.S., J.C.D., Religious Congregations in Their External Relations, 121 pp., 1916.
2. GALLIHER, REV. DANIEL M., O.P., J.C.D., Canonical Elections, 117 pp., 1917.
3. BORKOWSKI, REV. AURELIUS L., O.F.M., J.C.D., De Confraternitatibus Ecclesiasticis, 136 pp., 1918.
4. CASTILLO, REV. CAYO, J.C.D., Disertacion Historico-Canonica sobre la Potestad del Cabildo en Sede Vacante o Impedida del Vicario Capitular, 99 pp., 1919 (1918).
5. KUBELBECK, REV. WILLIAM J., S.T.B., J.C.D., The Sacred Penitentiaria and Its Relation to Faculties of Ordinaries and Priests, 129 pp., 1918.
6. PETROVITS, REV. JOSEPH, J.C., S.T.D., J.C.D., The New Church Law on Matrimony, X-461 pp., 1919.
7. HICKEY, REV. JOHN J., S.T.B., J.C.D., Irregularities and Simple Impediments in the New Code of Canon Law, 100 pp., 1920.
8. KLEKOTKA, REV. PETER J., S.T.B., J.C.D., Diocesan Consultors, 179 pp., 1920.
9. WANENMACHER, REV. FRANCIS, J.C.D., The Evidence in Ecclesiastical Procedure Affecting the Marriage Bond, 1920 (Printed 1935).
10. GOLDEN, REV. HENRY FRANCIS, J.C.D., Parochial Benefices in the New Code, IV-119 pp., 1921 (Printed 1925).
11. KOUDELKA, REV. CHARLES J., J.C.D., Pastors, Their Rights and Duties According to the New Code of Canon Law, 211 pp., 1921.
12. MELO, REV. ANTONIUS, O.F.M., J.C.D., De Exemptione Regularium, X-188 pp., 1921.
13. SCHAAF, REV. VALENTINE THEODORE, O.F.M., S.T.B., J.C.D., The Cloister, X-180 pp., 1921.
14. BURKE, REV. THOMAS JOSEPH, S.T.D., J.C.D., Competence in Ecclesiastical Tribunals, IV-117 pp., 1922.
15. LEECH, REV. GEORGE LEO, J.C.D., A Comparative Study of the Constitution "Apostolicae Sedis" and the "Codex Juris Canonici," 179 pp., 1922.
16. MOTRY, REV. HUBERT LOUIS, S.T.D., J.C.D., Diocesan Faculties According to the Code of Canon Law, II-167 pp., 1922.
17. MURPHY, REV. GEORGE LAWRENCE, J.C.D., Delinquencies and Penalties in the Administration and the Reception of the Sacraments, IV-121 pp., 1923.
18. O'REILLY, REV. JOHN ANTHONY, S.T.B., J.C.D., Ecclesiastical Sepulture in the New Code of Canon Law, II-129 pp., 1923.

---

* Below n. 100 only the following numbers are still available: Nn. 3, 4, 9, 25, 34, 57 and 75. Beginning with n. 100 only the following are unavailable: Nn. 100-111 inclusive, and n. 113.

19. MICHALICKA, REV. WENCESLAS CYRILL, O.S.B., J.C.D., Judicial Procedure in Dismissal of Clerical Exempt Religious, 107 pp., 1923.
20. DARGIN, REV. EDWARD VINCENT, S.T.B., J.C.D., Reserved Cases According to the Code of Canon Law, IV-103 pp., 1924.
21. GODFREY, REV. JOHN A., S.T.B., J.C.D., The Right of Patronage According to the Code of Canon Law, 153 pp., 1924.
22. HAGEDORN, REV. FRANCIS EDWARD, J.C.D., General Legislation on Indulgences, II-154 pp., 1924.
23. KING, REV. JAMES IGNATIUS, J.C.D., The Administration of the Sacraments to Dying Non-Catholics, V-141 pp., 1924.
24. WINSLOW, REV. FRANCIS JOSEPH, O.F.M., J.C.D., Vicars and Prefects Apostolic, IV-149 pp., 1924.
25. CORREA, REV. JOSE SERVELION, S.T.L., J.C.D., La Potestad Legislativa de la Iglesia Catolica, IV-127 pp., 1925.
26. DUGAN, REV. HENRY FRANCIS, A.M., J.C.D., The Judiciary Department of the Diocesan Curia, 87 pp., 1925.
27. KELLER, REV. CHARLES FREDERICK, S.T.B., J.C.D., Mass Stipends, 167 pp., 1925.
28. PASCHANG, REV. JOHN LINUS, J.C.D., The Sacramentals According to the Code of Canon Law, 129 pp., 1925.
29. PIONTEK, REV. CYRILLUS, O.F.M., S.T.B., J.C.D., De Indulto Exclaustrationis necnon Saecularizationis, XIII-289 pp., 1925.
30. KEARNEY, REV. RICHARD JOSEPH, S.T.B., J.C.D., Sponsors at Baptism According to the Code of Canon Law, IV-127 pp., 1925.
31. BARTLETT, REV. CHESTER JOSEPH, A.M., LL.B., J.C.D., The Tenure of Parochial Property in the United States of America, V-108 pp., 1926.
32. KILKER, REV. ADRIAN JEROME, J.C.D., Extreme Unction, V-425 pp., 1926.
33. McCORMICK, REV. ROBERT EMMETT, J.C.D., Confessors of Religious, VIII-266 pp., 1926.
34. MILLER, REV. NEWTON THOMAS, J.C.D., Founded Masses According to the Code of Canon Law, VII-93 pp., 1926.
35. ROELKER, REV. EDWARD G., S.T.D., J.C.D., Principles of Privilege According to the Code of Canon Law, XI-166 pp., 1926.
36. BAKALARCZYK, REV. RICHARDUS, M.I.C., J.U.D., De Novitiatu, VIII-208 pp., 1927.
37. PIZZUTI, REV. LAWRENCE, O.F.M., J.U.L., De Parochis Religiosis, 1927. (Not Printed.)
38. BLILEY, REV. NICHOLAS MARTIN, O.S.B., J.C.D., Altars According to the Code of Canon Law, XIX-132 pp., 1927.
39. BROWN, MR. BRENDAN FRANCIS, A.B., LL.M., J.U.D., The Canonical Juristic Personality with Special Reference to its Status in the United States of America, V-212 pp., 1927.
40. CAVANAUGH, REV. WILLIAM THOMAS, C.P., J.U.D., The Reservation of the Blessed Sacrament, VIII-101 pp., 1927.

41. DOHENY, REV. WILLIAM J., C.S.C., A.B., J.U.D., Church Property: Modes of Acquisition, X-118 pp., 1927.
42. FELDHAUS, REV. ALOYSIUS H., C.PP.S., J.C.D., Oratories, IX-141 pp., 1927.
43. KELLY, REV. JAMES PATRICK, A.B., J.C.D., The Jurisdiction of the Simple Confessor, X-208 pp., 1927.
44. NEUBERGER, REV. NICHOLAS J., J.C.D., Canon 6 or the Relation of the Codex Juris Canonici to the Preceding Legislation, V-95 pp., 1927.
45. O'KEEFE, REV. GERALD MICHAEL, J.C.D., Matrimonial Dispensations, Powers of Bishops, Priests, and Confessors, VIII-232 pp., 1927.
46. QUIGLEY, REV. JOSEPH A. M., A.B., J.C.D., Condemned Societies, 139 pp., 1927.
47. ZAPLOTNIK, REV. JOHANNES LEO, J.C.D., De Vicariis Foraneis, X-142 pp., 1927.
48. DUSKIE, REV. JOHN ALOYSIUS, A.B., J.C.D., The Canonical Status of the Orientals in the United States, VIII-196 pp., 1928.
49. HYLAND, REV. FRANCIS EDWARD, J.C.D., Excommunication, Its Nature, Historical Development and Effects, VIII-181 pp., 1928.
50. REINMANN, REV. GERALD JOSEPH, O.M.C., J.C.D., The Third Order Secular of Saint Francis, 201 pp., 1928.
51. SCHENK, REV. FRANCIS J., J.C.D., The Matrimonial Impediments of Mixed Religion and Disparity of Cult, XVI-318 pp., 1929.
52. COADY, REV. JOHN JOSEPH, S.T.D., J.U.D., A.M., The Appointment of Pastors, VIII-150 pp., 1929.
53. KAY, REV. THOMAS HENRY, J.C.D., Competence in Matrimonial Procedure, VIII-164 pp., 1929.
54. TURNER, REV. SIDNEY JOSEPH, C.P., J.U.D., The Vow of Poverty, XLIX-217 pp., 1929.
55. KEARNEY, REV. RAYMOND A., A.B., S.T.D., J.C.D., The Principles of Delegation, VII-149 pp., 1929.
56. CONRAN, REV. EDWARD JAMES, A.B., J.C.D., The Interdict, V-163 pp., 1930.
57. O'NEILL, REV. WILLIAM H., J.C.D., Papal Rescripts of Favor, VII-218 pp., 1930.
58. BASTNAGEL, REV. CLEMENT VINCENT, J.U.D., The Appointment of Parochial Adjutants and Assistants, XV-257 pp., 1930.
59. FERRY, REV. WILLIAM A., A.B., J.C.D., Stole Fees, V-136 pp., 1930.
60. COSTELLO, REV. JOHN MICHAEL, A.B., J.C.D., Domicile and Quasi-Domicile, VII-201 pp., 1930.
61. KREMER, REV. MICHAEL NICHOLAS, A.B., S.T.B., J.C.D., Church Support in the United States, VI-136 pp., 1930.
62. ANGULO, REV. LUIS, C.M., J.C.D., Legislation de la Iglesia sobre la intencion en la application de la Santa Misa, VII-104 pp., 1931.
63. FREY, REV. WOLFGANG NORBERT, O.S.B., A.B., J.C.D., The Act of Religious Profession, VIII-174 pp., 1931.

64. ROBERTS, REV. JAMES BRENDAN, A.B., J.C.D., The Banns of Marriage, XIV-140 pp., 1931.
65. RYDER, REV. RAYMOND ALOYSIUS, A.B., J.C.D., Simony, IX-151 pp., 1931.
66. CAMPAGNA, REV. ANGELO, PH.D., J.U.D., Il Vicario Generale del Vescovo, VII-205 pp., 1931.
67. COX, REV. JOSEPH GODFREY, A.B., J.C.D., The Administration of Seminaries, VI-124 pp., 1931.
68. GREGORY, REV. DONALD J., J.U.D., The Pauline Privilege, XV-165 pp., 1931.
69. DONOHUE, REV. JOHN F., J.C.D., The Impediment of Crime, VII-110 pp., 1931.
70. DOOLEY, REV. EUGENE A., O.M.I., J.C.D., Church Law on Sacred Relics, IX-143 pp., 1931.
71. ORTH, REV. CLEMENT RAYMOND, O.M.C., J.C.D., The Approbation of Religious Institutes, 171 pp., 1931.
72. PERNICONE, REV. JOSEPH M., A.B., J.C.D., The Ecclesiastical Prohibition of Books, XII-267 pp., 1932.
73. CLINTON, REV. CONNELL, A.B., J.C.D., The Paschal Precept, IX-108 pp., 1932.
74. DONNELLY, REV. FRANCIS B., A.M., S.T.L., J.C.D., The Diocesan Synod, VIII-125 pp., 1932.
75. TORRENTE, REV. CAMILO, C.M.F., J.C.D., Las Procesiones Sagradas, V-145 pp., 1932.
76. MURPHY, REV. EDWIN J., C.PP.S., J.C.D., Suspension Ex Informata Conscientia, XI-122 pp., 1932.
77. MACKENZIE, REV. ERIC F., A.M., S.T.L., J.C.D., The Delict of Heresy in its Commission, Penalization, Absolution, VII-124 pp., 1932.
78. LYONS, REV. AVITUS E., S.T.B., J.C.D., The Collegiate Tribunal of First Instance, XI-147 pp., 1932.
79. CONNOLLY, REV. THOMAS A., J.C.D., Appeals, XI-195, pp., 1932.
80. SANGMEISTER, REV. JOSEPH V., A.B., J.C.D., Force and Fear as Precluding Matrimonial Consent, V-211 pp., 1932.
81. JAEGER, REV. LEO A., A.B., J.C.D., The Administration of Vacant and Quasi-Vacant Episcopal Sees in the United States, IX-229 pp., 1932.
82. RIMLINGER, REV. HERBERT T., J.C.D., Error Invalidating Matrimonial Consent, VII-79 pp., 1932.
83. BARRETT, REV. JOHN D. M., S.S., J.C.D., A Comparative Study of the Third Plenary Council of Baltimore and the Code, IX-221 pp., 1932.
84. CARBERRY, REV. JOHN J., PH.D., S.T.D., J.C.D., The Juridical Form of Marriage, X-177 pp., 1934.
85. DOLAN, REV. JOHN L., A.B., J.C.D., The Defensor Vinculi, XII-157 pp., 1934.
86. HANNAN, REV. JEROME D., A.M., S.T.D., LL.B., J.C.D., The Canon Law of Wills, IX-517 pp., 1934.

87. Lemieux, Rev. Delise A., A.M., J.C.D., The Sentence in Ecclesiastical Procedure, IX-131 pp., 1934.
88. O'Rourke, Rev. James J., A.B., J.C.D., Parish Registers, VII-109 pp., 1934.
89. Timlin, Rev. Bartholomew, O.F.M., A.M., J.C.D., Conditional Matrimonial Consent, X-381 pp., 1934.
90. Wahl, Rev. Francis X., A.B., J.C.D., The Matrimonial Impediments of Consanguinity and Affinity, VI-125 pp., 1934.
91. White, Rev. Robert J., A.B., LL.B., S.T.B., J.C.D., Canonical Ante-Nuptial Promises and the Civil Law, VI-152 pp., 1934.
92. Herrera, Rev. Antonio Parra, O.C.D., J.C.D., Legislacion Ecclesiastica sobra el Ayuno y la Abstinencia, XI-191 pp., 1935.
93. Kennedy, Rev. Edwin J., J.C.D., The Special Matrimonial Process in Cases of Evident Nullity, X-165 pp., 1935.
94. Manning, Rev. John J., A.B., J.C.D., Presumption of Law in Matrimonial Procedure, XI-111 pp., 1935.
95. Moeder, Rev. John M., J.C.D., The Proper Bishop for Ordination and Dimissorial Letters, VII-135 pp., 1935.
96. O'Mara, Rev. William A., A.B., J.C.D., Canonical Causes for Matrimonial Dispensations, IX-155 pp., 1935.
97. Reilly, Rev. Peter, J.C.D., Residence of Pastors, IX-81 pp., 1935.
98. Smith, Rev. Mariner T., O.P., S.T.Lr., J.C.D., The Penal Law for Religious, VIII-169 pp., 1935.
99. Whalen, Rev. Donald W., A.M., J.C.D., The Value of Testimonial Evidence in Matrimonial Procedure, XIII-297 pp., 1935.
100. Cleary, Rev. Joseph F., J.C.D., Canonical Limitations on the Alienation of Church Property, VIII-141 pp., 1936.
101. Glynn, Rev. John C., J.C.D., The Promoter of Justice, XX-337 pp., 1936.
102. Brennan, Rev. James H., S.S., M.A., S.T.B., J.C.D., The Simple Convalidation of Marriage, VI-135 pp., 1937.
103. Brunini, Rev. Joseph Bernard, J.C.D., The Clerical Obligations of Canons 139 and 142, X-121 pp., 1937.
104. Connor, Rev. Maurice, A.B., J.C.D., The Administrative Removal of Pastors, VIII-159 pp., 1937.
105. Guilfoyle, Rev. Merlin Joseph, J.C.D., Custom, XI-144 pp., 1937.
106. Hughes, Rev. James Austin, A.B., A.M., J.C.D., Witnesses in Criminal Trials of Clerics, IX-140 pp., 1937.
107. Jansen, Rev. Raymond J., A.B., S.T.L., J.C.D., Canonical Provisions for Catechetical Instruction, VII-153 pp., 1937.
108. Kealy, Rev. John James, A.B., J.C.D., The Introductory Libellus in Church Court Procedure, XI-121 pp., 1937.
109. McManus, Rev. James Edward, C.SS.R., J.C.D., The Administration of Temporal Goods in Religious Institutes, XVI-196 pp., 1937.

110. MORIARTY, REV. EUGENE JAMES, J.C.D., Oaths in Ecclesiastical Courts, X-115 pp., 1937.
111. RAINER, REV. ELIGIUS GEORGE, C.SS.R., J.C.D., Suspension of Clerics, XVII-249 pp., 1937.
112. REILLY, REV. THOMAS F., C.SS.R., J.C.D., Visitation of Religious, VI-195 pp., 1938.
113. MORIARTY, REV. FRANCIS E., C.SS.R., J.C.D., The Extraordinary Absolution from Censures, XV-334 pp., 1938.
114. CONNOLLY, REV. NICHOLAS P., J.C.D., The Canonical Erection of Parishes, X-132 pp., 1938.
115. DONOVAN, REV. JAMES JOSEPH, J.C.D., The Pastor's Obligation in Prenuptial Investigation, XII-322 pp., 1938.
116. HARRIGAN, REV. ROBERT J., M.A., S.T.B., J.C.D., The Radical Sanation of Invalid Marriages, VIII-208 pp., 1938.
117. BOFFA, REV. CONRAD HUMBERT, J.C.D., Canonical Provisions for Catholic Schools, VII-211 pp., 1939.
118. PARSONS, REV. ANSCAR JOHN, O.M.Cap., J.C.D., Canonical Elections, XII-236 pp., 1939.
119. REILLY, REV. EDWARD MICHAEL, A.B., J.C.D., The General Norms of Dispensation, XII-156 pp., 1939.
120. RYAN, REV. GERALD ALOYSIUS, A.B., J.C.D., Principles of Episcopal Jurisdiction, XII-172 pp., 1939.
121. BURTON, REV. FRANCIS JAMES, C.S.C., A.B., J.C.D., A Commentary on Canon 1125, X-222 pp., 1940.
122. MIASKIEWICZ, REV. FRANCIS SIGISMUND, J.C.D., Supplied Jurisdiction According to Canon 209, XII-340 pp., 1940.
123. RICE, REV. PATRICK WILLIAM, A.B., J.C.D., Proof of Death in Prenuptial Investigation, VIII-156 pp., 1940.
124. ANGLIN, REV. THOMAS FRANCIS, M.S., J.C.D., The Eucharistic Fast, VIII-183 pp., 1941.
125. COLEMAN, REV. JOHN JEROME, J.C.D., The Minister of Confirmation, VI-153 pp., 1941.
126. DOWNS, REV. JOHN EMMANUEL, A.B., J.C.D., The Concept of Clerical Immunity, XI-163 pp., 1941.
127. ESSWEIN, REV. ANTHONY ALBERT, J.C.D., Extrajudicial Penal Powers of Ecclesiastical Superiors, X-144 pp., 1941.
128. FARRELL, REV. BENJAMIN FRANCIS, M.A., S.T.L., J.C.D., The Rights and Duties of the Local Ordinary Regarding Congregations of Women Religious of Pontifical Approval, V-195 pp., 1941.
129. FEENEY, REV. THOMAS JOHN, A.B., S.T.L., J.C.D., Restitutio in Integrum, VI-169 pp., 1941.
130. FINDLAY, REV. STEPHEN WILLIAM, O.S.B., A.B., J.C.D., Canonical Norms Governing the Deposition and Degradation of Clerics, XVII-279 pp., 1941.

131. GOODWINE, REV. JOHN, A.B., S.T.L., J.C.D., The Right of the Church to Acquire Property, VIII-119 pp., 1941.

132. HESTON, REV. EDWARD LOUIS, C.S.C., Ph.D., S.T.D., J.C.D., The Alienation of Church Property in the United States, XII-222 pp., 1941.

133. HOGAN, REV. JAMES JOHN, A.B., S.T.L., J.C.D., Judicial Advocates and Procurators, XIII-200 pp., 1941.

134. KEALY, REV. THOMAS M., A.B., Litt.B., J.C.D., Dowry of Women Religious, IX-152 pp., 1941.

135. KEENE, REV. MICHAEL JAMES, O.S.B., J.C.D., Religious Ordinaries and Canon 198, V-164 pp., 1942.

136. KERIN, REV. CHARLES A., S.S., M.A., S.T.B., J.C.D., The Privation of Christian Burial, XVI-279 pp., 1941.

137. LOUIS, REV. WILLIAM FRANCIS, M.A., J.C.D., Diocesan Archives, X-101 pp., 1941.

138. MCDEVITT, REV. GILBERT JOSEPH, A.B., J.C.D., Legitimacy and Legitimation, X-247 pp., 1941.

139. MCDONOUGH, REV. THOMAS JOSEPH, A.B., J.C.D., Apostolic Administrators, X-217 pp., 1941.

140. MEIER, REV. CARL ANTHONY, A.B., J.C.D., Penal Administrative Procedure Against Negligent Pastors, XI-240 pp., 1941.

141. SCHMIDT, REV. JOHN ROGG, A.B., J.C.D., The Principles of Authentic Interpretation in Canon 17 of the Code of Canon Law, XII-331 pp., 1941.

142. SLAFKOSKY, REV. ANDREW LEONARD, A.B., J.C.D., The Canonical Episcopal Visitation of the Diocese, X-197 pp., 1941.

143. SWOBODA, REV. INNOCENT ROBERT, O.F.M., J.C.D., Ignorance in Relation to the Imputability of Delicts, IX-271 pp., 1941.

144. DUBÉ, REV. ARTHUR JOSEPH, A.B., J.C.D., The General Principles for the Reckoning of Time in Canon Law, VIII-299 pp., 1941.

145. MCBRIDE, REV. JAMES T., A.B., J.C.D., Incardination and Excardination of Seculars, XX-585 pp., 1941.

146. KRÓL, REV. JOHN T., J.C.D., The Defendant in Ecclesiastical Trials, XII-207 pp., 1942.

147. COMYNS, REV. JOSEPH J., C.SS.R., A.B., J.C.D., Papal and Episcopal Administration of Church Property, XIV-155 pp., 1942.

148. BARRY, REV. GARRETT FRANCIS, O.M.I., J.C.D., Violation of the Cloister, XII-260 pp., 1942.

149. BOLDUC, REV. GATIEN, C.S.V., A.B., S.T.L., J.C.D., Les Études dans les Religions Cléricales, VIII-155 pp., 1942.

150. BOYLE, REV. DAVID JOHN, M.A., J.C.D., The Juridic Effects of Moral Certitude on Pre-Nuptial Guarantees, XII-188 pp., 1942.

151. CANAVAN, REV. WALTER JOSEPH, M.A., Litt.D., J.C.D., The Profession of Faith, XII-143 pp., 1942.

152. DESROCHERS, REV. BRUNO, A.B., Ph.L., S.T.B., J.C.D., Le Premier Concile Plénier de Québec et le Code de Droit Canonique, XIV-186 pp., 1942.

153. DILLON, REV. ROBERT EDWARD, A.B., J.C.D., Common Law Marriage, X-148 pp., 1942.

154. DODWELL, REV. EDWARD JOHN, Ph.D., S.T.B., J.C.D., The Time and Place for the Celebration of Marriage, X-156 pp., 1942.

155. DONNELLAN, REV. THOMAS ANDREW, A.B., J.C.D., The Obligation of the Missa pro Populo, VII-131 pp., 1942.

156. ELTZ, REV. LOUIS ANTHONY, A.B., J.C.D., Cooperation in Crime, XII-208 pp., 1942.

157. GASS, REV. SYLVESTER FRANCIS, M.A., J.C.D., Ecclesiastical Pensions, XI-206 pp., 1942.

158. GUINIVEN, REV. JOHN JOSEPH, C.SS.R., J.C.D., The Precept of Hearing Mass, XIV-188 pp., 1942.

159. GULCZYNSKI, REV. JOHN THEOPHILUS, J.C.D., The Desecration and Violation of Churches, X-126 pp., 1942.

160. HAMMILL, REV. JOHN LEO, M.A., J.C.D., The Obligations of the Traveler According to Canon 14, VIII-204 pp., 1942.

161. HAYDT, REV. JOHN JOSEPH, A.B., J.C.D., Reserved Benefices, XI-148 pp., 1942.

162. HUSER, REV. ROGER JOHN, O.F.M., A.B., J.C.D., The Crime of Abortion in Canon Law, XII-187 pp., 1942.

163. KEARNEY, REV. FRANCIS PATRICK, A.B., S.T.L., J.C.L., The Principles of Canon 1127.

164. LINAHEN, REV. LEO JAMES, S.T.L., J.C.D., De Absolutione Complicis in Peccato Turpi, V-114 pp., 1942.

165. McCLOSKEY, REV. JOSEPH ALOYSIUS, A.B., J.C.D., The Subject of Ecclesiastical Law According to Canon 12, XVII-246 pp., 1942.

166. O'NEILL, REV. FRANCIS JOSEPH, C.SS.R., J.C.D., The Dismissal of Religious in Temporary Vows, XIII-220 pp., 1942.

167. PRINCE, REV. JOHN EDWARD, A.B., S.T.B., J.C.D., The Diocesan Chancellor, X-136 pp., 1942.

168. RIESNER, REV. ALBERT JOSEPH, C.SS.R., J.C.D., Apostates and Fugitives from Religious Institutes, IX-168 pp., 1942.

169. STENGER, REV. JOSEPH BERNARD, J.C.D., The Mortgaging of Church Property, 186 pp., 1942.

170. WALDRON, REV. JOSEPH FRANCIS, A.B., J.C.D., The Minister of Baptism, XII-197 pp., 1942.

171. WILLETT, REV. ROBERT ALBERT, J.C.D., The Probative Value of Documents in Ecclesiastical Trials, X-124 pp., 1942.

172. WOEBER, REV. EDWARD MARTIN, M.A., J.C.D., The Interpellations, XII-161 pp., 1942.

173. BENKO, REV. MATTHEW ALOYSIUS, O.S.B., M.A., J.C.D., The Abbot *Nullius*, XVI-148 pp., 1943.

174. CHRIST, REV. JOSEPH JAMES, M.A., S.T.L., J.C.D., Dispensation from Vindicative Penalties, XIV-285 pp., 1943.

175. Clancy, Rev. Patrick M. J., O.P., A.B., S.T.Lr., J.C.D., The Local Religious Superior, X-229 pp., 1943.

176. Clarke, Rev. Thomas James, J.C.D., Parish Societies, XII-147 pp., 1943.

177. Connolly, Rev. John Patrick, S.T.L., J.C.D., Synodal Examiners and Parish Priest Consultors, X-223 pp., 1943.

178. Drumm, Rev. William Martin, A.B., J.C.D., Hospital Chaplains, XII-175 pp., 1943.

179. Flanagan, Rev. Bernard Joseph, A.B., S.T.L., J.C.D., The Canonical Erection of Religious Houses, X-147 pp., 1943.

180. Kelleher, Rev. Stephen Joseph, A.B., S.T.B., J.C.D., Discussions with Non-Catholics: Canonical Legislation, X-93 pp., 1943.

181. Lewis, Rev. Gordian, C.P., J.C.D., Chapters in Religious Institutes, XII-169 pp., 1943.

182. Marx, Rev. Adolph, J.C.D., The Declaration of Nullity of Marriages Contracted Outside the Church, X-151 pp., 1943.

183. Matulenas, Rev. Raymond Anthony, O.S.B., A.B., J.C.D., Communication, a Source of Privileges, XII-225 pp., 1943.

184. O'Leary, Rev. Charles Gerard, C.SS.R., J.C.D., Religious Dismissed After Perpetual Profession, X-213 pp., 1943.

185. Power, Rev. Cornelius Michael, J.C.D., The Blessing of Cemeteries, XII-231 pp., 1943.

186. Shuhler, Rev. Ralph Vincent, O.S.A., J.C.D., Privileges of Religious to Absolve and Dispense, XII-195 pp., 1943.

187. Ziolkowski, Rev. Thaddeus Stanislaus, A.B., J.C.D., The Consecration and Blessing of Churches, XII-151 pp., 1943.

188. Heneghan, Rev. John Joseph, S.T.D., J.C.D., The Marriages of Unworthy Catholics: Canons 1065 and 1066, XVI-213 pp., 1944.

189. Carroll, Rev. Coleman Francis, M.A., S.T.L., J.C.L., Charitable Institutions.

190. Ciesluk, Rev. Joseph Edward, Ph.B., S.T.L., J.C.L., National Parishes in the United States.

191. Coburn, Rev. Vincent Paul, A.B., J.C.D., Marriages of Conscience, XII-172 pp., 1944.

192. Connors, Rev. Charles Paul, C.S.Sp., A.B., J.C.D., Extra-Judicial Procurators in the Code of Canon Law, X-94 pp., 1944.

193. Coyle, Rev. Paul Raymond, A.B., J.C.L., Judicial Exceptions.

194. Fair, Rev. Bartholomew Francis, A.B., S.T.L., J.C.L., The Impediment of Abduction.

195. Gallagher, Rev. Thomas Raphael, O.P., A.B., S.T.Lr., J.C.D., The Examination of the Qualities of the Ordinand, X-166 pp., 1944.

196. Gannon, Rev. John Mark, S.T.L., J.C.D., The Interstices Required for the Promotion to Orders, XII-100 pp., 1944.

197. Goldsmith, Rev. J. William, B.C.S., S.T.L., J.C.D., The Competence of Church and State Over Marriage—Disputed Points, X-128 pp., 1944.

198. GOODWINE, REV. JOSEPH GERARD, A.B., S.T.B., J.C.D., The Reception of Converts, XIV-326 pp., 1944.

199. KOWALSKI, REV. ROMUALD EUGENE, O.F.M., A.B., J.C.D., Sustenance of Religious Houses of Regulars, X-174 pp., 1944.

200. McCOY, REV. ALAN EDWARD, O.F.M., J.C.D., Force and Fear in Relation to Delictual Imputability and Penal Responsibility, XII-160 pp., 1944.

201. McDEVITT, REV. VINCENT JOHN, PH.B., S.T.L., J.C.L., Perjury.

202. MARTIN, REV. THOMAS OWEN, PH.D., S.T.D., J.C.D., Adverse Possession, Prescription and Limitation of Actions: The Canonical "Praescriptio," XX-208 pp., 1944.

203. MIKLOSOVIC, REV. PAUL JOHN, A.B., J.C.L., Attempted Marriages and Their Consequent Juridic Effects.

204. MUNDY, REV. THOMAS MAURICE, A.B., S.T.L., J.C.L., The Union of Parishes.

205. O'DEA, REV. JOHN COYLE, A.B., J.C.D., The Matrimonial Impediment of Nonage, VIII-126 pp., 1944.

206. OLALIA, REV. ALEXANDER AYSON, S.T.L., J.C.D., A Comparative Study of the Christian Constitution of States and the Constitution of the Philippine Commonwealth, XII-136 pp., 1944.

207. POISSON, REV. PIERRE-MARIE, C.S.C., A.B., PH.L., TH.L., J.C.L., Droits Patrimoniaux des Maisons et des Eglises Religieuses.

208. STADALNIKAS, REV. CASIMIR JOSEPH, M.I.C., J.C.D., Reservation of Censures, X-141 pp., 1944.

209. SULLIVAN, REV. EUGENE HENRY, S.T.L., J.C.L., Proof of the Reception of the Sacraments.

210. VAUGHAN, REV. WILLIAM EDWARD, J.C.D., Constitutions for Diocesan Courts, X-210 pp., 1944.

211. LYONS, REV. JOSEPH HENRY, J.C.L., The Joinder of Issue in Canonical Trials.

212. BALZER, REV. RALPH FRANCIS, C.P., J.C.L., The Computation of Time in a Canonical Novitiate.

213. DOUGHERTY, REV. JOHN WHELAN, A.B., S.T.L., J.C.L., De Inquisitione Speciali.

214. DZIOB, REV. MICHAEL WALTER, J.C.L., The Sacred Congregation for the Oriental Church.

215. EIDENSCHINK, REV. JOHN ALBERT, O.S.B., B.A., J.C.L., The Election of Bishops in the Letters of Pope Gregory the Great.

216. GILL, REV. NICHOLAS, C.P., J.C.L., The Spiritual Prefect in Clerical Religious Houses of Study.

217. HYNES, REV. HARRY GERARD, S.T.L., J.C.L., The Privileges of Cardinals.

218. McDEVITT, REV. GERALD VINCENT, S.T.L., J.C.L., The Renunciation of an Ecclesiastical Office.

219. MANNING, REV. JOSEPH LEROY, J.C.L., The Free Conferral of Offices.